The Vibra

Universe

Harnessing the Power of Thought to Consciously Change

Your Life

by

Kenneth J. M. MacLean

The Vibrational Universe: Harnessing the Power of Thought to Consciously Create Your Life

Book #1 in the Potential of Consciousness series.

ISBN-13 978-1-932690-08-8

Library of Congress Control Number: 2005926179

4th Printing – May 2015

Typeset using the LATEX typesetting program.

Also by K.J.M. MacLean: *Dialogues: Conversations with my Higher Self*

Distributed by: Baker & Taylor, Ingram Book Group, New Leaf Distributing

The Big Picture is an imprint of: Loving Healing Press

Contact the author at www.kjmaclean.com

Contents

Foreword to the Second Edition   iii

Part I – THE BIG PICTURE

Chapter 1   The Big Picture   1
1.1   Introduction 1
1.2   Consciousness 2
1.3   What is Consciousness? 3
1.4   Quality vs. Quantity 4
1.5   Consciousness Is Eternal 6
1.6   Focus 9
1.7   A Short Diversion 11

Chapter 2   The Vibrational Universe   15
2.1   Looking at Matter and Energy from a Different Perspective 15
2.2   If Matter is Mostly Space, Why Do We See Anything as Solid? . . . 17
2.3   Emotions are also Vibrational in Nature 21
2.4   The Role of Emotions 22
2.5   The Impact of Thoughts on How You Feel 24
2.6   The Scale of Emotion 26
2.7   "Negative Energy" 29
2.8   Free Will 30
2.9   The Way You Think Affects the Way You Feel 31
2.10   Modeling the Human Energy Field 32
2.11   The Power of Self-Referencing 34

Part II – THE UNIVERSAL OPERATING SYSTEM

Chapter 3   The Operating System of the Universe   41
3.1   The First Principle: Consciousness 41

3.2   The Law of Free Will   43
3.3   The Law of Vibration   43
3.4   Your Broadcast Signal to the Universe   45
3.5   Subtle Energy   47
3.6   "Phantom DNA"   50
3.7   Oh, Really?   51
3.8   Non-locality   51
3.9   Coincidence   53
3.10 You Are the Modulator of Your Vibrational Signal   55
3.11 Looking at Life Energetically   56
3.12 The Law of Attraction   57
3.13 Consciousness, Feeling, and Action   61
3.14 The Law of Attraction, Continued   64
3.15 Luck   66
3.16 Desire Amplifies Your Signal   67
3.17 All Beings are Sovereign   67
3.18 Relationships   68
3.19 Victim and Victimizer   72
3.20 What You Give Your Attention to Grows Bigger for You . . .   73
3.21 An Illustration of the Law of Attraction   74
3.22 It is Easier to Think Positively than Negatively   75
3.23 Prosperity is Natural   79
3.24 The World Is In Perfect Balance   80
       3.24.1 The Hawk and the Sparrow   82
3.25 Diversity Is Vital In Order to Maintain Balance   82
3.26 The Law of Attraction: An in-depth illustration   83
3.27 Universal Forces   88

Chapter 4   Conscious Creation   93
4.1   The Role of Beliefs   94
4.2   Regaining Control   96
4.3   The Executive   97
4.4   What is The "Guidance System"?   98
4.5   How to Know What You Want 100
4.6   Be Selective When Consciously Creating 101

Chapter 5   The Law of Allowing (or, the path of least resistance)   103
5.1   Allowing is Loving 105
5.2   The Creative Process 107
5.3   The Power of Limits and the Creative Process 109
5.4   Everyone is Sovereign in Their Own Experience 112
5.5   It Is Not Possible to Create for Another 113
5.6   Failed Help 115

5.7   Feeling Good Is Always Appropriate 115

5.8   Creating Your Personal Reality 117

5.9   How Do You Allow? 118

5.10 What is Resistance? 119

5.11 Protection From Something Unwanted 120

Chapter 6   Group Dynamics and Sovereignty   123

6.1   Overview 123

6.2   Group Dynamics – Non Resistance and Politics 126

6.3   Non-Resistance and the Armed Forces 128

6.4   More on Group Dynamics 134

6.5   True Non-Resistance Comes From a Position of Strength 139

6.6   The Sovereign 140

      6.6.1   Mass Consciousness 142

      6.6.2   Characteristics of a Sovereign 143

      6.6.3   The Subconscious 145

6.7   Right and Wrong 148

Part III – APPLYING THE UNIVERSAL OPERATING SYSTEM TO LIFE

Chapter 7   Using the Universal Operating System in Life   155

7.1   Understanding the Emotional Scale 155

7.2   Barb and Jill 155

7.3   Rick and Sam 158

7.4   Enabling the Intellect 160

7.5   Fate vs. Free Will 160

7.6   Focusing 161

7.7   The Creative Process 162

7.8   Back to Fate 163

7.9   Risk 164

7.10 Judgment 171

Chapter 8   A New Perspective on Life   175

8.1   En-Joy 175

8.2   Joy vs. Selfishness 178

8.3   Happiness vs. Joy 180

8.4   How to Stay Positive in a Negative World 182

8.5   Integrity 185

8.6   Connecting With Source 186

8.7   Trust Yourself, You Are God 188

8.8   Control Equals Weakness 188

8.9   Passion 189

8.10 Being Different 193

8.11   The True Meaning of Selfishness   196
8.12   Giving and Receiving   200
8.13   Open Systems vs. Closed Systems   201
8.14   Is it Really "Better to Give than to Receive?"   202
8.15   Source Point vs. Result Point   202
8.16   Cause and Effect   205
8.17   The Myth of Objectivity   207
8.18   Challenge: An Empowering Look at Overcoming Obstacles   210
8.19   Sanity vs. Insanity   215

Chapter 9   The Creative Process and Manifestation   219
9.1   Identifying the Power within the Creative Process   219
9.2   What We Are Taught Is Backwards   220
9.3   The Importance of Being   222
       9.3.1   Inspiration   225
       9.3.2   Probability   226
       9.3.3   Being vs. Doing   226
9.4   Establishing a State of Being   229
9.5   Aligning Energy   231
       9.5.1   Introduction   232
       9.5.2   Stages in the Manifestation Process   233
               The First Stage   233
               The Second Stage   235
               The Third Stage   237
               The Fourth Stage   239
               The Fifth Stage   241
               The Sixth Stage   242
               The Seventh Stage   242
               The Eighth Stage   242
               The Ninth Stage   243
9.6   Manifestation and Delusion   244

Chapter 10   A New Approach to Problem Solving   251
10.1   Handling Problems   251
       10.1.1 The Physics of Problems   251
       10.1.2 The Physics of Handling Problems   254
       10.1.3 A Better Way of Dealing With Problems   256
       10.1.4 The Solution   256
       10.1.5 Raising Your Emotional Level   258

Chapter 11   What is Truth?   261
11.1   What Is Truth, Really?   261
11.2   What Is Truth Part II — Validity   263
11.3   What is Truth Part III — Prove It!   267

11.4   What Is Faith? 269
    11.4.1   Faith vs. Hope 272
    11.4.2   Holding the Vision 273
    11.4.3   Summary 275

Appendix A   Sampling and Perception   277
  A.1   Sampling 279
  A.2   Do we Perceive Digitally, or Continuously? 285

Appendix B   Thought Is the Basic Quantum Unit   289
  B.1   Comments: 290

Appendix C   Does Like Really Attract Like?   293

About the Author   295

Other Books by the Author   297

"The most beautiful thing we can experience is the mysterious. It is the source of all true art and science. He to whom this emotion is a stranger, who can no longer pause to wonder and stand rapt in awe, is as good as dead: his eyes are closed."

—Albert Einstein (1879–1955)

Foreword to the Second Edition

What is truth? Is life a crapshoot, or are there fundamental universal laws which apply to everyone? If so, what are they? How do I stay positive in a world that seems so negative?

I have been to many inspirational speakers, and taken lots of courses and seminars, only to come down after a few days. Personally, I could never figure out how to maintain that good feeling, and I have been searching for philosophies and techniques which could enable me to do so. This book is the result of that search.

In hindsight, I can see that the inspiration to write this book occurred when I was 4 years old, as my mother lay in a hospital bed, dying from leukemia. Later, at the funeral, I toddled up with my little sister to look at the body lying in the casket. I couldn't figure out why mom didn't get up and give me a hug! Incessant questions to my father and the rest of the family produced no satisfactory answers for me. One thing I did understand. Looking at the body before and after her death, I realized that the body was not the essence of a human being. Even at the tender age of 4, I recognized that there must be an energy which occupied the body, then, at death, left it. When that animating principle departed, only a physical husk remained. I have never forgotten that experience, and have been conducting my own personal investigation into the Big Picture (and the little ones as well) ever since.

In this book, I present a model of life based in the spirit-mind-body framework, which unabashedly places consciousness in a primary position. The discussion assumes, without proof, that consciousness has a non-physical basis, and therefore, that a human being is first and foremost a spirit associated with a physical body. I have found personally that when life is analyzed from such a perspective, mysteries are solved, explanations for the behavior of our fellow man become simplified and easier to comprehend, and living on planet earth becomes less stressful.

I am indebted to Robert Fritz, for his groundbreaking book *The Path of Least Resistance*. I am also greatly indebted to Jerry and Esther Hicks for their inspirational taped messages. From both of these sources I learned that even esoteric concepts can be explained in a practical and understandable way. I am standing on their shoulders, so to speak.

Thanks to all of my teachers, who are too numerous to mention.

This is a book of speculative thought. What is written here is simply my personal version of truth. I have borrowed freely from the great ideas of others, and I do not claim special or unusual insight. This book is simply a summary of what I have learned after 53 years on the planet. I am not a scientist and I do not quarrel with the discoveries of science, because I do not know enough to do so. Scientific inaccuracies in this book are unintentional and may be clarified by looking in your physics textbooks!

My purpose in writing the book is to share the realizations I have had on my personal path of growth, to have fun, and to present concepts that might stimulate new ideas from those who read it. And, I must admit, to rock the boat a little, to get people to question their bedrock beliefs, in a positive way. To jar people into becoming more mindful, more aware of the vast, unused potential that lies within every single person on this planet. I hope this journey will be as fun for you to experience as it was for me!

Kenneth James Michael MacLean

June 2006

"...my definition of Universe includes not only the physical but also the metaphysical experiences of Universe, which the physicists thought they had to exclude from their more limited definition of the finite physical portion of Universe. The metaphysical embraces all the weightless experiences of thought, including all the mathematics and the organization of data regarding all the physical experiments, science itself being metaphysical."

— R. Buckminster Fuller, *Synergetics*, (1975), p. 83

Part I – THE BIG PICTURE

CHAPTER 1

The Big Picture

1.1 Introduction

Have you ever wondered why the events in your life happen the way they do? Doesn't it seem sometimes that you have no control over what happens in your life? We're not talking about things like the weather, or the latest government policy, but things like, "Why don't I have enough money?" or, "Why can't I find that perfect relationship?"

It turns out that the universe, like a computer, has an operating system. A computer operating system is a series of instructions that allows the user to access the computer's components and to run the software programs that allow him or her to perform useful work. The operating system of the computer has rules that it must follow in order to make everything inside the computer work properly. The process by which this is accomplished is actually quite complicated, but the operating system takes care of it all, invisible to the user.

The universe also has an operating system, which I am calling the Universal Operating System. Is it possible, do you think, for an infinite creation like the universe to operate randomly? If you ponder that for a minute you can see that in order for anything to work properly it must be well designed. The telephone has a number pad and a display that allow you to use it; the stove has dials to control the cooking temperature. All devices, in other words, have an interface that allows the user to communicate with the machine and direct its proper function. Inside the device, the components are hooked together in the most efficient manner.

The universe is no different than your telephone, computer or household appliance, in the sense that it provides a way to interact with you in an intelligent fashion.

It turns out that *the universe has been designed to directly interface with your thoughts and feelings.*

The Universal Operating System is a subtle energy system that interfaces directly with each and every human being on the planet. Of course there is no way to prove this objectively, but there *is* a way to prove it to yourself. The purpose of this book is to describe the universe's interface so that you can use it to make your life better. In order to do this we have to start at the beginning, and talk about consciousness.

1.2 Consciousness

THROUGHOUT history, consciousness has been assigned a non-physical origin. It is only within the past hundred years or so that mankind, in his zeal to accurately describe the physical universe, has lost touch with his spiritual nature. In this book we say that self-awareness, being non-physical in nature, exists independent of physical structures or containers (bodies) and that it is eternal. We do this because when life is viewed from such a perspective it becomes easier to understand, and such assumptions, when fully understood, supply an inner feeling of power, joy, and well-being. These feelings are fundamental to life itself, and all beings, no matter how evolved, strive for them.

In this book, we take the position that the universe is well ordered and has been designed for well-being; that life is meaningful and can, and should, be joyful. We take the position that a human being has a physical, a mental, and a spiritual component and that the spiritual component, consciousness, is paramount in importance. Why is consciousness paramount? Because it is the animating and directing principle of the universe.

Science has already systematized the laws of matter and energy and we will not argue with them; however, in Chapter 2, we will propose an interesting twist on scientific laws that provide a new and empowering way to look at life and the universe.

Fortunately, just as there are laws describing the behavior of matter and energy, there are also a few general but powerful principles that describe how the universe responds to human beings (and other life forms as well). Knowledge of these fundamental principles can make life easier and a lot more understandable.

The universe's operating system provides a user interface, but it is a little different from a computer or a machine. However, the components are all recognizable and we will be describing them as the book goes along. By the time we are through you will have all the information you need to enjoy life more and worry a lot less!

You can and should test the principles in this book yourself to see if they work. The whole idea is to present material that a person can use in life to change conditions for the better; a bunch of theory that cannot be applied is, in my opinion, useless.

The good news is, you don't need to know any math, you don't have to be a holy man or a guru, you don't even have to be smart! All you have to do is follow some simple, but very powerful guidelines. It's so easy, even a child can do it.

When we say that you can use the Universal Operating System (UOS) to change conditions for the better, we are not saying that you can learn to levitate chairs, wave a magic wand and create a pot of gold, or create world peace. You can, however, learn how to improve the way you feel about yourself. And you can learn how to attract a good relationship, or find a better job, or get along better with your kids. These are things well worth achieving!

Learning about the operating system of the universe is a lot like learning a new software program. If you understand how to work the software, you can actually get results. If you do not, you are fumbling around with incomprehensible menus and just going by trial and error, and what you get is often totally the opposite of what you wanted. Understanding the universe's operating system allows you to be in control of the "software" that runs the universe, instead of it controlling you.

Because we are working in the spirit-mind-body framework, we have to make a few assumptions about the nature of consciousness itself in order to get a grip on how and why the UOS. works the way it does. So here goes!

1.3   What is Consciousness?

EVEN though it's impossible to say for sure what consciousness is, we can make some broad, general statements that most people can agree with. After all, every person is to some degree an expert, because if you are alive, you are conscious.

We will begin by saying that consciousness is the animating principle of the universe. The animating principle has been understood by every culture that has ever existed on earth, and has been called chi, prana, Spirit, Ka, life force, etc.

In our model, when a person or an animal dies, the animating principle leaves and the body decays. When a flower wilts, the consciousness of the flower leaves. When a one-celled amoeba dies, the consciousness of the amoeba departs. Everything that lives is conscious!

As human beings we don't really think that flowers and insects and amoeba's have consciousness. But for the purposes of this book, we will say that they do. The animating principle of consciousness is the Source behind all of the biological life on our planet.

1.4 Quality vs. Quantity

W E begin our discussion of consciousness by describing it as a static. A static is defined as something that is self-aware, but which has no moving parts and no mass; a pure potential or causative influence that has unlimited scope. In other words, consciousness exists independent of matter and energy, which means that all life forms continue after the body dies. This concept is ancient, and is known as reincarnation.

A quality is an observable characteristic, feature, or aspect of the animating principle. In physics we might call it a scalar, a dimensionless quantity with magnitude, but no direction (time is an example of a scalar). In this sense consciousness, although itself not measurable, may exert an effect or influence which is observable.

A quantity, on the other hand, is something that can be seen, felt, or heard by the senses of the body, and/or is measurable or detectable with instrumentation.

In the physical universe we can observe the qualities people exhibit. We say: "He has character" or "She is full of life." These are reasonable statements but they cannot be accurately quantified. If asked, "Why do you say she is full of life?" we may observe that she is always cheerful, has lots of energy, and participates in many activities. But it would be hard to write a mathematical equation to describe the quality called 'full of life.' The reason qualities cannot be accurately specified is because they stem from consciousness itself, which may change its mind at any time and so exhibit entirely different characteristics. For example, a person (let's call him Moe) who is angry a lot might decide to lighten up and take things less seriously, and will demonstrate remarkably different characteristics from that point on.

We cannot observe *how* Moe changed his behavior patterns because that process is invisible to us, but we can notice how much more friendly Moe is to his family, friends, and co-workers. We cannot know precisely why Moe changed either, but Moe does. Moe has used the most powerful tool of consciousness to alter his behavior and feel better about himself: he has made a new decision. One of the things we can say about consciousness is that it has the ability to think, to decide, to prefer. A decision or a preference leads to a new state of BEING, and from that state of being, a new way of feeling, and a new set of actions will result.

A decision, in other words, is a very powerful thing, because before one can act, one must have made a decision to do so. The content of this decision will determine what actions will be taken. If one wanted to bake a cake, one would not randomly throw ingredients together; one would operate off of a recipe. You would not walk across the street without thinking about the possibility of oncoming traffic. These statements are obvious but their importance is often missed.

All action is preceded by thought.

There has never been an action that did not involve a decision first, even if it's as simple as turning your car into your driveway. It is obvious that you could decide not to turn into your driveway after a day of work; you may decide, on an impulse, to go to the gym, or to the bar, or to see your girlfriend. To quote the Buddha, "All that we are arises with our thoughts. With our thoughts we make our world."

The importance of thought, and being, is mostly not understood. Action is considered far more important, for it is action, it is said, that gets results. Yet all of that action is based upon a state of beingness. For example, James might want to learn how to play the piano. First he assumes the beingness of one who can learn to play the instrument. In other words, you have to BE something before you can DO it. You have to have the idea of it, before you can start. The better James is at assuming this beingness, the faster he will learn. I assure you from personal experience and observation that if you cannot BE a person who can play the piano, you can never learn to play.

Before James knows how to play he says, "I want to be a piano player." After a few years of study and practice, he can say "I am a piano player." Both of these statements use a form of the verb to be. One might say, "Yes, but the only reason James can say he is a player is because he can *do* it." True enough, but that is not how we look at it! We say, "I am a piano player," we don't say, "I do piano playing." Why is that? It's because we instinctively recognize the power of thought and the primacy of consciousness as source for all of our actions. We understand that being encompasses doing; or, in other words, that action is a subset of being. Being is first, then action, then results. This might seem trivial and obvious, but it is not! In order to change your situation, you need to create a state of being within yourself exactly matching what it is you want to accomplish. Around this idea is a very important principle in the Universal Operating System, and we will discuss it in great detail.

Without a clear and firm decision about something, there can be no concrete results. We have all seen people who just drift along in life; they never seem to have a direction and wander aimlessly from one job to the next, from one relationship to the next. I remember asking such a person, "What do you want out of life?" At first she was startled, as if the idea had never occurred to her before; finally, after several tries, she shrugged and said, "I don't know."

Consciousness has the power to decide, and when a person does so, he or she creates a state of beingness, or orientation, which guides action. When James decides to be a piano player, we do not see him take saxophone lessons, or enroll in a martial arts class. Of course, he might do this as a result of other decisions he has made, but again, those decisions will guide his actions in those areas.

The conditions of your life are a precise combination of all of the decisions you have made.

Everything you do is preceded by a choice; your own choice. One might say, "Yeah, but if you're forced to do something by circumstances, or by physical violence, then it's not your choice." We will see later on that although this is an accurate statement on the surface, it hides a more fundamental truth. We will see that a person is always at source-point over his or her life! We will also see how the decisions you make directly affect your feelings and emotions, and how you can use the power of consciousness to feel better.

A decision, or a choice, or a state of being is an example of a quality. As we said before, it's impossible to observe a decision, we can only see the effects of the decision. However, a quantity is much easier to understand, for one can just look around and observe it. The chair you are sitting in, the floor, the tree in the backyard, the sun, moon and stars are quantities, for they can be seen and felt.

The difference between a quantity and a quality is that the former can be known directly from observation, and the latter cannot. The actions of James may be quantified, but not the motivations; we may say, "James practiced for 2 hours today," but that might not tell us *how* James practiced: we might have to write a book just to describe that!

Science has based its entire system of thought upon the idea that, "If something is observable, it is valid." And this is a good way to operate, because opinions vary. It is always possible to tell whether something is good or not by looking at it, and using it. However, we can get into trouble in life by always basing our decisions only on what we are able to observe, for if what we are observing is repellent, we are stuck! If there is not enough money for instance, then thinking and talking about the lack of money will not be beneficial. Later on, we will discover how to get out of that trap.

1.5 Consciousness Is Eternal

WE know that every person and every life form, in order to enter the physical universe, has to be born, and has to die. But what is birth and death? It's funny, but birth and death are the two single most important events in anyone's life, but they are largely ignored by science and in our schools. We say, "Well you're here, what difference does it make how you arrived? And there's nothing you can do about leaving either." That is true, but birth and death are ignored not because they are not extremely important, but because our scientific framework cannot agree on how and why these events occur. In the spirit-mind-body paradigm, however, the explanation is simple: birth is the animating principle entering a body, and death is consciousness leaving the body.

We look at the lifeless body and say, "Father is dead. He lived a good life, but now he's gone." However, all we know for sure is that the body is no longer alive. What happened to the animating principle, the personality we referred to as "father?"

Let's try to answer this question with an analogy…

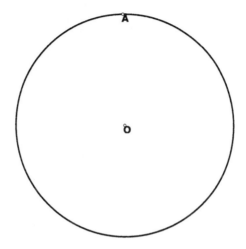

Figure 1.1: Life as a Circle

Let's say that a person's life is represented by a circle (Figure 1.1). When Dad is born, he is at point A on the circle. He travels along his life path in the physical body, around the circle and reaches…point A again, which is his death. Birth and death are at exactly the same place on the circle, for A is both the entry point and the departure point for something eternal, which we call consciousness, or self awareness. In other words, the animating principle enters the physical universe temporarily, and then leaves it.

Consciousness is a quality, meaning that it cannot decay, age, or die. Bodies die, because they are quantities, limited collections of material particles. If you leave your car out in the backyard for years and years, it will rust and eventually fall apart. My sister-in-law had a barn that she did not maintain, and over the years, it deteriorated and finally collapsed. This principle is known as entropy. In the physical universe, there is a tendency for matter and energy to naturally go from a state of order to a state of disorder. But consciousness is different.

Once consciousness achieves self-awareness, it's forever. To understand this, look at the circle again. Once you have completed it, there is no way to tell where it begins or ends. On a square, there are four easily recognized corners. Even on a curved figure, there are places that have sharper curves, and you can recognize beginnings and endings. A circle (and a sphere in 3 dimensions) looks the same no matter where you go on them. This perfection of form is a good representation of the animating principle, and is the closest physical representation to a quality I can think of.

In this book, we say that there really is no such thing as death, just a transition from one way of being and perceiving, to another. "Death" is experienced in truncated form during sleep. Consciousness departs for "dreamland," leaving the body behind.

However, you are conscious even when asleep, for dreaming is also a state of consciousness! In dreams, you see things and have experiences, just like you do in waking moments. These experiences may feel different, and sometimes they might be bizarre or even frightening, but they are real in the sense that you perceive them. In fact, I remember waking from a nightmare in a cold sweat, terrified. All during the next day I could not get the dream out of my mind, so for me, that dream was even more realistic than real life! I have also had positive lucid dreams that seem more real than "reality." I would bet that some of those reading this have had similar experiences.

We're sad when someone we love dies, for it is no longer possible to interact with them in a physical sense, but we don't have to be afraid for them, for they are still conscious and aware. Consciousness in its native, non-physical state feels wonderful and once the death process is complete, one re-emerges completely into the pure, positive life force energy of Source.

My sister, who is definitely not a new-ager, told me that mom appeared before her one day after work, 30 years after her death, as she lay upon the couch in her living room. Now of course we could simply say that my sister has a vivid imagination, but her excitement and certainty about the experience convinced me that she had actually seen our mother. Many, many people have had similar experiences, and if you checked around with your friends, I'd bet at least one of them would be able to recount something similar.

My friend Mark's father died a few years ago. At the funeral a young child suddenly cried, "I see grandpa!" pointing his little finger about ten feet above the casket. Remarkably, none of the mourners in this conservative Catholic family raised an objection, and many looked into the face of the child, awed, as he stared with his mouth open into the space above the coffin. At the most fundamental level, all of us instinctively recognize our divine nature.

Once a person gets the idea that he or she is an eternal being, life seems a lot less threatening, and world events do not seem to invoke the same fear and anxiety. If you know you are going to continue no matter what happens, you can worry a lot less and enjoy life a lot more.

Here's an interesting statistic:

There are approximately over 7 billion people on earth. Let's say that the average life span is 65 years, which means that on average, there are about 108 million deaths every year on planet earth, about 3 every second. Dear reader, there are beings shuttling in and out of here at an astonishing rate! And that doesn't even count animals and insects. Death is an entirely natural process, and is nothing to be afraid of.

1.6 Focus

WHAT about birth?

The idea of incarnation is important because it illustrates, on a broad scale, another characteristic of consciousness: focus.

Focusing is the concentration of attention. When working a crossword puzzle or reading a book, for example, a person focuses his or her attention on the material, thereby excluding awareness and perception from everything else. In the material universe, focusing occurs when matter and energy coalesces; as when water molecules in the air come together to form clouds.

The focusing of consciousness can be likened to what happens when you take a magnifying glass out on a sunny day. The glass focuses some of the billions of photons (marked with a "P" in Figure 1.2) into a beam of light which appears on the ground as a point of light. The point of light is analogous to an individually focused consciousness, with its unique personality, associated with a physical body.

The point of light is not different from the light that surrounds it, it just perceives from a different point in space/time. The ocean of light surrounding the point may be said to be more broadly focused, that's all. It has a broader awareness, a more expansive consciousness. In this analogy, the light that surrounds the point is the non-physical counterpart to the incarnated personality.

The beam may be likened to your connection to the non-physical part of your being. Without the beam, there can be no point of light in the first place!

Also, photons are constantly moving in and out of the beam and the point so it is always connected to the whole.

The point of light is focused very intensely, but has given up its complete connection to the whole; it has traded off its broader awareness of self so that it may have a series of temporary, but very powerful experiences. That is the purpose of incarnation.

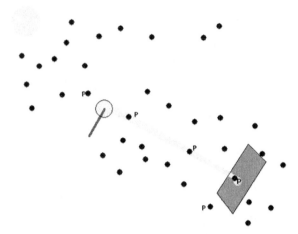

Figure 1.2: Magnifying Glass and Photons

At the amusement park, you go on rides which scare you to death and often provide a near-death experience. Why? To feel powerfully! When you're on that roller coaster going 100 miles an hour and you hit that sharp turn and you feel your body trying to slide out of your seat and fly into the air to certain death...well, all I can say is that a lot of people get off on that. It makes you feel so alive! What such experiences do is focus life force energy through you so fast and so powerfully that it just feels incredible. You become a powerful vortex for the energy of life!

When a being incarnates into a body there is always a connection to a broader consciousness, even though it sometimes feels that we are completely isolated into separate personalities. This broader consciousness is sometimes called "higher self," but regardless of the name that is placed upon it, it is the source of inspiration or intuition, and a permanent connection to the greater you to which you will return at the moment of "death."

Imagine a bathtub full of water. When the drain is opened, the water quickly flows through it and forms a vortex. The water in the vortex is focused very intensely and is moving very quickly in comparison to the tranquil water sitting in the tub. But it's the same water. Just as individual photons move in and out of the beam of light, so to do water molecules move into and out of the vortex. It's the gathering together of the water that creates something recognizable and distinct; the rest of the water is just sitting there in an unfocused condition.

When consciousness incarnates it sort of gathers itself together and experiences from a physical body. At death, a being lets go of the body and expands outward, like a gas released from a container or a shower room full of steam when you open the door. The steam wants to expand, it's a natural process. So is death. Death isn't a snuffing out of awareness, it's an expansion of awareness!

1.7 A Short Diversion

THE astute reader will notice that we have been contradicting ourselves for the last several pages. First we stated that consciousness is a static and that it has no mass, and now we are talking about the focusing of consciousness as if it were energy. Let's just say that consciousness, being a pure potential, is not limited by the restrictions of matter and energy. Being completely non-physical in nature, it has the ability to mold itself in any way it chooses.

We can certainly agree that consciousness has the ability to think and that thoughts have some kind of existence ("I think therefore I am" as Descartes said). Probably, most of those reading this book have, at one time or another, been able to pick up on the thoughts of another person; we call this intuition, or psychic ability, or ESP. If you have ever been able to do this, you know that a thought is discernable and tangible.

I have been getting quite good at knowing who is on the phone before I pick it up; for some reason I am able to receive the thoughts of the person calling. Two people in love may be in such great communication that each knows what the other is thinking before words are spoken; sometimes people who know each other intimately may finish sentences for each other. Somehow, thought and consciousness are able to interface. In the next chapter we will talk about thought, matter, and energy as being interrelated, each an aspect of the same thing.

We can speculate that although thought is so subtle that it cannot be detected or measured by any scientific instrument, it has the tiniest little bit of mass. In this conception, matter and energy are ultimately composed of thought, and all material things have a sort of quasi-consciousness, even though it may be different from human consciousness. In that sense, all things are alive. This doctrine can be (loosely) called Panpsychism.

Even though this idea has not been particularly popular with Western philosophers and has been adopted in a more religious or spiritual context, it can be associated broadly with a philosophy of process, which began with the Greek theoretician Heraclitus of Ephesus (born 540 B.C.) and in the twentieth century is often associated with the British mathematician and philosopher Alfred North Whitehead.

Today, modern physics imagines very small processes (quantum phenomena) combining to produce the physical objects that we can see and feel with our human senses.[1]

Interestingly enough, one of the bedrock laws of science is the law of conservation of energy. This law states that 'energy can neither be created nor destroyed.' If that is so, however, then all of the energy in the universe has existed, without reduction or increase, from the very moment of the beginning of the universe. In effect, it necessitates the adoption of some sort of "Big Bang" cosmology, which requires the creation of a whole lot of stuff instantaneously from nothing (a gigantic contradiction), or requires that the universe is eternal, having no beginning or ending (another gigantic contradiction).

Without the guiding, directing, and animating hand of consciousness, the origins of the physical world must remain a mystery.

All right, enough of that. Back to the subject!

Focus is just attention to something. When a person practices the piano, his or her attention is (hopefully) oriented to that set of activities. The more that person studies and plays, the better they get. A wise woman (Esther Hicks) once said that genius is just a lot of attention to a subject, and that is very true.

Focus is how someone gets from a decision and into effective action. If you are clear in your vision of what you want, your actions will be effective. If you are not clear, you may be working very hard and not getting anywhere, even with a strong will to succeed. How long and how hard you focus on something is a measure of your intention. Strong intent combined with clarity equals success!

Focusing automatically excludes that which is not relevant to the activity; in that sense, it is a tuning in, a narrowing of attention to a specific task. The ultimate example of focusing is birth, and the ultimate example of un-focusing is death, but life itself is a gradient scale of focus. The daydreamer never gets anywhere, for his attention is never on anything long enough.

Why do we need to know all this? Because the Universal Operating System responds to how we focus our thoughts. This is a strange concept for those of us rooted in the scientific method, for we have been taught that thought is ephemeral and irrelevant. While it is true that the operation of the UOS is invisible to our human senses, so is the operation of radio and television! We can't see the signals which our receiver

---

[1] For an excellent general treatment of these concepts, see the Stanford Encyclopedia of Philosophy, which is still, as of this writing, available free on-line.

picks up from the antenna on our roof, but we can't doubt the sound that comes out of our speakers.

Radio and television signals are examples of electromagnetic energy, which can be measured by instrumentation, but the implementation of the universe's operating system is a subtle energy phenomenon.

It turns out that the universe does respond to our thoughts, beliefs, and emotions, and does so very precisely and accurately.

The Vibrational Universe

2.1   Looking at Matter and Energy from a Different Perspective

SCIENCE says that everything in existence is made of atoms. In the atomic model of reality, an atom contains a nucleus surrounded by an electron cloud. The electrons are proportionately as far apart from the nucleus in an atom as the planets are separated from the sun in the solar system. So the atom is 99.9% space.

What is going on inside the atom? Well, electrons are located in orbitals around the nucleus, but it is not possible to pinpoint exactly where the electron is. So we use the term electron density, which is the probability of finding an electron in a particular part of the orbital. An orbital is an allowed energy state for an electron, with an associated probability function that defines the distribution of electron density in space.

This is just a fancy way of saying that electrons are oscillating madly around the nucleus, but not randomly.

The atom is vibrating within itself. All things vibrate, because all things are made of atoms and are therefore internally in motion. When something ceases to move, it dies. To understand this, look at a sample of dead tissue under a microscope. Or, go to the morgue and look at a cadaver.

In essence, an atom is a vibration!

The design of the atom can be understood from an examination of the solar system (see Figure 2.1). We know that the sun has (at least) 9 planets, orbiting in an elliptical fashion around the sun and themselves spinning upon their axes.

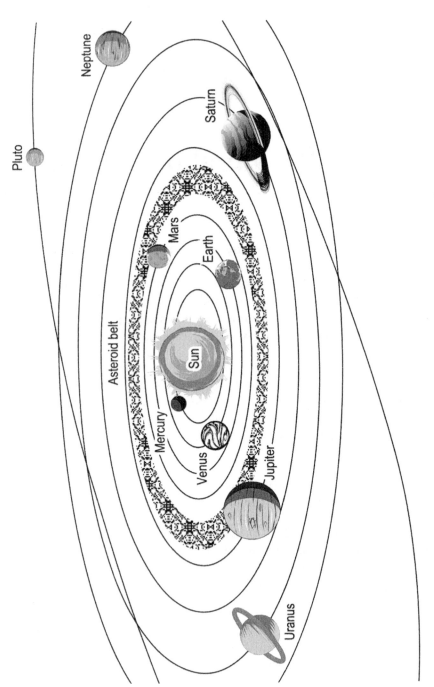

Figure 2.1: "Planets Orbiting the Sun." Image courtesy of pixshark.com

In the solar system, the earth is 93 million miles away from the sun, and it is considered one of the inner planets. If we consider the entire volume of space mapped out by the orbit of the planets, and compare that to the tiny volume of space occupied by the mass of all of the planets, we can see that the ratio in the solar system of space to mass is zillions to one. So too with the atom – it is almost entirely space. Now consider that the mass of the planets themselves are all made of atoms, which are mostly space... We can see that matter is very illusory, even though it appears quite real and solid to our senses.

Imagine that the actions of planets rotating on their axes (giving us day and night) and orbiting around the sun are speeded up, like a reel of film that gets drawn faster and faster through a movie projector. We would see the planets madly spinning and oscillating around the sun. If we speeded up the projector big time, the individual planets would become invisible to our eyes and the solar system, if shrunk to the size of an atom, might look like a tiny nucleus surrounded by an electron cloud.

In this analogy, the atom is just a bunch of tiny particles vibrating in space.

Matter and energy are composed of atoms, and atoms are themselves vibrational in nature. And so matter and energy may validly be regarded as vibrational. If that is so, then, since everything in the physical universe is made of atoms, we can say that the universe itself is vibrational in nature. Science tells us that the light that bounces off the objects in our world and reaches our eyes sometimes behaves as a particle, and sometimes as a wave. Waves are vibrations, so I think we are on solid ground in looking at the world vibrationally.

The material in the following chapters will be presented with this idea in mind. The reader should understand that I'm not trying to contradict the laws of science, because I don't know enough to do that. I'm just giving them a different spin! I'm doing this because I think it's fun to look at things from a different perspective. I have found that looking at life from a vibrational perspective leads to some very powerful, practical and helpful ideas that can simplify our understanding of life. So, with the understanding that our discussion is purely speculative, here goes!

2.2   If Matter is Mostly Space, Why Do We See Anything as Solid?

If something is vibrating very quickly, we cannot hear it. A dog whistle, for example, generates frequencies of sound that are too high for the human ear to detect. It's similar for a very low sound. The human ear can only pick up on vibrations in the range of about 20 per second to about 20,000 per second. When the tuner in your radio is set to 103 FM, it picks up only on the signals in that particular bandwidth, the rest are excluded.

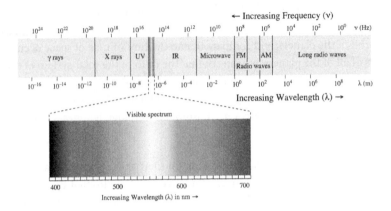

Figure 2.2: The Electromagnetic Spectrum (EM spectrum.svg). Image courtesy of Wikimedia Commons.

The electromagnetic spectrum is itself a scale of vibration. At one end are radio waves, which are very low frequencies and at the other end are gamma rays, which are very high frequencies. Actually the spectrum begins at 0 and goes to infinity, so we really don't know the full extent of it.

Light defines the visible universe, yet visible light is only a tiny portion of the electromagnetic spectrum. If this diagram were drawn to scale, the visible light section would be an almost invisible vertical line. The human senses can detect only a very, very small portion of the known range of universal vibration. With instrumentation, we can go out pretty far on the electromagnetic spectrum, but in order to make sense of it, the data must be arranged so that it resolves within the tiny bandwidth of the human senses. In other words, a gamma ray counter may beep, or display a mark on a graph, but we cannot really see or directly understand gamma rays:

The unaided eye perceives very little; but even with instrumentation, data from the broader electromagnetic spectrum must be transposed so that it can be understood (see Figure 2.3). Our science does a good job of guessing, but science still cannot see clearly beyond the range of the human senses. In fact, no one has ever directly observed an electron, or a proton, or a quark. The knowledge we have about the makeup of matter is composed of very clever educated guesses, and bolstered where possible by experimental testing.[2]

Therefore, our knowledge of the universe must always proceed from the prison of our human sensory information, and that is a good thing! It is a wonderful thing

---

[2] Richard Feynman, the Nobel prize winning physicist, has said, "It is not true that we can pursue science completely by using only those concepts which are directly subject to experiment." (Feynman *Lectures on Physics*)

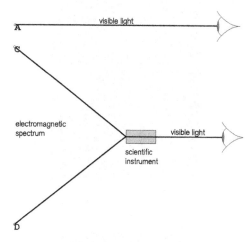

Figure 2.3: Mapping the larger electromagnetic spectrum into the range of human vision

to be human, but that should not devalue the experiences of other life forms. There are billions of galaxies out there, and probably lots of other intelligent life. It would be arrogant indeed to claim, from our limited human viewpoint, that we have all the answers. Many ideologues and dogmatists do so claim, but if you have ever been around one of these chaps for a while, you quickly grow weary of their rigid point of view.

Because the human senses directly perceive so little of the electromagnetic spectrum, our reality is really a narrow band of vibration within the vast, universal bandwidth. What would "reality" look like to a being who perceived in the X-ray or gamma range of the scale, or at the submicroscopic level? Probably a lot different than ours! Physicist Robert L. Forward wrote a fascinating book, *Dragon's Egg*, exploring this theme. Another brilliant writer, the mathematician Stephen Baxter, explores a similar idea in his novel *Flux*.

The following crude analogy (see Figures 2.4 and 2.5) demonstrates how something vibrational might be interpreted as solid. Consider a ball with a rod attached, mounted upon a shaft (top). When the shaft is rotated slowly, we can see the ball creep along its orbital path. But if we take that ball and rotate it fast enough, the ball turns into a solid torus, or donut (bottom).

The rotation pictured here is only going a few revolutions per second, but the ball, from the camera's point of view, has turned into a solid looking ring (a torus).

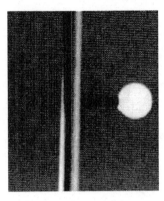

Figure 2.4: Ball mounted on shaft.

Figure 2.5: Ball rotating on shaft.

However, what if it were possible to rotate the ball so fast that it appeared, to our eyes and our touch, to occupy every position along the ring at the same time? The torus would be indistinguishable from a solid, motionless object.

We can say, from a vibrational perspective, that the solidity or reality of anything is a function of how fast or slow it is vibrating, relative to our senses. The three states of matter, gas, liquid and solid, reflect this idea, for we discern a decreasing amount of internal movement; the molecules of a gas are moving more quickly than those in a liquid, and in a liquid more quickly than in a solid.

The atom itself, being vibrational in nature, is the building block for matter. The senses of the human body are themselves composed of vibrating atoms; therefore, the perception of anything can be considered an interfacing of vibration. In this conception, what appears as solid and real is vibrational compatibility.

Just as the human ear is unaware of the existence of the dog whistle, once two vibrations become too distant from one another, it is impossible for one to perceive the other. Stated another way, we can say that only vibrations that are in the neighborhood of each other can see each other. This concept is extremely important, for it means that what we perceive as reality is simply a matching of vibration.

This idea seems strange, does it not? For it is clear that when we strike our hand upon the desk, our hand, and the desk itself, is very solid indeed. Solid objects appear to our senses as stationary; unmoving. The universe around us seems all too real; when we bang our foot into the wall, we become painfully aware of just how real it is. Nevertheless, the apparent solidity of our world is a vibrational interpretation of our senses.

Even a solid, seemingly motionless object must have a vibrational footprint. A simple experiment with a rotating wheel (see Appendix A) shows that when the frame rate of the recording device exactly matches the rate of rotation of the wheel, it appears to be motionless. In other words, if you had a camera that could record an image once every second, and you had a wheel that rotated once every second, the wheel would appear to be standing still. In this way, two exactly matching vibrations can appear solid and unmoving to each other. In this conception, anything that is perceivable must, in some way, be vibrationally active. So everything in the universe is, in some sense, alive.

Just as a radio tuner is only able to receive one station at a time, it isn't possible to be aware of all vibrations at once. The radio, by selecting or tuning in to one set of vibrations, makes that program "real," automatically excluding all others. And that is a good thing, otherwise we would hear 50 programs at once, causing confusion and sensory overwhelm. That is what the senses of the human body do. They focus perception into very narrow frequency ranges, so that all members of our species may have general agreement on what "reality" is. And of course, different species will see things differently, and will have a different reality. Certainly an ant or a fly or an amoeba or a plant will have a different experience than a human! Those experiences are a natural result of the way their bodies and senses have been designed.

For further discussion of this issue, see Appendix A.

2.3   Emotions are also Vibrational in Nature

WE'LL take our ideas one step further and suggest that human emotions are vibrational in nature. Later on, we will further extend the vibrational concept to thought. When the universe is viewed as vibrational, it is possible to apply the physics of vibrational interaction to simplify things that seem pretty complicated and mysterious.

If consciousness exists independent of physical bodies, then feelings/emotions must have a spiritual component. In other words, because consciousness continues its existence beyond the death of the body, it must perceive and feel independent of the body. In our conception, the physical reactions accompanying emotion are primarily the result of the effect of the animating principle on the body, just as in the idling automobile, an increase in the engine rpm is caused by the actions of the driver. In other words thought, emotion, and matter and energy itself are a vibrational continuum. In this conception, thought can have an important effect on how you feel, and even affect physical health. Of course, emotions can also be changed by the ingestion of chemical substances into the body, or indirectly by viruses or exposure to the environment. Nevertheless, anyone who is even remotely self-aware has been able to consciously change his or her mood by a change in attitude or belief.

The ability to directly and consciously change how you feel is an inherent ability of consciousness, and is the most important skill any person has. Like any skill, however, in order to gain proficiency, it must be practiced. This empowering theme will weave itself throughout the rest of the book; we have just been laying the groundwork for it. When you gain the ability to determine how you feel under any circumstances, you have achieved personal freedom; and that is something very precious indeed.

The ability to consciously change how you feel is only possible if one conceives of consciousness as an independent entity. In a purely mechanical view of consciousness, one is simply a victim of the vicissitudes of environmental or bodily conditions. When you feel crummy, there is a biological reason for it, so go get some drugs, or undergo expensive surgery, or just ride it out and hope you get better. Such a philosophy confuses cause and effect, and is promoted by those who want to control you. A person who believes he or she is a piece of meat is easily manipulated; one merely has to create fearful scenarios in the mass media to cause anxiety in the population at large. When the causative principle of consciousness is taken out of the equation of life, hierarchical societal structures are possible. Like lemmings, individuals submit to the latest news headline or crisis, meekly accepting the "solutions" that are offered, which usually involve some sacrifice by the populace. This is a great idea for those who like power and control, but a bad idea for the average Joe.

2.4   The Role of Emotions

EMOTION, like light and sound, has a range from low to high.

Someone at a lower level of emotion simply can't comprehend someone at a higher level. So it is futile to argue with someone who is "out of your range," for they cannot understand you.

Emotionally speaking, a person can always feel a little bit above and a little bit below where he's at, because we are usually not stuck in one emotion and, as conscious beings with free will, we have the ability to quickly adjust. However, it is very hard and almost impossible to make a big jump all at once from a negative emotion to a positive one, and vice-versa. Have you ever noticed how irritating cheerful people are when you're angry? You just want to smack them, or tell them to shut up and go away! That is because vibrations that are too different from each other clash, like two sour notes played on a piano.

When two people argue, it's a safe bet that vibrationally they are far enough apart so that each does not perfectly comprehend the other. I have heard people say, "I understand you, I just don't agree with you!" Certainly, it is possible to have understanding and also a difference of opinion, but true understanding should not cause upset. When vibrations get too out-of-whack they conflict. A classical music lover, for example, might not be able to appreciate the saxophone gyrations of Charlie Parker!

Your thoughts and your decisions not only can affect how you feel, but can literally determine what you perceive. Here is an example: Several years ago I remember doing some recording from my computer sound card, off an ancient VHS tape in another room. I had previously put my remote from the VHS on my computer desk, right in front of me. After working on the sound card, I needed the remote again. I remember I stared right at it for two minutes without seeing it. My thoughts were simply not tuned to "VHS remote." They were tuned to "computer sound card," because I was having trouble with it. I swear, I sat in front of my computer and looked directly at that darn remote without seeing it, wondering where it was. Only after I left the computer room, searched the TV room and came back, did I perceive it. By that time my thoughts were tuned to "TV remote." That which is real is that which is perceived, and that which is perceived is a match, vibrationally, to our thoughts! That is because our thoughts direct where conscious attention is focused. Even though the eyes of my body stared right at the remote, it did not impinge upon my awareness. If consciousness is purely biological, such a phenomenon is unexplainable.

Vibrational "tuning in" occurs all the time in life. When you are playing a game of tennis, for example, you aren't thinking about cooking a gourmet dinner. You are on the tennis court concentrating on your game. When a person "tunes in" vibrationally, he or she naturally engages in activities that are a match to the decisions he or she has made. This places people at different positions in space/time, depending upon the content of their thoughts. This may seem obvious and trivial indeed, but it isn't, for this principle is how the universe itself is organized. In other words, we live in a universe of attraction and combination. Things that are attracted to each other come together, and those that do not are excluded. This idea is reflected in the behavior of matter and energy; two atoms combine to form a molecule only if their atomic structure is compatible, which is to say, only if they are vibrationally compatible. Two people hang out if they like each other, and if they do not they avoid each other.

This idea can be expressed as like attracts like. This is the most important principle in the Universal Operating System, and we'll be talking a lot more about it later.

2.5 The Impact of Thoughts on How You Feel

Now we make one final assumption: that thought itself is vibrational, that it too is alive. A thought is alive because it proceeds directly from consciousness, which is the animating principle of the universe.

This is not a new concept. A meme, for example, is a self-replicating idea that is transferred from person to person. Richard Dawkins, who coined the term, says that a meme should be regarded as a living structure, not just metaphorically but technically. Examples of memes are tunes, catch-phrases, fashions, and ways of doing things. Dawkins would disagree with our use of the term, for he presents the meme as a biological entity, analogous to genes in biological evolution. Nevertheless, the meme is now recognized as a unit of intellectual or cultural information that can pass from mind to mind. In that sense, it is alive.

If thought is vibrational, and the universe around us is vibrational, then maybe the two can interact. In other words, maybe our thoughts and choices about things can actually influence the quality of our lives.

We have said that an atom vibrates within itself, and, we will say, so does a thought. Both are internally alive. If you don't believe that a thought is alive, perform the following experiment: flip to one of the pages of this book and put a thought on one of the pages: "Hi there!" or something like that. Go back to reading for a bit, and then, when you think of it, return to that page. Did you pick up on your thought?

Thoughts can be felt, even if they can't be seen or heard by the senses of the body, or measured by instruments. Thoughts come directly from consciousness, and can be picked up directly by consciousness. That is how remote viewing can occur. Rigorous protocols have been developed in this field; even the military has experimented with it in information gathering.[3]

All of us have probably experienced the impact of thoughts and emotions; it is often easy to sense a person's mood not only by the position of the body, but also by a detection of their emotional energy. In this book we accept the idea of the aura, or energy field, which surrounds the human body; in fact, it is essential to our presentation. Science does not accept the validity of the aura because it cannot be measured directly

---

[3] See the books *Mind Reach: Scientists Look at Psychic Ability* by Russell Targ and Dr. Harold Putoff, 1977; *Mind Race* by Russell Targ and Dr. Keith Harary, 1984, and *Mind Trek: Exploring Consciousness, Time and Space Through Remote Viewing* by Joseph Moneagle, 1993. Moneagle was an original participant in the now declassified U.S. government's Stargate psychic spying program.

with current instrumentation. Since it is only possible to directly measure and quantify the electrical potentials of brain waves, science says that mind and consciousness must exist in the brain. But EEG measurements do not measure consciousness, they only measure the brain's electro-neurological activity. In our vibrational model of the universe, the brain's electrical activity is an observable effect of the animating principle interacting with cellular structure.

Barbara Brennan, former NASA scientist, has documented the human aura in her books and calls it the Human Energy Field.[4]

In our model, the human energy field is a field of life force. Life force is a subtle energy phenomenon, which we'll look at in Chapter 3.

Even if it's not possible to accurately describe consciousness, or directly measure the Human Energy Field, it is possible to *feel* the energy around a person. If you have ever been confronted by an angry person, you know exactly what I'm talking about. If you have ever been in the presence of someone truly joyful, you know how wonderful it feels. And if you've ever felt love from another person, that feeling is unmistakable. Love is the quintessential communication between one conscious being and another! Love is what consciousness *is*.

It may not be possible to precisely quantify the human energy field and write equations about it, but it is surely real. Emotions can be felt at a distance, because emotions are vibrations and travel through space just like radio waves. So we will operate on the assumption that there is some sort of energy field surrounding a person, and that this field of energy can change its properties: anger feels different than joy, apathy feels different than grief, boredom feels different than exhilaration.

Without getting too involved or complicated, we'll say that the aura surrounding a person is a field of life force energy and is a product of the animating principle of consciousness, and that a person's thoughts, decisions, and preferences can change how he or she feels. This idea is common to all cultures that have ever existed on earth; in Hindu, Chinese, Mayan and our own Native American cultures, the animating principle was and is understood. It is only recently that the scientific method has eliminated consciousness and man's spiritual nature altogether from consideration. Although the scientific method has improved our society materialistically, its insistence that "only that which is observable is valid" has separated mankind from true knowledge of Self. It has placed the causative principle in the background, elevating the importance of matter and energy to a senior position. In this way, we have been taught that human beings are essentially victims, a slave to enzymes, chemical imbalances, and a harmful environment. One of the purposes of this book is to re-elevate consciousness to its proper position in the spirit-mind-body framework.

---

[4] In *Hands of Light* and *Light Emerging*.

2.6 The Scale of Emotion

F OR simplicity's sake, we will say that a pleasant emotion like joy is a high vibration, and a rotten emotion like fear or anxiety is a lower vibration. Each person can, through his beliefs, choices and thoughts, determine which emotion he or she feels.

Emotion can be graphed on a scale from lowest to highest[5] as shown in Table 2.1.

The scale from bottom to top represents an increasing feeling of positive emotion and less resistance to life experiences; from top to bottom it represents an increasing feeling of discomfort, stress, and negative emotion.

---

[5] Taken From: *Beyond Psychology: An Introduction to Metapsychology* by Frank A. Gerbode, M.D..

Emotion	Attitude
Apathy	"I give up."
Grief	
Propitiation	"I'll do anything to make it up to you!"
Sympathy	"I feel your pain."
Fear	
Anxiety	
Hidden Hostility	He's smiling in your face and stabbing you in the back. Says one thing and does another.
Callousness	"Tough for you. Just do it."
Anger	Out of control, lashing out at the world.
Antagonism	"Hey! Come over here and let me kick your butt!" Feistiness.
Boredom/ Complacency	Yawn
Conservatism	"Things are fine just the way they are"
Interest	"Hey that's cool!"
Enthusiasm	"Wow! Let's do that again!"
Exhilaration	"I feel fantastic!!!!!"
Serenity/bliss	Complete connection to Source, or God force, or life-force energy. This is the feeling consciousness has in its native, non-physical state.

Table 2.1: The Emotional Scale

As you descend the scale, you get dumber and dumber. As you go lower and lower emotionally, the intellectual function turns off. To understand this, remember the last time you felt apathetic. Thinking straight is almost impossible in the presence of that listless "I don't care" feeling. So not only does it feel rotten to be in the lower emotional vibration levels, it is also dangerous. Interestingly enough, intellectual intelligence has a lot to do with emotion, for the happier you are, the brighter you are as well.

Everyone is somewhere on this scale, because anyone who is conscious is feeling something. The scale itself is actually connected; it loops around from bottom to top. Remember our circle analogy from Chapter 1; birth and death are at the same place on the circle. So at death, a person leaves the body and re-emerges into a complete union with the totality of Self, fully experiencing consciousness in its native state, and going right to the top of the scale.

Life force energy, when it is not distorted or blocked by resistant thought, defaults to a feeling of joy and well-being. Positive emotion is experienced by consciousness in its native state. The emotional scale is essentially a measure of how much life force energy you are letting in and the degree of blockage or distortion of that life force. Therefore, simply eliminating resistant thought will make you feel better! This is the idea behind meditation. In fact, when the mind is completely quieted and there is no thought at all, it is possible to reach a deep, quiet place of serenity and power, and a feeling of oneness with self and with life; but that is another topic altogether. Life on planet earth with its incredible contrast and diversity forces you to make choices! Therefore, in practical living, it is not possible for most people to achieve a state of pure no-thought. It is vital, however, to understand the crucial importance of thought and its impact on how you feel.

"If the default is a feeling of well-being," you might say, "then why are so many people miserable?"

The answer to that question is different for each individual, but if you examine the religions and philosophies mankind has developed, most of them are negative:

- Souls are born with original sin (or karma). [tainted before you ever begin]

- You have to struggle and work hard for everything you get. [the universe is lined up against you]

- Challenge builds character. [only by overcoming the negative can you reach the positive]

- You'll get your reward in heaven. [you can't really find joy while on earth, so shut up and get to work]

- Human nature is animalistic and primitive; therefore, human beings need to be controlled and disciplined. [you can't know what's best for you, because your instincts are inherently flawed]

- If you don't behave you should be punished. [thus reinforcing negative behavior]

- Things never go as smoothly as you plan them [obstacles are inevitable]

- And finally, the formula that succinctly expresses mankind's worldview: All good things must come to an end. [But the bad stuff, that can last forever].

With belief systems like that, is it any wonder so many of us have difficulties? We have been taught to deny ourselves and disconnect from our divine nature. It's sad, but it doesn't have to be that way!

The only way you can feel a negative emotion is to mess up the flow of your own life force energy. I'll try to diagram this later on in the chapter.

One of the most important principles of the Universal Operating System says that *you can change the way you feel, simply by making a decision to do so.* The scale of emotions essentially shows the degree of presence or absence of life force energy. When thought is in alignment with your goals you feel positive emotion, and when it is not, you feel negative emotion. Therefore, self-limiting thought of any kind will always cause a descent on the emotional/vibrational scale. When you criticize your-self (or another) for example, you will always feel negative emotion, at least briefly. As you become aware of how you are feeling in response to your thoughts and de-cisions, you will become aware that you have direct control over every emotion you experience. Understanding this begets an inner feeling of power and self-confidence.

In our model, the human energy field is a cocoon of life force that surrounds and penetrates the body's cellular structure and keeps it functioning. Contained within it is the programming for the body's cellular structure, and for perfect health.

Have you ever wondered how the body can breathe at night? What keeps the body going when you aren't there? Science says that the autonomic function maintains the body, but that is just putting a label on something without explaining it. Life force energy (animating principle) is the engine that powers the body's biological systems, and is the source of the "autonomic function." In the spirit-mind-body framework, we place spirit as the causative force, not biology!

In the non-physical model of consciousness, *thought interfaces directly with the life force energy that flows through your human energy field*, causing a rise or fall in emotion and also affecting the body's health. In other words, life force and thought are both creations of consciousness; both are aspects of the animating prin-ciple. Your thoughts are therefore the steering wheel that drives the vehicle of your body/mind/spirit system.

2.7 "Negative Energy"

SIMPLE observation shows us that dark is just an absence of light. There is no *source* of darkness, there is only a source of light! Darkness is not a force, and it has no power unto itself.

If you think about that for a while, examine your own life, and observe others care-fully it really starts to make sense. You will discover that in every case, the experiences you have are a direct result of your patterns of thought and belief, not negative (or random) forces. You begin to see the causative principle alive in your life, and in the lives of others. You begin to discover more about who you really are. You begin to understand and properly assign cause and effect, and that makes you more intelligent and powerful in your own life.

Once you get the idea that life is supposed to be a positive experience and not a negative one, you can turn your life around. You can prove this to yourself by simply quieting your mind, opening up, and relaxing into yourself. I learned how to do this, oddly enough, by observing my cat. One day while watching a baseball game on TV, the little guy settled down about five feet away, closed his eyes, relaxed, and began to purr. I could see him literally open up to something that obviously felt really good, but what was it? After trying it myself a number of times during meditation, I got it. It's an opening up to what I can only call a feeling of well-being that seemed to surround me and exist within me. Eventually, I realized that feeling of well-being *is* me! In this way I personally made a connection with my own life force and discovered its inherently positive nature.

The validity of the assertions in this book must be personally tested in your own life. Looking to the experiences of others for proof will not work, for what works for another may not work for you. The Universal Operating System, in other words, is entirely subjective. Later we will see that a vibrational universe is responsive to the thoughts of every individual in it.

2.8 Free Will

THE principles of the Universal Operating System make no sense at all unless there is free will. If your choices have little or no effect on your life, then why bother to live at all?

However, if free will exists, then why do we experience so much of what is not wanted?

My observation of people has shown me that happy people never doubt the existence of free will. Almost always, those who doubt the idea simply have experienced a life in which the fulfillment of their desires has been frustrated to a greater or lesser degree. Happy people are happy because they have been successful attaining their goals.

Observation of this phenomenon has led many people to conclude that life is a crapshoot, and that good or bad luck is the reason some are successful and others aren't. Or perhaps it's heredity, or the circumstances of one's birth, or natural talent. All of these factors are outside an individual's control, which naturally negates free will. But if free will has any meaning, then why can't everyone be successful?

We will discover the answer to that question in detail. In a nutshell, you always get more of what you focus on. The Universal Operating System responds to what you have your attention on, and that is very often not the same as what you want. Remember, the nature of our universe is vibrational (or, at least, can be viewed that way without contradicting the laws of science). Thought and emotion are also vibrational, and action follows thought. The environment and the people in it respond to the vibrational pattern you set up within yourself, by the way you think and feel about life. This assertion is testable in the laboratory of life; knowledge of the state of your being and observation of how others react to you is sufficient to confirm it. The only prerequisite is enough self-awareness to know what you are thinking and how you are feeling.

The way you feel is always a precise indicator of your true state of being. Inside of you is a flawless guidance system called the emotions, which tells you precisely how much life force you are letting in, and what you are doing with it! By paying attention to how you feel, it is possible to guide yourself smoothly and effortlessly through the river of life.

Observation of others is also instructive. You will find that an individual always causes the responses of their environment, even if that person is not conscious enough to understand it.

The principle "What you focus on you get more of," is the reason some succeed and some fail. It is the reason that a business that looks so promising at the start can wilt and die, and another that starts from nothing can prosper. It is also the reason that a person can work and work and work and never get anywhere.

2.9   The Way You Think Affects the Way You Feel

Let's look at an example of how thoughts can direct feeling.

Barb is depressed. She and her boyfriend Thorpe had a fight and he said some nasty things to her. He told her that she was a shrew, that her nose was too big, and accused her of not liking any of his friends.

Barb now has a choice: she can either believe what Thorpe said about her, or stay within herself. Barb has decided that what Thorpe said is true: she went to the mirror in the bathroom and sure enough, her nose does stick out a little too far. And maybe she is a shrew; after all, Thorpe just wanted to go out with his buddies, even though he promised her he'd take her to dinner and a movie last night. And Thorpe is right: she doesn't like most of his friends. One of them is unemployed and the others drink too much.

Then Barb begins to think about her life and realizes that she has had a succession of relationships with the same kind of man: unsupportive, selfish, and unloving. So here we find Barb sitting alone on the couch when the phone rings; it's her friend Jill.

"How are you Barb?" Jill says.

"I feel like crap."

"Don't tell me: Thorpe," Jill says instantly.

"You got it."

We'll postpone the rest of Barb and Jill's conversation until Chapter 4, and just say that during their talk Barb makes three new decisions: firstly, that she's going to dump Thorpe. That gives her an immediate lift. The second decision she makes is that from now on, she won't even look at a guy unless he is genuinely interested in her. And the third decision she makes is that her nose is just fine, thank you, and if some guy doesn't like it, too bad!

Just before she hangs the phone up Barb says, "Jill thank you so much! You saved my life!" While it's true that Jill was a sounding board for Barb and might even have made some helpful suggestions, Barb raised her emotional vibration solely on the basis of the decisions she made. Barb did it all: first she made herself depressed, then she made herself happy again, even though the reality of her relationship with Thorpe is still unchanged.

This little example is just one of thousands we could discuss, but the important point is that thoughts determine feelings. Self-limiting thought makes you feel rotten, but you can change all of that by getting some new ones!

Of course, when your life is really messed up, it's harder to get more positive thoughts because the reality surrounding you is so negative. Nevertheless, we will see that there is nothing intrinsic to reality that *forces* anyone to feel good or feel bad. Feeling bad is a learned habit that can be easily and safely broken.

2.10 Modeling the Human Energy Field

L ET's finish our discussion about thought by modeling the human energy field. We're going to show a couple of diagrams as analogies; I'm not saying the Human Energy Field looks like this, although some psychics say that they see meridians of energy in the aura:

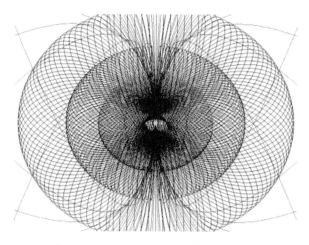

Figure 2.6: Artist's conception of a Human Energy Field with meridians

(Note: this is a computer generated image). In this conception, which is based on the geometric figure called the torus[6], life force energy enters and exists through the top and bottom, swirling around, bathing the body's cellular structure in life force energy. Because thought is at the same fantastically high vibration as life force energy, thoughts can directly affect the condition of the human energy field.

Imagine the body lying within the center of this diagram, fed by life force. Every thought you think affects the meridians of energy, blocking or distorting, or opening up the spigot and allowing it to flow smoothly and freely. The default condition is a feeling of happiness and well-being, because that is the quintessential nature of life force energy. It is divine, and so is every life form on the planet (and the planet itself).

Emotions (energy-in-motion) are a direct reflection of the condition of the energy meridians. Self-limiting thought adversely affects your own life force. The most important relationship in your life connection is the one between you, and you!

In our model the human energy field is the source of the autonomic function. Within it are the design templates for human DNA. One cannot construct a building without a blueprint, for all physical structure originates from a template of thought. The human body is a physical structure; therefore, the design of the body must also proceed from thought.

As you can see from Figure 2.6, the human energy field is self-contained. The energy within it is constantly recycling, coming back upon itself, and refreshing itself. It is self-referencing.

---

[6]Arthur Young suggested that consciousness can be modeled on the torus, and I have used this brilliant idea as well.

In this model, illness results from a blockage or a distortion of life force energy to an area of the body. If there is a long-standing pattern of negative thought, it will be reflected in the body. A change in thought allows the human energy field to re-adjust and bounce back into proper shape. Life force energy *wants* to flow smoothly and evenly because that is the way it has been designed.

Every human energy field is connected to the universe at large; individual personalities interface with a universal field or medium of consciousness, just as the vortex in the drain is fed by the still water in the bathtub. This postulated field of consciousness permeates all things and exists from one end of the universe to the other. In a vibrational universe, thought is transmitted instantaneously within this medium.

2.11 The Power of Self-Referencing

Figure 2.7: The Worm Ouroboros, a serpent eating its tail (Aztec).

THIS symbol was known in Egypt, China, India, Africa, North and South America. It has traditionally been represented as the eternity of time, or condensation and distillation, or death and renewal, etc. I believe the symbol is also a metaphor for the self-referencing nature of consciousness.

The ability of something to influence itself is called self-reflexiveness. Self-reflexiveness can be observed in nature. For example, when a plant is moved, it automatically adjusts the position of its leaves to get as much sunlight as possible. A tree grows a fruit that contains a seed, which then grows into another tree, continuing the cycle. The natural life processes of nature mirror the design of consciousness.

This idea is used in the construction of fractals. A fractal is made by defining a relationship and setting up a precise set of initial conditions for the relationship, using mathematics. Then the relationship is tested, and the result is plugged back into the relationship, which is again tested and the result plugged back in, over and over. This is done for a predetermined number of tests, or until the result of the testing reaches a conclusion. Just as the thought of a conscious being may influence the life experience of the thinker, so too does the result of the fractal testing influence the next test. Mathematicians call this procedure iteration, and it is identical to what we said occurs in the human energy field. If you look at the fractals below you can see that the idea of self-referencing is very powerful, for it can be used to generate images which look completely real. (I had to eliminate the color information for publishing, but these still look pretty real.)

Fractals are generated by constantly re-referencing a defined relationship. Fractals show up in nature, from ferns to landscapes to clouds. The self-referencing nature of consciousness is mirrored in the construction of everything we observe in our world.[7]

One of the properties of fractals is worth noting. If you had a computer program to look inside any of them, you would see, upon magnification, similar patterns repeating themselves no matter how deeply you went. The patterns are never identical, but they are enough the same to be noticeable. This property is called self-similarity. We see this all the time in life. When you get stuck in a rut, the same old things, people, and situations seem to appear and reappear. The situations are rarely identical, but similar enough to make you tired of it. I knew someone who left town because she was sick of her job, her boyfriend, and her apartment, but it was hardly a year later when I heard, through a mutual acquaintance, she had quit her job in the new city and broken up with another boyfriend. Life itself is self-referencing!

---

[7] First four fractals from *The Science of Fractal Images* by Peitgen and Saupe, Springer-Verlag, 1988. The last fractal is Barnsley's fern.

Table 2.2: Fractals

"The intellect has little to do on the road to discovery. There comes a leap in consciousness, call it Intuition or what you will, the solution comes to you and you don't know how or why."

—- Albert Einstein

Part II – THE UNIVERSAL OPERATING SYSTEM

The Operating System of the Universe

THE fundamental assumption of the Universal Operating System is that consciousness is the animating and directing principle of the universe, and that consciousness designed the universe to be responsive to itself. Otherwise, life is random and our choices have no meaning.

An observant person will, by applying the principles herein, be able to determine the truth or falsity of the above statement. It is an experiment well worth undertaking, for one eventually discovers the joy and power that lies within Self.

THE UNIVERSAL OPERATING SYSTEM

A model describing how the universe at large interfaces with consciousness

3.1 The First Principle: Consciousness

1. Consciousness is pure, positive, creative potential. Consciousness is the animating and directing principle of the universe.

2. Consciousness by definition is self aware. Self-awareness is eternal. Everyone reading this is an eternal being. The body you occupy will eventually die, but you will BE forever!

3. The product of consciousness is thought. A thought is a postulate, a consideration, a decision. In our model, thought is vibrational in nature (see Appendix).

4. In our model, space is not empty, but filled with a subtle, universal medium composed of thought energy. Thought travels instantaneously within this medium from one end of the universe to the other.

5. All matter and energy in the universe is vibrational in nature, and is ultimately composed of thought. A thought can be considered energy; the fundamentally smallest quanta of energy in the universe (see Appendix B).

6. All thought is conscious, being a creation of consciousness; so all things in the universe are, on some level, conscious. This means that your thoughts interface directly or indirectly with everything in the universe!

7. The decisions of consciousness are meaningful; that is, the universe and everything in it is responsive to the decisions you make.

8. The fundamental characteristic of consciousness is choice. In other words, what consciousness does, in every moment in its interaction with the physical universe, is choose, prefer, and decide. Choice is a necessary result of living in a physical universe, for one is constantly presented with a variety of objects, people and situations.

9. The quintessential nature of consciousness is a feeling of well being, a knowing of itself as perfect, and an understanding of itself as unlimited.

10. Because consciousness is a pure potential, it cannot be quantified or directly measured; only the products or effects of consciousness can be measured. We define consciousness to be non-physical in nature.

The statements above mean that your decisions determine your experiences.

Consciousness is inherently pure, positive and blissful in its native state. This is self evident to anyone who has felt a true connection to his or her inner self, for it evokes a feeling of power, joy and confidence. Negative attitudes, beliefs and feelings simply vanish in the presence of such understanding, just as a light illuminates the darkness. It is impossible to prove this scientifically, for all answers to questions about consciousness is consciousness itself. Consciousness is "the alpha and the omega."

Consciousness is eternal because it is a potential (or an energy which is so refined that it cannot be measured), and so cannot age or decay. Consciousness is eternal because it is self aware, and once self aware, is eternal.

These statements are appropriately circular, for something that is eternal has no beginning or ending and cannot be described intellectually.

From this inherent knowledge of well-being, and the desire to experience itself in all possible ways, all of existence flows forth.

From the First Principle comes the interface to consciousness, the Universal Operating System.

3.2   The Law of Free Will

THE Law of Free Will states that every conscious being is free to choose, in every moment, for it is not possible for one person to think, feel, or act for another. In other words, every conscious being has the ability to decide for himself or herself, without interference from anyone else. This is guaranteed by the design of consciousness itself, which is self-referencing and self-reflexive.

Consciousness – and your own self-awareness – is non-physical and eternal: therefore, you are completely free from harm. IF you understand this your decisions can be based solely on personal integrity. Harm only applies to your body. Nothing permanent to your SOUL can ever happen to you in a physical lifetime.

The Law of Free Will allows a conscious being to change his or her state of being, or conception of itself, at any time, through the exercise of conscious choice.

Free will is meaningful because the universe at large, including all consciousness within it, will respond appropriately to your choices. This statement cannot be proven broadly, only personally.

Free Will allows a person to be a deliberate, conscious creator of his or her experience. Because others also have free will, it is not possible to create in the experience of another, except by another's conscious consent.

The Law of Free Will is inseparably bound with its two compatriots, the Law of Vibration and the Law of Attraction. Together they guarantee ultimate personal freedom, if properly understood and applied.

3.3   The Law of Vibration

THE Law of Vibration states that all things can be considered to be vibrational in nature.

Since thought is a vibration, then a conscious being, through thought, is a vibrational transmitter and receiver. This phenomenon occurs subtly and subjectively, at the level of consciousness itself, and cannot be directly measured or objectively verified. Nevertheless, anyone who has ever had a sudden hunch or inspiration, or used his or her intuition, has experienced it.

A sound is a vibration, carried upon molecules of air. An activated thought is also a vibration, carried upon a universal energy created by consciousness. This energy has been traditionally called chi, prana, or life force energy, and has been known and understood for thousands of years by many cultures on our planet. Everything conscious in the universe is interconnected.

In the Universal Operating System, only activated vibrations are important. In other words, think of a tuning fork. In its deactivated state, a tuning fork which resonates to "A" has a potential vibration, but a quiescent tuning fork sends forth no signal. Only when the tuning fork is struck does it emit its characteristic sound.

The implications of this are enormous, for a person may have many subtle and fleeting thoughts, but only the ones that are continually activated will have any effect.

For example, a person may have been negative his entire life, and the ratio of his thoughts and actions may be 100 to 1. He may have thought millions of negative thoughts and only a relatively few positive ones. He may be known by all as a complete cynic, and unsuccessful in life. Nevertheless, at any time, he may deactivate the old patterns of thought by ceasing to place his attention upon them. Then, like the vibrating tuning fork, they will gradually die away, and there will be an immediate improvement in the way he feels, and subsequently, in the conditions of his life. It is simply a matter of using the inherent power of consciousness to shift focus from the unwanted vibrations to the wanted ones; the negative vibrations will deactivate and the positive ones will become dominant.

It is often thought that if a person has been negative in the past, he or she will continue to have negative experiences. It is said that negative thinking and negative behavior build up over time and has led to the idea of karma. However, if you look at things from a vibrational standpoint, you understand that a newly struck note on the piano, for example, will quickly drown out the old, sour notes which gradually die away. In other words, a new thought or decision can quickly nullify old decisions.

The Universal Operating System is dynamic and instantly responsive to activated vibrational content. It is infinitely subtle and will respond to you according to the vibrations which you have activated within yourself, via your thoughts, beliefs, and feelings. Therefore, when a conscious being changes his or her beliefs, he or she broadcasts a new vibration which feels different, and to which the rest of the universe responds. In a vibrational universe, every conscious being can be in control of the way he or she feels, and how others respond to him or her.

It may seem fanciful to say, "change your thinking and you will feel better," but I guarantee you from personal experience that it works. Thought may be ephemeral and immeasurable, but the character of your thought has a powerful effect on the emotions. You can test this premise by thinking negatively about yourself for a while, and noticing your position on the scale of emotions presented in Chapter 2. Now try some uplifting thoughts. You may find that it is difficult at first to even think anything positive, but once you do, you should find yourself moving up the scale.

There is one other very important implication of the Law of Vibration, namely, that it is impossible ever to deactivate a vibration by trying to fix it. For as soon as one places one's attention upon something, one has activated it.

Try not to think of an elephant!

Most therapies involve wrestling with problems and difficulties in an attempt to get rid of them, but all this does is activate the unwanted vibration more and more! As long as the tuning fork is continually struck, it will continue to emit a sound. The only way to deactivate the tuning fork, or any thought, or any feeling, or anything unwanted, is to cease to pay attention to it. This is what Jesus meant when he said 'turn the other cheek.' (Such therapies can be effective, but only because the client eventually takes attention off the uncomfortable vibration, deactivating it).

This is an enormously powerful and significant datum, one which occupies a primary position in the Universal Operating System. Such an assertion may seem absurd, but I assure you that it can be tested, and I invite you to do so. A theory is worthless unless it can be applied!

In short, every conscious being is sending and receiving vibrational signals to and from the rest of the universe. These signals are carried upon a medium of subtle energy, which in our model is not visible or measurable with instruments, but which impinges in every moment at the level of consciousness itself. Your personal signal is the result of activated vibrations within you as a direct result of your thoughts, beliefs and feelings. Even the dullest person is thinking and feeling something!

3.4 Your Broadcast Signal to the Universe

WHAT does it mean to say that a person is broadcasting a "vibrational signal" to the universe? Think of each thought as a combination of waves, each of a certain shape, amplitude, and frequency, like a sound wave. Many of us have seen the waveforms that a piece of music will make when it is graphed on a computer screen. Likewise, consider that a thought also generates a unique pattern of vibration. As an analogy, consider the experiments in vibration conducted by the German researcher Hans Jenny, who used sound, electricity and other vibrational stimulation to produce clearly defined visual models of vibrational effects.[8]

---

[8] *Cymatics Vol. II* by Hans Jenny, Basilus Presse, Basler Druck– und Verlagsanstalt German Edition (English translation), pp. 103, 105.

Figure 3.1: Images produced by vibrational stimulation of various liquids.

Figure 3.2: Image produced by vibrational stimulation of various liquids.

How is thought transmitted from one place to another? A vibration needs a medium through which it can propagate. Light, for example, is a wave (and a particle), and it would seem that there must be some universal background substance that allows light waves to move through the universe. However, a famous and cleverly designed experiment by Michelson and Morley in 1887 was unable to measure it, and the fabric of space was assumed to be a vacuum. Now we know that physical space is actually a seething cauldron of particles and anti-particles winking in and out of existence from the quantum level, even though we have been unable to directly measure it.

(In fact, in order to make quantum mechanics consistent with general relativity, the mass density of the vacuum is required to be around 10^{94} grams per cubic centimeter! If true, there would be about one trillion times more intrinsic energy within the volume of one hydrogen atom than is contained in the physical mass of planets and stars, out to a radius of 20 billion light years.)[9]

In an attempt to explain immeasurable phenomena such as intuition, remote sensing (ESP), remote viewing and quantum entanglement (non-locality), a few scientists have postulated the existence of a subtle force which is not yet directly measurable, but whose effects can be seen. This is not such a startling concept, for scientists already theorize that more than 90 per cent of the matter in the universe is invisible, and can be detected only by its gravitational effects on stars and galaxies.

3.5 Subtle Energy

T. M. Srinivasan, Ph.D. (Co-Founder International Society for the Study of Subtle Energies and Energy Medicine, Science Editor, International Society for the Study of Subtle Energies and Energy Medicine) defines subtle energy this way:

> The term Subtle Energy (SE) is of recent origin…Several scientists in the United States (Tiller, Bearden, Rein, Putoff, Green, Srinivasan) have studied SE and its effects. Though each has developed his own nuanced theory of SE, in general they all tend to concur that SE phenomena is related to a type of unified energy, and is not just a physical field of very low magnitude.
>
> Contemporary quantum physics has mathematically described and predicted the presence of a unified energy which underlies conventional

---

[9] Source: Dr. William Tiller, "A White Paper on the Law of Cause and Effect." These calculations have led some to propose the existence of "zero-point energy," or "vacuum energy," and people get really excited about finding a way to somehow extract this energy. However, no one knows whether this energy really exists, and if so, how much of it there is. Most mainstream scientists scoff at such an idea. Astronomers calculate the mass density of the vacuum to be around 10^{-28} grams per cubic centimeter, or basically zero! Only a competent scientist understands the reasoning behind these calculations. As laymen, we have to assume that the vacuum density of space is undetermined.

transverse electromagnetic (EM) vectors. The concept of a subtle energy underlying EM fields was first introduced by Bohm and Aharonov in describing quantum potentials as an implicate order "embedded in" our normal 3-D space. It has recently been proposed that an additional implicate order is embedded within the quantum potentials. This higher-dimensional space is composed of an energy which has been called time-reversed waves, non-Hertzian waves, longitudinal waves, scalar waves, or zero-point energy.

The classical EM fields have been under investigation since the laws of Maxwell were established more than 150 years ago in England. We know all about the physical fields; we can generate, manipulate and use them for purposes such as long distance communication, computer applications and measurement techniques that are proliferating all around us. However, our knowledge regarding SE fields is expanding slowly.[10]

Paul Von Ward, a researcher and writer in the fields of consciousness and frontier science, suggests that subtle energy is a conductive medium through which consciousness acts on matter and energy. He writes, in his article titled "Subtle Energy in Human Senses and Powers," that

subtle energy appears to contribute to many processes not currently explained by conventional science: telekinesis, remote sensing, gut-feelings or heart-based intuition, healing by prayer or other psychic means, bio-communication between species, etc. Since these processes have tangible effects that can be documented, but not explained by the known principles of the electromagnetic force, they require that we hypothesize another force through which conscious intent acts on the affected objects, senses, and cells.[11]

Dr. William A. Tiller, Professor Emeritus at Stanford University, in the May/June 1999 edition of the journal *Science & Medicine* (Vol. 6, No. 3) writes,

There is now a large body of experimental data in the general area of psychoenergetics associated with the directed focus of human intention. Remote influence experiments with healers, remote viewing experiments, investigations of psychokinetics, clairvoyance, homeopathy,

---

[10] From "A Subtle Energy Technology for Noise Reduction in Physical and Psychophysical Systems", Jan, 1999, By T. M. Srinivasan
[11] See Paul Von Ward's website at www.vonward.com.

and other phenomena confound the established picture of natural laws but attest to the existence of processes requiring the involvement of emotional, mental, spiritual, and other inadequately understood domains of nature.

Because these domains are incompletely understood, they might best be grouped into a category called 'subtle energies.' Future research may delineate and distinguish the various characteristics of these energies and their usefulness in medicine. For now, subtle energies can be defined as all those energies beyond those presently acknowledged in physics.

In the paper, Dr. Tiller describes six scientific experiments using directed intention, all of which produced noticeable (and sometimes extreme) recorded effects on the human body and/or physical objects. In one experiment, Dr. Tiller created a gas discharge device surrounded by dielectric (non-conducting) coated electrodes, and connected to a power source that applied a 450 Hz AC voltage. The system was "tuned" to keep voltage peaks 10 to 15 percent below the breakdown threshold of the gas, and electron microavalanches passing through the gas were monitored by a pulse counter that could be set to record any pulse over a predetermined size. Dr. Tiller writes,

> Typically, the pulse counter was set so as to just miss the largest microavalanches traveling across the gas. Thus the system was poised but yielding a zero count for many hours until a human subject attempted to influence it. Most of a thousand or so experimental runs involved a person holding his hands about six inches from the device and intending to increase the count rate. Over a five-minute period, the number of recorded pulses was often in the range of 50,000. If the subject's hands were not held near the device but the intention was still to increase the rate, total counts could be increased from zero to the range of 10,000 to 20,000 within five minutes. If the subject's intention was directed away from the device by being focused on a different mental task, no change in the count rate occurred.[12]

The effects of subtle energy are clearly demonstrated in the work of Cleve Backster, who discovered in 1966 that a person's thoughts and emotions can affect the cells of plants. Using a polygraph detector hooked up to a leaf of a dracaena cane plant, and standing at a distance of five feet or so from it, Mr. Baxter formed a picture in his mind and thought, "I am going to burn that plant leaf," immediately noticing a wild agitation on the polygraph equipment. This discovery has been confirmed many

---

[12] Dr. Tiller holds several patents, and he has written four books and more than 300 papers. For a more detailed report on the experiments, see the article or visit www.tiller.org.

times over the years by Backster and others, and is often referred to as "The Backster Effect."

Robert Stone, in *The Secret Life of Your Cells*, shows how in the 80s and 90s Mr. Backster conducted hundreds of hours of experiments with leukocytes (white cells). It was found that even when these cells are separated from the body, they can be affected by a donor's thoughts, and especially by negative emotion, even though the donor may be miles away.

Backster's plant experiments show that positive emotion has no effect on the testing equipment, but in the presence of negative emotion, the equipment shows immediate bursts of electrical activity. This is a fascinating phenomenon, for not only does it indicate awareness on the part of the plant; it also indicates that well being is the norm! And it's also cautionary, for if your thoughts can affect cells at a distance, then there's no doubt they can permeate every cell of your body as well.

In this book we say that the human energy field is a nurturing field of subtle energy. Our thoughts, beliefs and feelings have an enormous impact on how we feel, and can even affect our health. Misalignment and blockages in the human energy field can cause stress and eventually physical illness. People who hold grudges often get sick, because, in their upset with another, they continuously hold themselves in vibrational disharmony.

3.6 "Phantom DNA"

EXACTLY what is subtle energy? No one really knows, only that it may be responsible for effects currently unexplainable by science.

In 1985, a Russian physicist, in experiments with DNA, noticed a peculiar "phantom effect" when it was exposed to coherent laser light. When the DNA was removed from the scattering chamber and the space measured, a distinct pattern was still present. If the space was left undisturbed, the effect was observed for up to a month. The author of the experiment concluded that "some new field structure is being excited from the physical vacuum."[13] This phenomenon was only observed when DNA molecules were tested.

Perhaps this phenomenon is the precursor to the recognition and indirect measurement of the subtle energy of life force energy. (This is just speculation on my part, and not a conclusion of the experimenter. It is interesting nevertheless).

---

[13] "The DNA Phantom Effect: Direct Measurement of A New Field in the Vacuum Substructure" by Dr. Vladimir Poponin. http://twm.co.nz/DNAPhantom.htm

3.7 Oh, Really?

M AINSTREAM science scoffs at the idea of subtle energy, understandably, because it cannot be measured. The alternative, however, is a strictly biological basis for consciousness, which many of us simply find unacceptable. There is simply no way to objectively show the existence of subtle energy, or the nature of consciousness, one way or the other. People will believe what they want to believe!

An experiment that purported to show the stupidity of those who believe in a non-physical basis for consciousness was performed a few years ago. A psychic who claimed to see auras was placed in a room with several compartments, whose doors were closed. The psychic claimed to see auras behind every doorway. When the doors were opened, the number of people present was less than the number of compartments, proving that the psychic was a fake.

Implicit in this experiment however, is the assumption that only a physical being has an aura. No allowance is made for the claimed properties of consciousness itself, which is said to exist independent of physical bodies. In other words, if consciousness is indeed non-physical in nature, then non-physical personalities certainly exist, but the parameters of the experiment simply assume that consciousness comes in "lumps" associated only with physical containers. It is not permissible to disprove something simply by ignoring it!

Of course, by the same token, it is impossible to prove empirically that consciousness does exist, for there are no points of reference for it in the physical universe. It is not measurable. A non-physical basis for self-awareness is simply assumed and assigned to something ephemeral called "consciousness," which is also impermissible experimentally. It is claimed without objective proof that although consciousness cannot be measured, its effects on physical objects are measurable. This empirically illogical reasoning (coupled with the fact that charlatans are known to exist) naturally drives some scientists and skeptics batty.

Nevertheless, we must admit a draw in this debate, for there are plenty of data "fudgers," swindlers and con artists even in medical and scientific disciplines. In short, if consciousness has a non-physical basis, it is automatically outside the realm of scientific proof or disproof.

3.8 Non-locality

W E could say that the Universal Operating System responds to individuals according to the principle of non-locality. A good definition of non-local is, "unmediated action at a distance." To mediate is to act as a go-between. Therefore, a non-local interaction between object A and object B (or person A and person B) would not touch anything measurable. The key word in the last sentence is measurable! Experiments have shown that two subatomic particles can affect each other over great distances. If it is possible for subatomic particles, it surely is possible for consciousness. What if the vibrations of thought are carried within a universe wide subtle energy field, or medium, compatible with consciousness itself, connecting all things in existence? If thought is indeed the building block of matter and energy, such experiments become more understandable.

Another way to understand non-locality, or "spooky action at a distance" as Einstein referred to it, is to recognize that in physics, time is given a separate axis, along with the three physical dimensions, and can be considered as a separate dimension.[14] If this is so, then it is obvious that time, being a scalar and present everywhere in the universe, is in instantaneous contact with every point in space.

Just as radio waves are invisible to human senses yet can be detected by a radio receiver, so too can the impulses which carry the subtle energy of thought be detected by human consciousness. We've already talked about how easy it is to pick up the strong emotions of anger, hatred, grief, and joy, but it should also be possible, if our theory is correct, to detect thought impulses as well.

There are times when a person has a premonition of a future event which then comes true, and which cannot be explained by observation. For example, knowing who is calling on the telephone before you pick up, or knowing when a guy is going to turn into your lane and cut you off. There is a certainty that accompanies these events which brings them from the realm of "educated guesses," to absolute knowing. You just feel it, and know it beyond a shadow of a doubt.

And there are times when life-threatening situations put a physical being in contact with non-physical energy. Recently, a NASCAR driver claimed he was rescued from his burning racecar by a non-physical presence. These guys are not what you'd call new-agers, but in a story I copied from my local newspaper, the driver claimed that someone carried him out of the car, even though observers saw no one. Such claims may be assigned to an overactive imagination, but I prefer to take a person at his word.

> NEW YORK (AP) Dale Earnhardt Jr. has trouble remembering those
> frantic seconds when he escaped from his burning racecar. He believes,
> however, that his late father figured in his survival.

---

[14] The mathematician Hermann Minkowski first proposed this in 1908; Einstein used Minkowski's approach to develop his general theory of relativity in 1915.

"I don't want to put some weird, you know, psycho twist on it like he was pulling me out or anything, but he had a lot to do with me getting out of that car," the NASCAR star said. "From the movement I made to unbuckle my belt to lying on the stretcher, I have no idea what happened."

Earnhardt recalled that perilous July day in Sonoma, Calif., during an interview with correspondent Mike Wallace for *60 Minutes* that will be broadcast Wednesday on CBS.

Earnhardt's father was killed three years ago during the final lap of the Daytona 500. The son insists he felt his father's presence on the day when he scrambled out of his flaming car and was left with second-degree burns on his legs, neck and chin. In fact, he said, when he reached safety, he began inquiring about the "person" who helped him from the car.

Earnhardt told *60 Minutes* he grabbed one of his representatives by the collar, "screaming at him to find the guy that pulled me out of the car. He was like, 'Nobody helped you get out,' and I was like, 'That's strange because I swear somebody ... had me underneath ... my arms and was carrying me out of the car.'"

Wallace asks whether that was his father.

"Yeah, I don't know," Earnhardt said. "You tell me. It ...freaks me out today just talking about it. It just gives me chills."

3.9 Coincidence

In a vibrational universe, coincidences are not accidental, but a precise vibrational matching of your signal with others that are compatible.

It is instructive to analyze the word "co-incidence." "Co" is a prefix and my dictionary has four entries, all of them applicable: "1. a) *together, with* as in *co-operation*, b) *joint*, as in *co-owner*, c) *equally*, as in *co-extensive*, 2. A prefix formed from *complement*, meaning complement of, as in *cosine*." "Incidence" comes from the word incident, which means "something that happens, event, occurrence." – *Websters New World Dictionary.*

The word coincidence is telling us that two events are intimately bound up with each other in a non-random way, yet when you look up the word "coincidence" in the dictionary it says "2. An accidental and remarkable occurrence of events, ideas, etc., that sometimes suggests a causal relationship." That is how we use the word: accidental. But the composition of the word is precisely the opposite. Two coincident occurrences cannot take place accidentally; they must be co-responsible for their meeting.

We say the two events are happenstance because we do not perceive the non-localness of vibrational interaction!

The concept of co-incidence can be stated in the following way: *Vibrational proximity determines proximity in time and space.*

You have control, in a broad sense, of those who come into your experience. To illustrate this concept, imagine two guys who work at the same company, getting up in the morning to go to work. One of them is joyful, hops out of bed, gets himself ready and drives to work. The other guy wakes up grumpy. On the way, the joyful guy encounters a few red lights, but finds himself in pockets of traffic which are moving smoothly, and arrives at the parking lot with a couple of minutes to spare. The grumpy guy gets behind a slowpoke, misses all the lights, and in general finds himself in frustrating, slow moving traffic, and gets to work 10 minutes late. Why did the joyful guy encounter a smooth ride and the grumpy guy have problems?

"Coincidence," you say. "Bad luck," another says. "That's life," replies a third. "You gotta take the good with the bad."

I say that the joyful guy matched up with those who envisioned a smooth ride to work, and the grumpy guy matched up with those of like mind, and all received precisely the content of their vibrational signals to each other.

There's no way to prove this assertion other than on a personal basis. You *can* prove it to yourself, however, in this and many other ways. You can perform life experiments and satisfy yourself that you really do have a vibrational signal, and that others respond to it! When you get this idea, you discover within yourself a feeling of power and confidence that you might not have known you possessed. It's fun!

Think of your vibrational signal by imagining that every thought causes the human energy field as a whole to vibrate, or pulse, somewhat like one of the computer animations that come with CD and mp3 players nowadays. The vibrational content of every thought is sent out to the universe at large. Because thought is so subtle, there are usually no immediately noticeable effects, unless the thought is amplified by intense desire or intention. However, over time, continuing focus in an area can cause emotional effects and eventually result in a co-incident event or manifestation.

In this model, it's impossible to con the universe at large. It is possible to fool others with our words, and even fool ourselves, but we cannot fool the universe, because everyone and everything in it is responding exactly to whatever is being focused upon in thought. In other words, the system has integrity. Honesty and truthfulness are built right into it. From this idea we can understand that a person who claims to be happy and prosperous and talks a good game, yet drives a run-down car, is grouchy and irritable and has trouble paying his bills every week, has a gap between the words he is speaking and the true vibration he is offering.

People who work hard but never get anywhere are not primarily focused on the positive aspects of the desired goal. In other words, a lot of people attempt to create their lives by going into action; but action cycles will not solve the misalignment of their thoughts and beliefs. This tells you, amazingly enough, that thought is more important than action in reaching the goal! Or rather, that a little attention to lining yourself up energetically can save a lot of toil. "Work smart, not hard," is what my friend Dave always says.

The easiest way to understand your vibrational signal is to notice how you feel and how others react to you. Your emotions are a direct reflection of your thoughts, and you can, with a little conscious effort, observe that the response of others is not random, but a reflection of your own emotional state. This may seem obvious, but I assure you it's quite profound when you begin to apply this data to your life. You begin to realize that you are determining the precise nature of every relationship in which you are involved, and that evokes an internal feeling of power and confidence.

3.10   You Are the Modulator of Your Vibrational Signal

You are in control of the way you feel and how others respond to you. Just as your ears can pick up on sound waves in the air, so too can conscious beings pick up on subtle energy transmissions of others. Sometimes these transmissions are very subtle, as when you sense a delicate change in mood, or get a hunch; and sometimes they are not so subtle, as in the case of hatred, anger, or other demonstrative emotions. Let's dismiss the fiction that a person's demeanor is determined solely by observing body movements and positions, for this places effect before cause. The movement of the body is caused by the decisions and intent of the conscious being that inhabits it.

An analogy to the vibrational signal of a conscious being is a radio transmission. An AM or FM broadcast transmits a carrier wave, which is then modulated by another signal which represents the content of the program (AM stands for Amplitude Modulated, FM stands for Frequency Modulated). A radio signal can transmit a rock-and-roll concert, a philosophy lecture by Alan Watts, or anything at all, depending upon how the content of the program modulates the carrier. The carrier wave acts somewhat like a horse that carries its rider. The horse may carry a beggar, a king, a lady, or a sack of coal, just so long as the passenger is compatible in size and shape with the carrier.

In the transmission of radio signals, the carrier wave is of much higher frequency than the modulating signal (the signal which contains the information), because it is much easier to transmit a signal of higher frequency, and the signal will travel further. Therefore, a carrier wave of infinitely high frequency would not only travel infinitely far, but would do so instantaneously and with perfect ease. These are the characteristics of a pure potential, or quality, which is how we have been describing consciousness and life force energy. So life force energy, even though we have categorized it as subtle, is very powerful indeed.

In this analogy, life force energy is the carrier wave that is being transmitted through your human energy field at all times, and your modulation of that carrier wave is what you feel inside your skin, and what others feel when they are in contact with you. Emotions, intentions, attitudes, the subtleties of mood and demeanor are all observable and feel-able, from one conscious entity to another.

The content or modulation of your personal signal is determined by your thoughts, attitudes, and beliefs. The strength of your signal is determined by the power of your intention. Interestingly enough, only those who are "tuned in" to your signal can respond to it; just as the more precisely a radio dial is set to a program, the clearer it is heard. So if someone is in your face, you have both dialed each other in very strongly!

No one can tune your personal radio dial except you, so the only way you can perceive something is to already be vibrationally receptive to it. In short, you determine who and what comes into your life and how others respond to you.

Most people would say that if someone is yelling at you, it's the other person's fault. "He's the one shouting, not me!" On the surface this seems reasonable, but underlying the physical manifestation is the attracting nature of your vibrational signal. You are, in every moment, a broadcasting tower to which the rest of the universe responds.

The vibrational model of the universe places a conscious being at complete cause-point in life. The more consciously a person can establish his or her thoughts and beliefs, the greater the likelihood of success.

3.11 Looking at Life Energetically

THE experiences of life can be modeled as a sequence of energy flows. Please pay close attention to the Energy Flows summary below since we'll be revisiting it occasionally throughout the book.[15]

---

[15] From Frank A. Gerbode, M.D. in *Beyond Psychology: Introduction to Metapsychology.*

Energy Flows

- **Reflexive flow** is self to self. These things include your thoughts and be-liefs, your emotional state and the exact nature of your vibrational signal, all of which are directly under your control. Activities involve the things you prefer to do alone, like meditation, artistic expression, working out, etc. The energy flow here is completely within self.

- **Inflow** is others to self: These events are things people do to you or for you, brought to you by the Law of Vibration and the Law of Attraction. The energy flow here is from the outside, toward you.

- **Outflow** is self to others: Teaching, counseling, socking somebody, etc. The energy flow is from you, outward to the universe.

- **Crossflow** is others to others: Watching a baseball game, observing your children at play, etc. Here you are an observer of the actions of others and the energy flows are outside of you.

Your interactions with the physical universe are a combination of one or more of these energy flows. When you play a game of tennis you're engaging in inflow and outflow, for instance; and if you're like me, an internal battle is raging on the reflexive flow!

All of the other flows originate with the reflexive flow. In our society, many people think that outflow is dependent upon inflow. "I did it because he did it to me first," etc. Inflow is often assigned to probability, luck, or coincidence. Crossflow is considered very dangerous, for it includes the entire universe outside of your sphere of influence. However, in this book we are reversing the standard paradigm! We're saying that an individual consciousness is not just a tiny cog in the great machine of the universe, but a powerful co-creator (along with the Universal Operating System) of his or her experience. That is not obvious at all, which is why it has gone unnoticed. It's not obvious until you consciously begin to change your state of being and observe the changes in your life.

When you begin to look at life as a series of vibrational interactions, you begin to understand the primacy of consciousness in the spirit-mind-body framework, and acknowledge your personal power source.

3.12 The Law of Attraction

How is the interaction of vibrational signals managed?

The answer is, through the all-powerful universal law known as "like attracts like," which is also called the Law of Attraction.

The Law of Attraction states, "That which is like unto itself is drawn."[16]

It means that whatever you decide to bring your attention to will be drawn more and more into your experience. In our model, thoughts are magnetic and so attract to them more vibrations like it. It's a subtle energy phenomenon. One might say, "So what? Subtle energy is ephemeral, without substance or importance. It's not real." Well, if you continue to dwell on something your vibration becomes more and more powerful with respect to it. "Coincidences" occur in your life, as you are vibrationally attuned more and more powerfully to the content of your thoughts. The more you dwell on something, the more energy you give to it, increasing the strength of your signal, and the more your activities reflect your orientation. You find yourself meeting people of like mind and finding yourself in situations that are a precise match to what you're thinking and feeling. It takes time for this to happen of course, but because we have not been taught about the power of thought, often we assign our experiences to luck, or chance. We don't make the connection between what we've been focused upon and what occurs in our life, because of the insulating buffer of time. In fact, we often place effect before cause and say, "my thoughts and beliefs are dependent upon what I observe."

Thorpe, for example, says he wants to be wealthy but instead spends 99% of his time bemoaning a lack of money. His signal of "not enough money" is matched up with all other signals of the same kind and therefore, gradually over time, Thorpe finds himself associating with people who do not have enough, and in situations in which there is not enough (like at the end of the month, when there is not enough in the bank to pay the bills), over and over. Unsurprisingly, Thorpe begins to assume that "not enough money" is a natural law of his life.

But this is not true at all: Thorpe lacks money because that is where his attention is all of the time! Thorpe continually creates his life from what he observes, and because he observes the same things, he continues to mindlessly activate the same vibrations and send the same signals over and over again, by the sameness of his thoughts. His action cycles never change, and he attracts into his life the same old stuff. Thorpe's life is a self-fulfilling prophecy, what I call a self-fulfilling idiocy. However, if you explained the subtle energy phenomenon of matching vibration to Thorpe, he will laugh and say, "I think about being poor because I *am* poor, not the other way around." Poor Thorpe. He's got the cart before the horse, and his life will never change until he gets a new way of thinking.

---

[16] From the brilliant lecturer Esther Hicks.

Thorpe says, "My life never changes." But this isn't true at all. Thorpe's life is constantly changing, but it is always changing into the same thing. Thorpe's life is circular, or rather, self-similar. He never experiences exactly the same things because life itself is dynamic, powered by the changing preferences of consciousness. Nevertheless, Thorpe's life is similar enough so that he gives up trying to make it better. What Thorpe doesn't understand is that he always takes his *weltanschauung* (world-view) with him. Like an old acquaintance of mine, she may move to a new city and get a new job, but if she does not change her vibrational pattern, her life in the new city will begin to eerily resemble the old.

The good news is, it is possible for Thorpe to change his mind. This opportunity presents itself in every instant, but Thorpe has no clue that his thoughts and beliefs have any relevance at all. (Mostly when guys like Thorpe change at all, it's because of an accident or life crash, which forces them to alter their way of thinking. When you hit rock bottom, sometimes you see the connection between your state of being and the experiences you have).

Thorpe is not very bright, but IQ is not relevant; the UOS does not care how smart or dumb you are. A change in your state of being will result in a new and different vibrational signal. You become inspired to take different actions and begin rendezvousing with new people. Nothing is ever forever. If there is something in your life that is not wanted, don't wait until the situation becomes a crisis! The universe is a logical place; it isn't random, uncaring, or chaotic. What you focus on, you get.

There is a subtle twist to the Law of Attraction, as Thorpe found out: it does not matter whether you desire the thing you are focusing upon. That which you are thinking and feeling will be drawn into your experience regardless. That is why the rich get richer and the poor get poorer. It is why things seem to snowball, for better or for worse. It's why fighting something you don't want will always draw it into your experience. It's the underlying principle behind the saying, "You eventually become that which you despise."

The Law of Attraction says that it is important to focus on what you want, and avoid focusing on what you don't want. Simple, idiotic really, but hard sometimes to put into practice. Many people, when reading this, will think to themselves, "Focus on what you want, yeah that sounds good." Then they will think about that new relationship, that new job or whatever, and try to get a new attitude. After a few minutes, they realize their thoughts are right back where they were before! After doing this for a while they give up and say, "It's too hard!"

It's hard only because your habit of thought is geared toward what you already have (or don't have). You look around at the old car, you drive the old car, and you naturally can't help but think of the old car! Your vibrational inclination has set you up to only receive thoughts and interact with those who believe just as you do. In addition, your action cycles are all vibrationally geared toward the unwanted condition.

We have often heard people say that it is easier just to keep doing the same thing, even if it feels rotten. This is not irrational at all, in fact, it is entirely logical. Once established, a pattern of thought, belief or feeling will be difficult at first to overcome, because the Law of Attraction is working to match you up with more thoughts and feelings of like kind.

What to do?

Practice noticing and thinking about stuff that makes you feel good. Appreciate what you have. Observe the environment and force yourself to discover things you like, even if it's something as trivial as cloud patterns through the windshield of your car in the middle of rush hour traffic, or the sun coming through the window at work. Find something, anything, that pleases you or about which you can adjust your attitude from negative to positive. If you do this for a little while you'll discover that these things aren't trivial at all, but profound and joyful. Eventually, you'll discover that no matter what you observe, you can feel good about it. And when you do your life will start to change for the better.

The advice in the above paragraph are really tired old bromides; but the fact is, there is no magic wand, no pill, no crystal, no magic healing technique or self-help process that will halt the flow of your own self-limiting thought. In order to change, you have to work at it! However, this work can be conducted joyfully, in the knowledge that *the entire universe is set up to support your choices!* That is the amazing fact of life on planet earth. No matter what you have been taught, the universe exists to supply you with everything you have ever wanted. You just have to know how to ask for it, and then ask for it!

This vibrational work can be conducted primarily on the reflexive flow (which can save you a lot of toil), and it must precede the actions you take. The purpose of this book is not to outline a magic formula for success (that is impossible), but to give the reader an understanding of a few fundamental and powerful principles that he or she can use to improve their personal life situation. I did not make these up because I'm not that bright; and in fact, these principles have been known for thousands of years.

It is only negative thinking which makes you feel rotten and which messes up your life experience. In other words, all of the events from the world around you, all of your emotions and everything you feel is experienced on the reflexive flow, and only you have control over that. Think of a polarizing filter on a camera lens. In order to reach camera memory (or film, in a standard camera) and be recorded, light must first pass through the filter. So the quality of the picture is dependent upon how the filter is adjusted.

I used to observe life with the attitude of a critic: my polarizing filter was always twisted. On the way to work I would critique the driving skills of my fellow travelers, or the make and model of their cars. At work I would do the same with people, categorizing them according to their deficiencies. And my family! Well, all of them were dolts. In fact, nothing was immune from my censure! This way of thinking began to carry over to my view of myself as well; or was I always that way, slopping the pigsty of my personal self-criticism onto others? Either way, it was a hard way of living, and a lot of work besides.

If you want to feel better, you have to find things to feel happy about, and no one can do that but you. However, it is an incredibly rewarding and exciting adventure. Imagine feeling good ALL the time. Seem ridiculous or impossible? Well, it's possible, for your birthright, as consciousness, is a feeling of joy. It's hard at first to change, but that's only because the Law of Attraction is bringing you more of what you have told the universe you wanted. In order to change your life (inflow, outflow, or crossflow), you have to first change yourself (reflexive flow). In fact, the reflexive flow is the key to everything, for you will discover that when you feel better about yourself, the environment will begin to reflect your new vibration back to you in the form of new relationships and manifestations. You'll feel inspired more and more of the time, instead of just going through the motions.

If you are a mostly negative person, as I was, you have to actually practice feeling good. It took me years to establish a critical and jaded world outlook, and when I first began to look on the bright side, it was extremely difficult. But I discovered it's so much easier to change from negative to positive, than from positive to negative, because feeling good is the default for consciousness everywhere! All you have to do is overcome the inertia of habitual thought, and the rest will follow. There is no source of negative energy working against you. You have all the tools you need to feel better about anything, starting right now.

3.13 Consciousness, Feeling, and Action

LOOKING at a human being primarily from the viewpoint of consciousness, and assuming that consciousness is non-physical in nature, we can define 'feeling good' as a default attribute of the subtle energy of consciousness itself. This will seem unsatisfactory indeed for those interested in objective proof, but it can be proven by anyone to himself or herself, subjectively.

When resistant or self-limiting thought is eliminated, you will feel better.

The above statement is true without exception, and I invite you to try it.

It's the reason why meditation is so effective. It will work on any condition or area of life, no matter how serious. Notice that this definition has nothing to do with others changing their behavior, or the environment around you altering itself to please you. Feeling better is completely under your control.

When I figured this out, it amazed me. I was taught that human nature is primitive, barbaric and difficult to change, but it turns out that the only way you can feel bad is a denial of self. It's your own self-limiting thought that sends you down the scale into the lower emotions. One might say, "A good feeling isn't going to pay my bills." That's true, but would you rather be poor and miserable, or poor and happy?

What you will find is that when you get happy, good things begin to flow into your experience, and the unwanted condition begins to change for the better. The subtle but extremely powerful operation of vibrational interaction will begin to tune you in to a different set of people and circumstances, and you will become inspired to new action cycles.

If you suffer from any unwanted condition, you don't want to hear someone telling you to just cheer up and everything will magically get better. But if you want things to improve, you must first start with improving yourself; and that involves feeling better about yourself. It's nice to know that feeling better isn't such a hard thing! If your life is in a rut, you are continually matching up with the same kinds of people and situations, so there is a lot of inertia to overcome. However, unless you change your state of being, nothing in your life will change much, no matter how hard you work at it.

Many people will say that change occurs solely because of action cycles and that a state of being, or "vibrational" effects, has nothing to do with it. Well, the two are inextricably linked. Action follows effortlessly from a state of being that is perfectly aligned to it. The hard work comes when you're trying to *force* a result from a vibrational misalignment. Then, you cannot make enough phone calls or knock on enough doors. Then, you have to sweat and slog for every positive outcome. When someone tells you that an energetic alignment to the goal can make the job much easier, you want to say, "Shut up! Roll up your sleeves and get to work, or leave me alone." The proof is right there in front of you: piles of printouts, phones ringing off the hook, people coming and going like mad. "You see that? If it's so easy, let's see you do it." Objective evidence all points to the same conclusion, but the physical evidence is there only because it is a direct reflection of your state of being. That is the difficulty with objectivity. It can only prove that which already exists!

A business sends out a mailing because it believes that mailings will reach many prospective buyers, but reading a piece of paper or hearing a commercial doesn't alter your inclinations, unless there is something that really connects with you. And that can't happen unless there is a proper vibrational connection between sender and receiver. In our model, anything physical is itself a collection of vibrations, and a representation of the consciousness of the sender.

"You're making this way too complicated," you say. "I send out a mailing because statistically I know that I will get a sales return of 0.7%" Well, nothing statistical or probabilistic is written in stone. Statistical analysis and probability theory are oriented toward the general, and individual results always vary.

Roy H. Williams, bestselling author of *The Wizard of Ads*, describes a study conducted by the Wharton School of Business which attempted to answer the question, "If I invest x dollars what will be my exact rate of return?" A number of large corporations funded a 7-year study which monitored the return on investment in advertising of several dozen small businesses. There were only 3 conclusions reached:

1. There is no correlation between dollars invested and sales return,

2. Results are directly linked to the message, and

3. Results increase with repetition.

It was discovered that two advertisers can invest the same amount of money to the same target audience and one will get no responses whatsoever, while the other will be wildly successful. The key is the content of the message, and then repetition.

The content of the message, however, is vibrational. It is a direct reflection of the consciousness of the sender, and will resonate (or not) with the receiver according to the law of like attracts like. There may be many methods of presenting the message, but these are just the medium that carries the content. In a sense, what is occurring in advertising is simply a vibrational communication between conscious beings, using physical media.

If actions alone determine the outcome, then it should be possible to systematize all activities so that everyone can get the same results, but it does not work that way in the real world. The "X" factor in any set of actions is the subtle, invisible interaction between consciousness.

During Biff Bifferson's seminar detailing his successful sales formula, Biff outlines the precise steps necessary to get the desired outcome, yet results vary widely among the participants. Biff always claims, "You didn't follow my instructions precisely, which is why you didn't get the result." However, the actual reason is that Biff's vibrational orientation cannot be taught to his students, only the actions that proceed from his state of being can be taught.

That recalls to mind the story of the Master and the student. Every morning the Master would lecture. He took off his cap, placed it precisely in the middle of the table, took three deep breaths, and began to speak. On his deathbed, the Master tells the student, "Be faithful to my Teachings and you will have no difficulties." On the morning of his first presentation, the new Master is asked whether he has a full grasp of the Teachings. "Oh yes," he says, "it's easy. The first thing you do is take off your cap and place it in the middle of the table. Then you take three deep breaths..."

A state of being or a vibrational orientation has a great deal to do with how you feel, for if you are properly aligned toward your goal, you will feel positive emotion. How you think determines how you feel and how you feel determines what you do, but no one ever does anything without the *expectation* that it will feel good.

Feeling good is the reason for everything we do, and is the end result of doing anything. You play the game to win the game, and when you win, you feel good. You put out the mailing to increase sales, and when sales increase, you feel good. When more money comes in you feel good because you can buy some new stuff, and when you get the new stuff it's fun to play with it. But you play with it because it makes you feel good! And when it's no longer fun, you throw the stuff in the basement, or in the garage, and call it junk. The point is, if there was something intrinsic in physical objects which made them pleasing or displeasing, we would buy something and be happy with it forever.

Again, we come back around to the circularity of the First Principle. Consciousness is the causative agent of the universe, and it occupies the primary position in all physical activities.

3.14 The Law of Attraction, Continued

WHY is the principle of like attracts like so important? Because we live in a universe which is attraction based. You hang out with people you like, not with people you don't like! In the physical sciences, atomic elements clump together in defined, organized relationships. Sodium atoms come together with chloride atoms to form salt, two hydrogen atoms and an oxygen atom are perfectly suited to combine and form water. A magnesium atom, however, never combines with an argon atom. The Periodic Table helps us to determine which elemental combinations are valid, and which ones are not.

In life, we may take an instant dislike to another person. We say "that guy rubs me the wrong way," meaning that there is a subtle, vibrational/emotional clash. A good salesman in a roomful of people can often immediately recognize those with whom he will have the most success. These are all feel-able phenomena, even though it is impossible to quantify how it happens.

The Law of Attraction can be stated simply: things that are attracted to each other come together, and those that don't remain apart. We apply this principle to consciousness with the understanding that a human being is entirely free to choose the thoughts, beliefs and attitudes that determine his or her vibrational makeup.

The Law of Attraction is inclusive, for it simply matches vibration. It is like an obedient servant, always taking you literally. It is logical, not random. If you focus your attention 99% of the time on A and 1% of the time on B, you should experience 99% of A and 1% of B, no matter what you say you want. And that's what happens. In order to change that ratio, it's only necessary to get a grip on what you give your attention to.

Our friend Thorpe, for example, is so upset about his financial state that he can't stop complaining about it. Many of us do the same thing, and it's a completely natural reaction. Why? Because we know, deep down inside, that life is supposed to be good! If human nature is inherently bad (as some of our earthly philosophies assert) then when we felt bad we'd want to feel worse and worse. But of course that is absurd. We all understand that to feel bad is a sort of insanity, and most of us will do anything in an attempt to feel better, even actions which appear to an observer as irrational!

Unfortunately, when you get into the lower emotions you get dumber and dumber and it's harder to remember who you really are, but that is also when the need to feel better is greatest. Strange as it may seem, even the most irrational act is motivated by the desire for improvement. Understanding this idea helps generate a more forgiving attitude toward our fellow man.

Anger is not always destructive. Anger is only detrimental if you descend to it from a higher emotion. If you have reached anger from a place of apathy, grief or fear, then it feels pretty good! If you have to vent, then vent! Just don't make a habit of it, as Thorpe has, unless you want to keep experiencing the object of your anger. Allow the experience of what you don't want to guide you to what you do want, and begin to focus on that.

How can you always focus on what you want? How do you even know what you should want? I often found myself saying "I don't know what I want!" The answer lies in the emotions. Choosing a path that will serve you will always generate positive emotion, and vice-versa. So if you are confused as to what path you should take, just consult how you are feeling about it. Anything that brings you joy when you think about it will be a valid path, for your emotions are your communication line to your soul.

Far from being irrelevant, the emotions may be compared to the monitor of a computer system, which is the user's interface to everything that is happening within the computer. Running a life without consulting the emotions is like trying to operate a computer without a monitor; there is simply no way to tell what's going on! The mind, through conscious choices, chooses the parameters within which the life path will run. The mind forms the train tracks of your life path. When you get too far out of alignment, your emotions will tell you that you are going off the rails. The great thing about this mind-emotion system is that it is fully integrated and flexible, for one may always change his or her mind about where one is going, and so build a new set of tracks. By always consulting the emotions during this process, one will always be in alignment, and find inner balance.

3.15 Luck

WHY are some people lucky, and others unlucky? It's because "lucky" people are focused on what they want, and "unlucky" people are not. It's as simple as that. An instructive exercise is to look at an area of your life which isn't going well. Write down the particular problem or difficulty you are having as succinctly as you can. Then list all of your thoughts, beliefs and attitudes about this non-optimum area, as soon as they come into your mind, without "editing." If you are honest with yourself, you will find that there is a perfect correspondence between your thoughts and beliefs on a subject, and what you are experiencing in life. In fact, if you simply observe how you think and react during the day, in all areas of your life, you will soon find that you do indeed, "create your own reality," irritating as it might sometimes be! (It's never fun when somebody says "you brought this on yourself," even if it is true.)

When I did this on the subject of money, I was shocked what came out of my head and on to the paper. Stuff like "people who are rich are really screwed-up," "money is filthy and is used to control people," etc., etc., so it is no wonder I was having so much trouble making money, for I was mired in poverty consciousness.

If you do this exercise and find that your thoughts and feelings match precisely with the reality you are living, it is tempting to say, "Well of course! I have these thoughts because that's the way it is. My thoughts just mirror reality." But such a mindset guarantees that you will get more of the same. People sometimes say, "What's real is real and there's nothing you can do about it." But that's like driving your car always looking in the rear view mirror. You have to keep your eyes on the road ahead if you want to get anywhere.

3.16   Desire Amplifies Your Signal

DESIRE for something increases the strength of your signal regarding it, somewhat like turning the volume up on your stereo. Desire = intent. Strong intention just means strong focus on the goal. A person with strong desire is easily recognizable, for he or she seems to exude an energy of purposeful intent.

Any desire is always accompanied by emotion; more resistance to the goal = lower emotion, less resistance = higher emotion. Even though "serious" intent (putting your game face on) is often favored over lighthearted action, more resistance = more difficulty.

Desire is easy to see. Desire is life force. The more life force energy a person is allowing, the more he or she is animated and excited.

People who are good at manifesting have lots of desire and self-confidence. Their action cycles are effective because they are in alignment with the goal; people and resources seem to rendezvous with them effortlessly.

Persons with lots of desire usually feel very strongly, and sometimes their lives can be very dramatic. Those with little desire experience lives without much change or excitement.

3.17   All Beings are Sovereign

A very important consequence of the law of like attracts like is that it is impossible to create in the experience of another. It is impossible to make another happy, or healthy, or prosperous, or change another's attitudes or worldview without their agreement. One may provide things for another, but only with that person's consent, otherwise the proffered items will be rejected. One may hate another and attempt to do him or her in, but these actions can have no effect if the object of these efforts is not vibrationally in range. For example, there are more laws on the books outlawing pornography than you can count, yet pornographers flourish all the same.

It is possible to do anything you choose, so long as you do not resonate to those who wish to impede you. It seems fantastic, but the Law of Vibration and the Law of Attraction supersede all man made laws.

You might say, "That is all fine and theoretical, but what about Pete the criminal who uses violence to force Joe to do his bidding?"

On the surface, it is clear that the use of coercion or violence is a direct violation of the Law of Free Will. However, one must ask, "How did Joe paint himself into that corner with Pete in the first place?" If it were possible to undertake an analysis of Joe's thoughts, it would show a series of free will decisions right down the line, leading Joe to his rendezvous with Pete. In a vibrational universe Joe, in order to meet co-incidentally with Pete, has to have carefully matched vibrational signals with Pete. Fear, worry, and anxiety are great ways to align yourself to something you don't want!

Have you ever noticed how even obnoxious or outrageous people can still attain success? The loud-mouthed salesman or the hypocritical televangelist lives in luxury and it just doesn't seem fair! There is a factor common to them all, however: such persons do not care what others think of them. When you do not concern yourself with the opinions of others, you do not include their thoughts, beliefs and judgments within your personal vibrational signal. Back in the 60s, a strange fellow named "Tiny Tim" appeared onstage with long unkempt hair, lipstick and makeup. He played a ukulele very badly and sang "Tiptoe Through the Tulips" in a shrill screech. Yet this no-talent performer made himself famous!

I am not advocating that you make a spectacle of yourself, I'm only pointing out that when you look at the universe vibrationally, it is possible to comprehend a lot of previously unexplainable behavior.

3.18 Relationships

THE Law of Attraction is very important in relationships. For example, if your boyfriend has 10 nice characteristics and 3 irritating ones, the tendency is to focus on the 3 undesirable traits and try to fix them. But the Law of Vibration tells us that doing so will only activate them more in you and so draw those irritating behavior patterns out in him as well, when he interacts with you. In other words, trying to fix someone else just activates in you what you hate about the other person!

Have you ever noticed how children or pets respond differently to different people? A friend of mine has a daughter that is nasty to her, but when the baby sitter comes, she is a perfect angel. Another friend can get even the nastiest animal to lie down on its back to get its tummy scratched.

Let's say your boyfriend has a habit of chewing very loudly. The more you try to get him to stop, the more he does it. The only way out of this dilemma is not to change him, but change yourself. In other words, he already knows what you want. Now you have to get to a place where you change the way you feel about him to something that feels better. If you can change the way you feel about him to a more positive place, you will see an improvement in his behavior. This may seem a completely irrational statement, but I assure you from experience that it works like magic. It is a logical outcome of the Law of Vibration and the Law of Attraction.

The way to do this is to focus on the ten good traits and ignore the three bad traits, when he is with you. In this way you deactivate the three bad vibrations within yourself, and so your signal no longer finds a matching vibration within him. So if you don't want to do it for his sake, do it for your own peace of mind!

This does not mean he won't eat like a barbarian when he is with other people. It just means he will willingly change the way he eats when he dines with you, not because you have scolded him into it, but because you have changed the way you feel about your boyfriend from one of irritation to one of good feeling, and you get a matching response. Of course this may take a little time, because it always takes a little while for a vibration to fade away, and your boyfriend has a habit of thought and action already established. But in the meantime you feel better.

Of course you could always leave the guy. That is what often happens. There is so much attention to the three bad habits that they become strongly activated within you, and within him. There is no longer any place for feeling good, for those vibrations have been squeezed out by the focus on the bad stuff. You draw out the bad stuff in him, and he does the same with you. End of relationship. And that's too bad, because the ratio of good qualities to bad started out at 10 to 3.

Here is a conversation we might have with the woman about her boyfriend and his bad eating habits:

"Why don't you ignore his bad habits and focus on his good ones?"

"Because I just can't get up and walk away every time we sit down to eat. His chewing is disgusting and I can't help but notice it."

"Then notice something about him you like. After all, you're with him because there is more you like about him than not."

"That's hard to do when he is chewing so loudly."

"It's hard because you have a habit of noticing what you don't like about him. Instead, notice what you like, and the stuff you don't like will gradually go away."

"Huh? When he's eating, it's revolting. That's the truth! I don't live in a fantasy world."

"It's only the truth because you have activated the vibration of what you don't like about him within you, and he is responding to it. There are lots of truths about him, but you have just decided to focus on a negative one. Find another truth."

"But that's the way it is!!! I can't change his behavior, and it is profoundly irritating to me."

"Yes, that's the way it is. Now you have to figure out whether you like the way it is, or whether you want to change the way it is. You can't force him to change his behavior, but you have complete control over how you feel. Do you want to be truthful about a situation you don't like, or do you want to feel good?"

"I just don't believe I can affect his behavior by changing mine."

"Even if you can't, does it feel better to notice the stuff about him you hate, or to notice things about him you like?"

This little conversation is an example of what gets experienced so many times in life. It is so easy to become fixated on the present reality; we forget to create something better. That is because the Law of Attraction continues, inexorably, to match up signals. When you feel a certain way, there is vibrational *entrainment* in your interaction with others. So it is easier to feel crummy about something unwanted, than to try to find things about it that feel better.

Entrainment is defined as the tendency for two oscillating bodies to lock into phase so that both vibrate in harmony. It can also be defined as a synchronization of two or more rhythmic cycles. For example, when two pulsing heart muscle cells are brought close together each begins to pulse synchronously. The discovery of entrainment is linked to the Dutch scientist, Christian Huygens. While working on the design of the pendulum clock, Huygens discovered that when two clocks were placed on a wall near each other and their pendulums swung at different rates, they would eventually wind up swinging at the same rate. This occurs because of their mutual influence on one another.

Have you ever been involved in a relationship in which you were expected to behave in a certain way? I used to have a hair-trigger temper and whenever something did not go right I felt my wife cringe, waiting for an angry explosion. One day I dropped a glass and it shattered on the floor. I was OK with it, however, and calmly began to walk towards the hallway closet for the broom and dustpan. However, I felt such a strong expectation from my partner that I actually *did* lose my temper, even though she said nothing! If you have ever been in a situation like that you know what it feels like.

I constantly scolded my wife when she did this, unaware that it was my own strongly activated vibration of anger that naturally caused her negative expectation. We were both reinforcing each other, even though it felt to me that she caused me to lose control. In such a situation a positive solution is possible if only *one* of the players finds a different resonance.

When I changed my act from anger to the higher emotions, my wife, magically, no longer reacted in this manner.

These situations are sometimes assigned to "karma," but it is much more elegantly explained by vibrational interaction and the law of attraction. In a vibrational universe, it is possible for one vibration to entrain another. For example, one bell in a room full of bells, when struck, will generate a sympathetic response from all of the bells attuned to that note. It has been discovered that a more powerful vibration entrains a weaker one. It is also true that positive emotion is a more powerful vibration than negative emotion. Therefore, the adoption of a positive vibration must inevitably diffuse, or subsume, a lower emotion. That is why we have the saying "love always conquers hate." Hate is a lower harmonic of the vibration of love.

All negative emotion finds its power in positive emotion.

Many of us have been taught that if something *is*, then it is *real* for all time. But the only reason something unwanted is experienced is the direction of thought toward it! You see, we have it all backwards. We have been brought up to tell the truth and to be honest, and mostly that is a very good thing, but telling the truth about something unwanted is pointless. It is so easy to give chapter and verse about how we got to an uncomfortable place, and why it happened, and all of the events leading up to it, etc., but all this does is continue to activate the vibration which brought about the unpleasant circumstances. Talking about problems doesn't alleviate them! If feeling angry, frustrated, or worried about something helped the situation, we would all be living in paradise.

One more point about our conversation deserves mention: if chewing loudly did not bother you, then you would never notice it. That's the funny thing about 'reality' – it is utterly dependent upon you and what you choose to pay attention to. If you did happen to notice your boyfriend's chewing but didn't have a hot button about it, the conversation might go something like this:

"Would you do me a favor and eat a little more quietly?"

"I didn't know I was bothering you."

"No big deal, but I'd appreciate it."

"OK."

End of story.

When you ask your boyfriend to chew quietly from a place of irritation, your signal to him is very strong, evoking a similar reaction:

"You know, you eat like a barbarian. Would you masticate a little more quietly please?"

"I don't eat like a barbarian!"

"Yes you do, and it's bothering the hell out of me."

"No I don't."

"Dammit, would you do this one little thing for me, just for once?"

"What's wrong with you? I only got up 15 minutes ago and you're all over me"…

etc.

The reality of a relationship can be changed, but it has to start with you! While it is obvious that if your boyfriend would just shape up and fly right you could be a lot happier, doing so is disempowering, for now your happiness is utterly dependent on his actions. If he is feeling uncooperative then you are doomed to misery!

All conscious beings inherently possess free will; and most people will object very strongly when told that their behavior is inappropriate and must be changed. It is so much easier, and feels so much better, to exercise the power that lies within you to change the way you feel. And when you do so, you are rewarded, for the property of vibrational matching is now working in your favor. When you try to change another, your attention is on the stuff about them you do not like; therefore, the Law of Vibration and the Law of Attraction are now working to bring you more of the unwanted stuff! You are always fully empowered in anything you undertake, including a relationship; even though most of us have been taught that in order to feel good about someone, that person should change his or her behavior first. This often does not work because it is backwards.

3.19 Victim and Victimizer

ACCORDING to the Law of Attraction, the victim of a crime has attracted the victimizer, as insensitive as that seems. The victim and victimizer are co-creators in the crime, for without a matching signal, the victim cannot become entangled with the criminal. A person afraid of being mugged may attract a mugger just as a buyer attracts a seller. The victim is afraid of being robbed, the robber wants to rob. Common factor: robbery. Simple, but powerful!

"Well then," you might say, "if thought controls experience, what are you supposed to do with a mugger in your face? Good luck trying to think him away."

The answer is, if you are getting mugged you have already, in your past, been focusing so negatively that you are now forced to take action. However, if you had spent the last year, or the last month, or even the last day, intending that as you go through your day you will only interact with those who are in harmony with you, your experience would have been a lot happier! It is easy to argue against something by arbitrarily placing a person into a difficult situation, ignoring the decisions he or she has made which brought him there, and saying, "OK, what do you do now?"

Politicians who wish to regulate behavior use this sort of argument all the time. When a child fell off a bicycle and was seriously injured, my city passed a law mandating the use of helmets for everyone. My state has passed a law mandating the use of seat belts. The list goes on and on, but what is not understood is that what happens to a person is a precise mirror to his or her state of being. In other words, you are not necessarily safer in a car because you have a seat belt on, unless you believe that being safe results from seat belts! A person without a seat belt who feels perfectly safe is not going to match up with careless drivers, for there is no vibrational co-incidence.

The more mindful you can get regarding your vibrational signal (reflexive flow), the more control you are going to have over your life (inflow, outflow, crossflow). What has been said about victims may seem brutal, unfair, and ridiculous, but if you honestly look around at the world and observe your own experiences and those of others, you may begin to see the truth of it.

3.20   What You Give Your Attention to Grows Bigger for You

My friend Craig is really into world peace. He used to hold 24-hour world healing meditations and is very focused on being and living peace, which I find admirable. One day, however, being a little depressed about the world political situation, he began to describe his attempts to transmute what he felt was an enormous increase of fear in the world. He was so worried that he couldn't stop talking about it. "I know that by talking about FEAR I am getting more fearful, but I heard on the news yesterday...," then he would say: "OK , I know I am just being part of the problem, but what about the war we are about to get into? People are really AFRAID and what about the poor blokes who have to fight..." then he would realize he just activated the vibration of fear even stronger within him. This went on for a little while. Finally he just said, "OK, I'm going to just be peace, because whenever I think about this stuff I feel worse and worse." My friend is very wise, and this little example serves to illustrate what happens when you begin to focus on something you don't want. The vibration just gets bigger and bigger within you! That is how problems grow until they become unmanageable. That is how things get to the point where you encounter a mugger. It appears that the cause of the difficulty is coming from outside of you (it's the mugger's fault, obviously!) but the origin of the problem is being generated from within you.

Fear, anxiety and worry is the best way to focus upon what you don't want, because you keep the unwanted thing continually activated, feeding more and more energy to it, making it bigger and bigger. If you do this for a long enough time, you get a manifestation in your life of the unwanted thing.

For some reason, many people would rather get rid of something unwanted, than create something desired. Like war, for instance. During the Persian Gulf War I saw a lot of "No War" and "War Is Not the Answer" signs, along with a few "Peace" signs. Some well-intentioned people get so upset by war that their attention goes immediately to it. I guess they feel that being peaceful cannot stop war, but resonating to the vibrations of war just makes you a carrier for it. You become a cancerous growth in the mass consciousness, amplifying the vibrations of war. The only way to experience peace is to be peaceful. Fighting war (or fighting anything) aligns you to conflict, and therefore, precisely to those who support and create war. That's what happens in a vibrational universe where free will reigns supreme.

Similarly, those who like war get angry at those who disapprove of it. But their efforts to stomp out free speech and action just mobilizes more opposition! The bottom line is that most people will not tolerate constraints on their freedom for very long, because freedom of choice is fundamental to consciousness itself.

3.21 An Illustration of the Law of Attraction

How does the Universal Operating System help one to get "matched up" with the people and resources you need? Well, let's take Rick and Sam. Both of them are tired of their job as salesmen for a big corporation, and both want to start a new business. Sam thinks that it would be a great idea, but that it's really impossible. Rick decides that although he has no employees, infrastructure, or money, it's going to happen. On the way home from a conference in another city, Sam is sitting next to Bill. Sam is tired and grumpy, thinking about his crummy job and how he wants out. Bill leans over to start a conversation but Sam turns away, looking out the window. After the plane lands Sam is waiting for his ride when a woman bumps up against him. "Sorry," she says, and is about to make chit-chat, but Sam is irritable and moves away.

When Bill leans over to talk to Rick, however, Rick is receptive, for he has been making plans during the entire flight and is feeling juiced. They shoot the breeze for a while and Bill mentions that he's about to retire after 30 years from a well paying executive position. It turns out that Bill, in his late middle age and with a fat bank account, finally wants to take some risks in his life; he's tired of his corporate job and is looking for a challenge in his retirement. Bill, in his fantasies, has always dreamed of managing a small start-up but never had the guts to do so before. Now he's ready. Rick and Bill get excited about Rick's new venture and exchange addresses.

What happened? Sam's very strong desire for a new business put him within vibrational reach of Bill, but Sam's decision that it's hopeless sabotages the opportunity. The woman who bumped Sam is a software engineer who is also looking for a new opportunity, and might have made a good employee or partner in Sam's business.

That's how the law of like attracts like works. Through a series of seeming "coincidences," based upon the content of your conscious vibrational signal, you meet up with people with matching, or similar, desires to yours. It's your free will decision to take advantage or not, but one thing is for sure: Rick is going to have a lot easier time of it than Sam creating his new company.

The thing is, you never have a clue about how this works unless you are vibrationally ready for it! A guy like Sam would say that it's total nonsense. And for him, it IS nonsense! He is always vibrationally out of range of those who can help him, even when they are sitting across from him.

Rick and Sam illustrate an important point about the Law of "like attracts like" and the Law of Vibration, which we will use later on in an analysis of problems: you can only perceive within a limited range, so you can only come together with those who are in your range. If Sam continues to focus more on his crummy job than on the new business he wants to create, he will no longer even meet up with people like Bill, for they will be completely outside of his vibrational bandwidth.

The Law of Attraction, for effective results, requires conscious application.

Can you run a business using these principles? Well, the Law of Free Will guarantees that you only have control over the content of your personal experiences. However, it is possible to use the power of your example and your ability to persuade, cajole, coerce or inspire, to get others to line up with your vision. Those with leadership ability understand this very well. Those who are truly wise, however, understand that the power of any group is based solely upon the agreement of individuals within it.

3.22   It is Easier to Think Positively than Negatively

JUST as it is easy to fall into the trap of negative thinking and experience negatively, it is even easier (and more profitable) to get into the positive habit of thinking about what you want.

A few years ago I was very upset at our neighbors because their big golden retriever would come right up to my house and bark loudly. This would often occur during the early morning hours, waking me up too early. I went over there and did a lot of yelling and screaming at the owners, with little effect. The more I resisted that dog, the more he came around! Well, this went on for a year or so until I finally got smart and realized that the dog was not the problem. I was the problem. So one day I sat down, cleared my space, and imagined my neighbors and their dog as friendly to me and I toward them. This took quite a bit of work, for I had built up such a heavy vibration that it was a long time before I was able to think a charitable thought, or feel a good feeling, about the whole situation. But I persevered and actually got myself to a place where I felt, genuinely, no anger whatsoever toward them or the dog.

What happened after is interesting, because I was hoping for a magic response from the bloody dog; like, all of a sudden he would just be friendly toward me. That didn't happen, but something even more remarkable did: whenever the dog came into the yard, I felt no hostility whatsoever, and, in fact, got quite a bit of amusement out of his crazy barking. The dog came around less and less, and the neighbors began to keep a close watch on him. Soon after they bought an invisible fence, and now everyone is happy.

As long as my vibration was one of resistance, and my actions hostile, I drew forth from my neighbors and their dog a matching response. It took a while to get over my human tendency to blame others for my situation. For some reason, my first reaction was one of powerlessness. When I felt powerless, I naturally assigned blame to something outside myself. It was only when I wised up and began to see that others responded towards me precisely as I felt about them, that I was able to gain control over myself and the situation. And the neat thing is, all of my action, all of my blustering and threats, didn't do anything except make a bad situation worse. That damn dog kept coming around even more, despite all of my frenzied activity. Only when I aligned my energy toward that of harmony did I get any positive results. The problem, essentially, resolved itself.

The First Principle, the Law of Free Will, the Law of Vibration, and the Law of Attraction automatically orient a conscious being at source point. This is by design. Whatever is happening to you that you don't like, can be changed for the better. Apparently, the laws of the Universal Operating System are simply woven into the fabric of the universe. Once you begin to apply these principles to your own life, there will be a feeling of confidence and power. You will begin to realize that it is possible to modify the conditions of your life at will. You will begin to experience magic in your life.

The Law of Attraction acts as a protective buffer when you take the time to create a positive reality; the unwanted vibrations are deactivated when attention is placed elsewhere. This concept is not broadly understood. We feel that the good can only be attained if the bad stuff is eliminated first (or at least regulated); "common sense" tells us that if evil is not eradicated, it will eventually overwhelm us. History books tell us how peaceful, happy civilizations were overrun by barbarian hordes. All of this is a misinterpretation, however. It is not possible for a truly harmonious and peaceful population to attract violent killers into their midst, for there is not a vibrational matching. Violent killers will not attack peaceful people, *unless* the peaceful ones decide that there is danger. What passes for historical forces is just a lot individuals agreeing on the same thing.

Only those things you place your attention on can come to you. This means, for example, that if thought is directed exclusively to health, health will be the result; that is true even if a person is ill. I am willing to bet that there are very, very few people on this planet who have never had a thought about illness! "Of course," you say, "that is because there is so much illness it is impossible not to notice it. Throughout history illness and disease have been prevalent in human societies. Illness must therefore be a common denominator of human existence." Well, I will make an outrageous statement, but one that is in full accord with the Universal Operating System: It is not possible to become ill unless there is a vibrational proclivity for it. Even though the body ages, its systems are designed for health and vitality. However, it is always possible to orient oneself in the opposite direction. If you examine society and especially the media, you will see the proportion of attention that is devoted to illness vs. health. A few hours of watching television will be very instructive in this regard. If you watch television consciously, you will be amazed at what you see and hear! The point is, the vibrational playing field of mass culture is tilted in favor of the negative over the positive. Personally, I have given up on television, except for the Food Channel and the occasional sporting event.

Historically, mankind has been wedded to tradition, preventing changes in consciousness. The power of thought has never been understood on our planet except by a very few, who have secluded their knowledge from the common man. A way of thinking and being that has been prevalent for thousands of years does not validate its worth. In other words, the *value* of something is not indicated by its longevity, its existence has continued only because so many have given it their attention.

Speaking personally, I used to be so negative about myself and the world political situation that it began to affect my health. It was only after a number of scary experiences that I began to wake up to my true self. Once I began to travel along the road of less resistance, I began to realize that within me was a core of beautiful energy, a positive, uplifting, soaring, powerful energy that was fundamentally who I am. When I really began to understand the law of like attracts like, I realized that no matter how crazy things got out there, I could lead a life of joy if only I began to concentrate exclusively upon what is wanted, and utterly neglect that which is unwanted. This is easier said than done, but really, would you rather pay attention to stuff that makes you feel good, or stuff that makes you feel bad? It's a no-brainer. What is interesting is that after I began to practice focusing my attention in this way, things that were formerly upsetting – like national and international politics – were no longer so.

Focusing exclusively on what is wanted may sound suspiciously like burying one's head in the sand, but I prefer to think of it as removing one's head from the muck – the muck of negativity, depression and anger! I found out that joy feels a lot better than anger. Now this might not seem like such a revelation to you, dear reader, but I used to be a fellow with a hair-trigger temper. Anger felt wonderful, and I would love to get myself in situations where I could explode at people, or put them down. If you have ever been there, you know what I'm talking about. It made me feel powerful! But I discovered that it was a false power, a power based on my own fears and insecurities.

Being formerly a political junkie, I found it difficult at first to take my attention off current events, until it became clear that personal knowledge of these events was unimportant in my life.

For example, I was often very concerned about the state of the national debt and its effect on the economy and, indirectly, on my business. However, I found that by ignoring the news, I no longer resonated to negative information, and my business became more successful!

There are probably many readers who can focus positively on politics, and who actually work in politics to make the world a better place, but I was not one of them. I use this example from my life merely to illustrate that whatever upsets you can safely be ignored. And when it is ignored, your personal situation regarding it will improve. Like everything else in this book, this assertion must be tested; otherwise, it may seem delusional. Nevertheless, as you begin to experiment with the vibrational universe concept it becomes obvious that the universe is, and has always been, responding to your every thought. You begin to realize that it is possible to be, do, or have anything you desire. Once you accept these principles it is no longer possible to whine or complain for any length of time, for such a philosophy places you in the driver's seat of your life.

The first thing you will notice in experimenting with the vibrational concept is a change in your attitude, on the reflexive flow. Then gradually, conditions around you will begin to change as you line up with your newly activated vibration. A curious phenomenon sometimes occurs: right off the bat, all hell breaks loose in your life! Do not despair; this is perfectly natural. If you have a habit of holding life at arms length, it may come crashing down on you! This is particularly true in relationships; as you begin to change, others who are comfortable with the "old" you may have difficulty adjusting to your new orientation. This is a good sign, because it means you are truly adjusting your vibration enough for others to notice.

If you have spent the past twenty years creating negatively in an area, your dominant vibration is mostly negative, but it is still possible to see small results very quickly, and bigger results if you just stick with it for a little while. My health didn't improve all at once. But over a period of two or three years, I noticed I felt better and better, and got sick less and less. That is not to say that you *couldn't* turn your situation around immediately. All it takes to completely change your life is a definitive alteration of your vibrational signal. If you could immediately change a signal that was mostly negative to one that was purely positive, you would see instantaneous and far-reaching positive manifestations in your life. Medical miracles, for example, sometimes occur when a person has reached a health crisis and the person is able, somehow, to completely let go of all resistant thought. Often this is accompanied by a spiritual awakening of some kind. But please don't wait until you've hit bottom to try it!

The success or failure in applying the vibrational universe concept is strictly personal, and is mainly dependent upon establishing a state of being that is in positive alignment with your life path. The only thing I can tell you, from years of personal experience with this material, is that *your life will always accurately reflect the content of your true vibration.*

It is not difficult to figure out what to do with your life! In some circles, a great mystery is built around uncovering your life mission, or your life lessons. Seminars, techniques, and accessories of all kinds are promoted to increase spiritual growth and awareness. The efficacy of all of them is dependent on only one thing, however: your personal state of being with regard to it. Here is a little secret I learned after participating in some of them: All you have to do is find something to feel good about and pursue it! In this way, you align with your divine self, and find joy. If you want to find success, eliminate mysteries. The truth isn't "out there," it's been inside you all along, and it doesn't have to take lifetimes to find it. There is no past life karma to overcome. You are free, right now, to change your life and the operating system of the universe exists to back you up. You are the pilot of your ship of consciousness, so set a destination and grab onto the rudder! Just remember that it's supposed to feel good.

3.23 Prosperity is Natural

WHEN first exposed to this philosophy some are concerned that it promotes selfishness. What would happen, they ask, if everyone in the world began to selfishly demand prosperity? The earth is already polluted; if it were mined and dredged so that all 7 billion can live as we do in the West, our poor planet would be irreparably harmed.

Well, a vibration of prosperity cannot possibly lead to harm. Prosperity is a vibration entirely compatible and in alignment with source energy, and will generate activities in support of well-being. Life is not a zero-sum game! Life is a win-win game. At present mankind uses scarce fossil fuels, but there is no natural law which says that energy must come from non-renewable energy sources.

The main reason we have economies of scarcity is because of a consciousness of scarcity. The vast majority of human beings on the planet earth believe that there are not enough resources for all to live prosperously. And that is true *if* we assume that energy must come from fossil fuels. The present planetary economies are a perfect match to the human consciousness of scarcity and lack. This consciousness is woven through many of our religions, philosophies, and political systems. It is endemic in the thinking of mankind and is constantly reflected back to us in the manifestations we receive. Therefore, we observe scarcity and continue to align our thoughts to it. After all, it is real! However, this is really a mindless and stupid way to create a planetary environment. It's like a hamster on a walking wheel. Once the little guy gets it going, his own momentum forces him to keep moving his feet. But he may decide to stop creating the momentum that makes the wheel turn, simply by a conscious thought to do so.

Surely there are more efficient and cleaner ways to generate energy than with fossil fuels. As the consciousness of mankind moves away from belief in scarcity, new sources of energy will be developed in response. One thing is certain. A vibration of scarcity cannot support clean and abundant energy, for the two are not a match. Ironically, the more emphasis on conservation, the more a consciousness of scarcity is maintained, for the dominant vibration of conservation is 'not enough.' Vibrationally speaking, conservation can only lead to a continuing emphasis on fossil fuels.

It is now theorized that the vacuum of space is not empty at all, but filled with a seething cauldron of subatomic particles which constitute a universal background energy. According to current theory at the time of this writing, the light emitting matter and energy of the universe (planets, stars, galaxies, etc) make up only 4% of the known matter and energy in the universe! Where is the other 96%? Scientists call it dark matter and dark energy, but no one really knows what it is. According to the latest estimates, dark energy makes up about three quarters of the universe and dark matter around 23%. Interestingly enough, dark energy appears to be massless, occupying space uniformly throughout the universe. These ideas have led some frontier scientists to revive the "aether" concept, wherein space is filled with a material substance which causes the formation of matter and energy and is responsible for visible phenomena. This is the material equivalent of a single unifying principle, which we have referred to in this book as "life force energy," or "source energy."

3.24 The World Is In Perfect Balance

THE question sometimes arises, "If everyone is selfishly getting what they want, who will do the work of the world? Grow the food and pick up the garbage and man the cash registers?" The answer lies in the fact that the Law of Vibration and the Law of Attraction ensures that the world remains in balance. In our vibrational model, each receives precisely according to the content of his or her thoughts and beliefs, so there can be no experiential mismatches. This sounds awfully like "fate" but it isn't, for the Law of Free Will is always in operation. It's funny, but those who do not believe in free will have the free will choice to do so; one may choose slavery if that is desired. Fate is just the continual creation of your life from what you are observing; over and over and over again, like a stuck CD.

If you have something to sell you can always find a buyer (if you don't believe me, look at the Oriental Trading catalog!) And if you manufacture too much of your product, it will remain unsold, causing you to come back into balance. An economy like the one in the old Soviet Union was doomed to failure, for it produced tons of stuff nobody wanted. Eventually such a system must collapse, for it is modeled on activities that promote imbalance.

As a species, human beings assume that change is dangerous and disruptive. However, if people are changing positively, the universe will respond positively! Change is only disruptive when it is resisted. We have a saying: "Better to live with the danger you know than the one you don't." What is the dominant vibration in this sentence? Danger! It epitomizes the human mindset perfectly – the world is fundamentally a negative place, and the only way to survive in it is to struggle along with the current reality, even if that reality is uncomfortable, because who knows what evil is lurking just over the horizon. But of course, maintaining such a negative vibration only ensures more of the same; it is a self-fulfilling idiocy.

The idea of balance poses a question that seems to contradict the Law of Attraction. How come, in relationships, a shy guy will be attracted to an outgoing woman, or vice-versa? The answer lies in the fact that the shy guy wants to be more outgoing, therefore his focus is on an outgoing person, and so by Law of Attraction attracts the outgoing woman, or vice versa. The seller is focused on finding a buyer, and the buyer is focused on finding a seller, and so balance of energy is achieved; like attracts like.

Science has come up with the "opposites attract" explanation for attraction and repulsion to explain the interaction of matter and energy. This concept was demonstrated a long time ago in experiments with a simple electrometer (See Appendix C).

We see balance everywhere, at the microcosmic and macrocosmic scales. Kepler's laws of planetary motion show geometrically how the orbits of each planet are kept in perfect proximity to the gravitational pull of the sun. In chemistry, atoms bond according to strict rules that keep a balance within the molecule. All natural systems operate in balance. Chaos theory shows how self similarity is a natural occurrence in nature. Weather is a good example. Even though conditions never remain exactly the same, everything is kept in balance within defined parameters. The temperature in my hometown, Ann Arbor, Michigan, never gets above 105 degrees Farenheit and never goes below −25, and usually it ranges from −10 to 95 no matter the season. If the design of the universe did not reflect balance, it could not demonstrate the well-ordered-ness we observe in nature. Without balance, there is just random behavior, without purpose.

3.24.1 The Hawk and the Sparrow

HERE is a little story to illustrate how the world is already in perfect balance. The Emperor was sitting on his throne in the Great Hall. Suddenly, a little sparrow flew in. "Help me!" it said. "The hawk is trying to kill me!" A couple of seconds later the hawk flew in. "Be gone, hawk!" the Emperor said. "Today your killing stops! The sparrow has chicks to feed and a mate to take care of."

The hawk was angry. "But why do you deprive me of the food God has designated for me?" the hawk replied. "This sparrow is mine!"

"I am an enlightened ruler," the Emperor replied. "It is my job as a human being, who have been given dominion over the planet, to watch out and protect more helpless species." The hawk replied, "Then you condemn me and mine to starvation! I also have a mate and chicks to feed. You cannot deprive me of the food that is my God-given right."

The King realizes that the hawk is also a deserving life form. So he tells his men to find food for the hawk, and they wind up killing a lot of sparrows. The moral of the story is that the world is already in a perfect place, given the level of consciousness present for all concerned. In other words, the world is always balancing the needs and desires of everyone to the highest possible advancement, given the thoughts, beliefs, and desires of all life.

3.25 Diversity Is Vital In Order to Maintain Balance

DIVERSITY maintains balance at a high level of sophistication. If everyone thought like an engineer, our society would be well regulated and all devices and ma-chines would operate efficiently. Bringing your car into the shop would actually be a pleasurable experience! But say the engineer wanted to listen to some good music. Who would be there to compose, play and record the music? Nobody. Who would be there to make entertaining movies? Who would play the baseball and basketball games the engineer likes to watch on TV? This is a crude example, but you get the picture. On planet earth, we have people interested in so many different things that it is easy to get your needs met, no matter how outlandish, and find different or unusual things to do.

My friend Dave makes keyboards, and he often must rely on the skills and resources of others. One time he needed a welder, another time a computer-aided lathe, another time an expert on metalworking. If all were like Dave, there would be perfect agreement and harmony, but he would never be able to accomplish his goal of building a keyboard with its unique design. Dave has certain skills, but he is utterly dependent upon those with different ideas, skills, and resources. The more diversity the better, for the more ideas there are, the more interesting society becomes.

In order to illustrate the Law of Attraction more fully, I have included a more extensive example, loosely based on something I experienced in my life.

3.26   The Law of Attraction: An in-depth illustration

LET's introduce Joe Doakes, a muscular, solidly built guy who likes to lift weights and who enjoys sports. Mr. Doakes has, some would say, the unpleasant quality of being belligerent. Mr. Doakes is a warrior. When we look at him we can immediately see a "high volume" kind of guy.

Joe chooses to find an outlet for his aggressive impulses in the joys of conflict. To Joe, nothing in life is finer than a good fight. For Joe, it is of little consequence whether his opponent is fairly matched in skill or strength; it is the joy of battle which sustains him. Joe has little leaning toward fair play or morality. It simply is not in his makeup, and if confronted with the ethical dilemma of a "fair fight" Joe would simply laugh. We make no judgment of Joe, and neither does the universe. The Law of Attraction states that like attracts like. Joe will naturally find circumstances and people in alignment with his preferences. Since Joe frequents bars and gyms, this is where the preponderance of his quarrels ensue. Joe lives in a world where everyone he meets is perfectly matched up with him.

Now let's introduce a person with an exactly opposite set of preferences. Let's call him Cecil Aldershot, a man of delicate sensibilities, steeped in metaphysical knowledge, and an avid supporter of peace on earth and harmony in relations between all living things.

Again, there is no judgment by the universe of Cecil's preferences. The Universal Operating System does not consider Cecil's preferences better than Joe's, or Joe's better than Cecil's. They are simply different.

What are the chances of the two of them ever meeting each other? Exactly zero. The Law of Vibration and the Law of Attraction guarantee that only that which is like unto itself can be co-incident. Yet we will show how the two of them can come together in the dance of vibration that is life.

During his childhood Cecil, of a frail constitution, was always the loser in any physical confrontation which he so unwillingly took part. Cecil learned that hatred and violence were abhorrent to him, in fact were opposing his own thoughts and feelings completely. Cecil learned to avoid those brutes, as he called them, who seemed to enjoy nothing more than the infliction of pain and misery on other life forms. Cecil has worked avidly in the refining and raising of his consciousness, and associates with many people of like mind; we can say confidently that Cecil enjoys his life very much. The same thing can be said about our belligerent friend Joe. Joe and Cecil merely express their joy differently. Joe expresses himself in what we will call an undisciplined manner (Society calls it undisciplined. To Joe it is entirely natural). Observing Cecil, on the other hand, one immediately perceives a much more subdued and balanced demeanor.

One day during a meditation for global harmony at a local metaphysical bookstore, a hostile bully broke up the gathering with threats, taunts and insults. After this confrontation, Cecil was reminded of those incidents in his childhood when he was confronted by the very same sort of violence. He began to ponder on this, wondering why he should have attracted such a one. As he began to devote more thought to it, the old feelings of intimidation and victimization began to be activated once more within him.

Let's pause a moment. If Cecil had dealt with this incident as he normally would have, going over it briefly and resolving for himself the disharmonies within it, he would have quickly returned to balance. But because the contrast to his everyday experience was so great, Cecil felt he had to have an answer for this unfortunate incident. It went against his nature as a student of metaphysics and a seeker of truth to leave the mystery of it unexamined. As a consequence of placing his thoughts and feelings in the old vibrational pattern, however, it became reactivated within him.

Cecil and his friends are typical of many who seek a joyous experience on earth. In observing the world around them and its incredible diversity and often powerful contrast, they reasoned that if all were in harmony, then everyone on the planet could enjoy a happy physical experience, not just a privileged few. After all, is it fair, they would say, for millions of fellow humans to be living lives of poverty, misery and desperation? Why should all not benefit from the higher vibrations of peace, joy and abundance? And so Cecil and his friends would meditate every day, volunteer their services to charitable organizations, and generally make themselves helpful to what they called the greater good. In order for someone to feel good, they reasoned, there should exist an environment comfortable to all. Then all could experience comfort! What better idea for comfort than harmony and abundance for everyone?

If we were to ask Joe Doakes this same question, however, we would get an entirely different answer. You see, Joe would not agree at all that harmony and abundance was an environment to be desired. To Joe, this would be a nightmare of boredom. In an environment of harmony, Joe would immediately look for ways to liven things up! And what better way to entertain himself, he would think, than to start an argument or provoke a test of physical strength. To Joe, this test of strength makes him feel so alive!

Joe likes to work hard for what he gets. He revels in action and physical movement, in the challenge of overcoming obstacles. If Joe meditated, he would meditate for global conflict – not world war or anything of that nature, but a world where laws were less restrictive, protection for the weak and innocent was less severe. Joe would wish to live in an environment like the old west, where fighting was understood and appreciated, and cowardice and physical weakness was punished severely.

Both Joe and Cecil do agree on one thing: in order to feel as good as possible, the environment should be pleasing. Joe hates the fact that his aggressive impulses are restrained, that the only outlet for his kind of physical expression is in a gym, or in the military. He would like very much to be able to provoke anyone he sees on the street at any time.

Cecil dislikes the "meanies" of the world, considering them to be of a "lower" vibration, and would like very much to see others behaving toward him with the same consideration he bestows on them. This is a reasonable assumption, is it not?

But in order for the environment to be pleasing to all, all must agree on a pleasing environment. And that is an impossibility. Cecil would like it very much if people like Joe would just disappear. In his support of animal rights, environmental harmony and peace on earth, Cecil and his group are constantly butting heads with short-sighted people who couldn't care less for anything or anyone but their own selfish pleasure. Even though he tries to love all, Cecil truly cannot understand how the infliction of pain on another life form can be tolerated. However, there are over 7 billion humans living on earth, and if each one of them is trying to get the others to act in a manner pleasing to them, what is the likelihood of success? Not very high! In fact, it is a job even God does not want to undertake. That is why God permits all thought and all action, for by limiting some thought or action, the all-that-is is also limited. An understanding of the Law of Attraction makes this dilemma unnecessary.

Let's go back to our original statement: how do Joe and Cecil come together, even though their natural vibrational patterns are opposing? We have seen how Joe likes to pick fights and his indifference as to his opponents. We have also seen how Cecil has reactivated the vibration of fear toward bullies. Now, Law of Attraction goes to work. Normally Joe would never find Cecil. It is up to Cecil to attract to him such a

CHAPTER 3 — THE OPERATING SYSTEM OF THE UNIVERSE

one as Joe. Only by Cecil's continued attention to his fear of bullies can this occur. As Cecil continues to focus upon the incident at the peace meeting, his vibrational signal becomes more aligned to bullies.

One day soon after Cecil is walking down the street from the metaphysical book-store, and in his musings unwittingly takes a right instead of a left and goes walking down toward the gym. At this time it just so happens that Joe has completed his workout and is feeling rather sprightly and aggressive. Joe looks around at all of the others passing and vibrationally feels Cecil. Cecil's vibration is saying "Do not come to me, bullies. I do not want to fight. Please do not send me a bully, I do not like violent people." etc., etc., etc. Out of all of the dozens of people who are passing by at this moment, only Cecil is a vibrational match to Joe. So what happens? Joe gets a taunting smile on his face and that old devil takes over. He feels the joy of battle, and the comfort of the life force surging through him. Joe sees immediately that Cecil is physically delicate and decides that he will have a little fun with him.

"Hey meat – yeah YOU!" he says to Cecil.

"Who, me??"

Joe bumps up against Cecil and sees the fear turn on in Cecil's eyes. This is music to Joe's senses.

"Hey you bumped into me!" Joe says, all the while shoving Cecil backward.

You get the idea. A conflict of greater or lesser proportion will ensue depending upon how strong Cecil's fear of conflict is. In this case, it has less to do with Joe than with Cecil. Although it takes two to tango, for Cecil it is entirely up to him how far this encounter will go. If Cecil is fearful enough of fighting, his vibration is now more and more powerful, and more and more of a match to Joe's always very powerful desire for conflict. In other words, Joe's vibration is always for a fight, and in order for Cecil to encounter Joe, Cecil must bring his vibration toward Joe's.

This is simply the law of like attracts like at work. It is a situation often described as "karmic." Karma is simply Law of Attraction. Those situations which seem to mag-netically pull you into the middle of them are simply your own attention to, and focus on, a vibration matching the situation, in the present. Your attention to the person or situation now being experienced actually attracted it to you, not the other way around. It's not someone else, or the universe, imposing itself into your life, even though it sure feels like it! It is always and only your free will offering of vibration that attracts whatever is in your experience, to you.

You might say, "But Joe's actions are terrible! What if everyone were like Joe?"

But everyone is *not* like Joe. Every being incarnated on earth is unique. If there were two people exactly alike, one of them would be superfluous! There are over 7 billion humans, all with our own unique set of preferences. We are all different. We attract unto us that which is consonant with our preferences. That is how the universe works. This planet is in absolutely perfect balance. For every vibration of hatred, there is a like vibration to match it. For every vibration based in love, there is one of like kind to match it. In the case of Cecil and Joe, there is Joe's love of spirited conflict to exactly match Cecil's fear of spirited conflict. The common denominator is spirited conflict! Cecil remembers the delight of the neighborhood bully, in his pushing and shoving and taunting of him; his utter dismay that there existed persons in the world with (to Cecil) such a crude and brutal worldview. It is the apparent joy of conflict for some people, and his utter inability to deal with it, which is uppermost in Cecil's consciousness. That is what attracted Joe to him! Joe and Cecil are an exact vibrational match, like two waveforms of the same frequency and phase, augmenting each other. Cecil's vibration attracted Joe's vibration and they fit together like a key going into a lock. Thus we see that it is the victim of a crime that is more responsible for the crime than the perpetrator. Without a like vibration to match to, no criminal could ever find a victim! This outrageous, offensive, and counter-intuitive statement is fully supported in a vibrational universe.

The Law of Attraction never misses. It is infallible, because it is woven into the very fabric of the universe.

Many people think that it would be a good idea if the world would just shape up and others would behave themselves. Then it would be easy to be happy, for we could just look around and see pleasant things! So well-intentioned people form groups and organizations to fight poverty and cancer and war, and stamp out corruption and pornography and many other things as well. However, things get messy very quickly, for when everyone in the world is acting to control others, many toes are stepped on. If you desire that others should act in a way which is comfortable for you, be sure that they are feeling the same way about your activities! Now we have a recipe for conflict. There are now lots and lots of people all acting to control you, in their fear that you might do something to threaten them. And you are doing the same. I'm sure that you have, at some point in your life, tried to accommodate the wishes of a group of people, whether it be family, friends, or co-workers, and you very quickly came to understand the difficulty of pleasing everyone. But such grotesque circumstances can be avoided, with a clear understanding of the Law of Attraction.

Let's look again at the portrait of Cecil and Joe.

Joe is happy with his bar fights and his sporting encounters in the gym. Cecil is happy with his metaphysical friends. Each can live harmoniously in his separate world without ever attracting the attention of the other. Because Joe would be merely inconvenienced by a metaphysical discussion, whereas Cecil would be seriously incommoded in a fight, Cecil has the most at stake. But Cecil, if he understood the Law of Attraction, would know clearly that it is his perfect guarantor of safety and protection. The solution for Cecil is to keep focused on what he wants. By focusing only on peace, harmony and abundance, he attracts these into his life and automatically places himself in a position where Joe cannot ever reach him, for unmatched vibrations are never co-incident.

This is a much more elegant way to run a universe! Now, instead of each person having to control the actions of everyone else, it is only necessary for each person to control his or her own vibrational space. Now we can dispense with the inevitable conflicts that ensue when people are trying to stick their noses in each other's business. Joe can have his bar fights, Cecil can have the group which feels most comfortable to him, without there ever being a conflict. If Cecil is focusing on his desires for peace and harmony, he does not take that wrong turn and so never encounters Joe.

Where the Cecil's of the world get into trouble is when they try to limit or constrain the Joe's of the world. By pushing against the Joe's they only get more of them. What you resist will persist in your experience.

3.27 Universal Forces

WHAT appears to be luck, coincidence, or uncaring universal forces is actually the Law of Attraction at work, in company with its cohort, the Law of Vibration. Here are two more illustrations of the Law of Attraction. The first is taken from the life of a friend, the second, from a personal experience.

Inga is depressed. At work she can't seem to get along, at home she is irritable with her boyfriend. Considering herself a spiritual person and on a path of personal growth, she feels blocked. Meditation, healing work, none of her tried and true techniques can break the spell. So she goes to her local astrologer, and all is explained. Her charts show that she is in the middle of a three or four week period of difficulty, especially with members of the opposite sex. Inga is relieved but she isn't looking forward to more trial and tribulation! During that period she has two big arguments with her boyfriend Bob, gets into several work-related fights with fellow employees, and becomes even more depressed about her weight than usual. But she weathers the storm until the following month, when things straighten out. Interestingly, she notes that her recovery is almost date coincident with the information on her chart.

Do we say the astrologer was correct in her predictions about Inga? Do we admit that the forces of the universe can impose themselves into our experience, against our free will choices? Or do we say that Inga created the whole thing? It's up to you I guess, but I prefer explanations which place a conscious being at cause over his or her life.

I prefer to say that it was Inga's agreement with the astrologer that placed her vibration in such a way as to exacerbate an already difficult situation, and promote conflict with Bob and her workmates. Inga has the ability (as do we all) to draw into her experience anything she places her attention on. It just happened that she decided to go into agreement with the astrologer, and therefore created more conflict in her relationship.

However, in talking with Inga it is clear that she believes differently. She believes that the forces of the universe align in certain ways to affect everything in it, and when that happens, it is foolish to struggle against them. This idea is common in some circles. Even though it is based correctly on the idea of interconnectedness, it strips a person of his or her personal power.

Such an attitude, however, has been prevalent throughout history. Even kings and queens have been seduced by the idea that universal forces can be directed or predicted by astrologers or magicians; that somehow the forces of nature can be aligned for or against you, and there is nothing you can do about it. A famous historical example is that of Catherine de Medici, wife of Henry I, King of France, who, it is said, used the talents of her personal astrologers, (among them the famous Nostradamus) to rid herself of the king's longtime mistress, Diane de Poitiers (the Duchesse de Valentinois), and her political enemies.

The point is, even if we admit that astrology is a valid subtle energy phenomenon, it seems more likely that a person's own vibrational makeup will have a far greater influence on personal behavior than stars and planets whose effects do not even impinge on the conscious awareness. Simply stated, a firm belief in something will bring more of it into your experience.

Let's look at another, more practical example. Take Ralph, a guy who loves fast cars. Ralph has saved up enough for a down payment on a new sports car. He is really getting juiced thinking about showing it off to all his friends, and anybody else that will notice. He gets to the dealer breathless with anticipation and when he sees that beautiful machine he thinks: "Man that thing looks so great. I hope nothing ever happens to it." He begins to get anxious about scratches and dents, and idiots running into him. Anyone who has ever bought a new car knows how Ralph is feeling right now! Anyway, Ralph completes his paperwork and is anxious to get out of there and get his car safely in his own garage. He is driving down the street when Thorpe, (Barb's old boyfriend) who just quit his job and got his last paycheck, is headed off to the bar. Thorpe is really feeling his oats and comes out of the parking lot hell-bent-for-leather. He doesn't even see Ralph as he jerks his rig out into oncoming traffic and turns right in front of Ralph, putting a big dent in Ralph's brand new car.

Did Ralph just have bad luck? Was there some evil force that directed Thorpe to mess up Ralph's new car? Or was it simply "one of those things" that occur when millions of people are jostling each other in cities across our planet? If we accept these explanations, we have to assume a universe where either things just randomly happen, or where there is a diabolical source of negative energy that, like a boogeyman or devil, decides to mess us up. Neither of these explanations makes any sense to me. In our vibrational model of the universe where consciousness can directly affect what it experiences, the universe is well ordered and so no random events ever happen. Ralph was a perfect vibrational match to Thorpe, for Ralph was worried about irresponsible people banging into his new car, and Thorpe is, well, irresponsible! And so they came together, exactly according to the thoughts, beliefs and feelings which were uppermost in each of them at the time. Ralph was worried about his car getting dented, and Thorpe was in just the right mood to want to run into somebody. BAM! A perfectly orchestrated event, with Ralph and Thorpe as both actors and directors. Ralph and Thorpe meet at a precise location in space/time in a non-random, co-incident event.

You might ask, "How come Ralph got his new car dented so quickly?" There is supposed to be a time lag between the thought and the manifestation! The answer is, Ralph has been carrying around the vibration of new stuff getting wrecked for a long time. When Ralph was younger, he saw a kid in a hot rod run into the station wagon of his father's best friend. Ralph got the idea that even adults don't have control of their lives. Ralph knows that he himself is a careless driver sometimes and figures accidents can happen to anyone. Ralph is so hyped about his new car that fear for its safety is by far his dominant vibration, amplified by his emotional state. A pure, powerful vibration can be answered almost instantly if it is strong enough. Remember, the universe does not discriminate! It regards all vibrations as equally valid.

"OK," you might say, "I'll give you that one. But what about a person who wants to start a new business in the middle of a big recession, or what about a baby that is born into the middle of a war zone? Here we have one person against the world. How can one person overcome the will of everyone else?"

If you want to start a business and the economy is in bad shape, you can either think like Inga and believe the pronouncements you hear on the news, or from the Federal Reserve, or from other people you consider to be experts, or you can simply canvas your market, get a business plan together and get going. If you keep a positive vision of your business venture, you will inevitably be drawn to the needed people and resources. Depending upon the strength of your desire and the clarity and purity of your vision, your business will either succeed or fail, but the success or failure has nothing to do with the state of the economy, or the decisions of anybody else. As the old investment saying goes, "The time to buy is when blood is running in the streets." People experience abundance even in the most dire of times! The pronouncements of talking heads on the news regarding the state of the economy are about as relevant as Inga's astrologer. All of the facts marshaled by the latest economic reports and news bulletins have the same relevance as Inga's planetary alignments. What comes to you has nothing to do with "the facts," or what others believe or do! Successful people will tell you this without hesitation.

If you believe it is impossible to do something, you will fail. It's as simple as that. That is a rigorous definition. As Mike Ditka, the Super Bowl winning coach of the 1985 Chicago Bears expressed it, "If you don't think you can win the Super Bowl, you can't win it."

If you believe you will succeed, and continue to believe it, eventually you will. Ask any successful person in any field and they will tell you that their success was directly proportional to their belief in themselves. Talk to unsuccessful people and you will find the exact opposite. (By successful I don't necessarily mean monetary success. A homemaker with five children may be spectacularly successful as a mother, wife, and nurturer, and may live a life so full of love that it boggles the mind).

You only get into trouble when you believe one way, put a happy face on top of it, and plunge in anyway. How can you tell when it's a good time to plunge in and when it's a good time to lay back? By how you feel. If you feel anxious, worried, scared, or any of the negative emotions, you are probably going to meet up with some challenging situations. That is not a reason to avoid going forward anyway, but it is a sign your vibe is not up to speed yet, and that you are probably going to encounter difficulty. Even elite athletes feel butterflies before a big game, but their anxiety is a thin layer over a vibration of confidence.

The repetition of affirmations, for instance, will have no effect unless there is a change in the way you feel. As we've said before, your emotional state is the primary indicator of your state of being, and the state of your vibration. If you are in the habit of glossing over the way you feel, life is going to present a lot of challenges. If that is the way you like it, then carry on! Most of us would rather travel our life path without a lot of drama and strain.

Someone who truly understands the Law of Attraction can work in the contagious disease ward and never get sick. It's how a master can walk the battlefield, and never take a bullet. You don't have to be a saint or a guru to get good at vibrational alignment, however. It just takes practice! After you have practiced for a while, you never even meet up with people and situations that were formerly anathema. In other words, you have purified your vibration to the point where you now interact with an entirely new set of people.

For example, Barb decides she is tired of dating men who are good looking but shallow. She reads somewhere about the law of like attracts like and realizes that she likes attractive men but has a belief that handsome guys are always charming and small-minded. She changes her belief just slightly and makes a new equation: Barb's guy = good-looking + deep. Lo and behold, at work, a new hire gets assigned to her section and he pretty much fits the bill. Barb is astonished, for she has never seen a man like this, didn't even know they existed! To Barb's friend Jill, Barb's "new" discovery about men is laughable, for Jill has been introducing Barb to wonderful guys without success for a long time, and has herself been happily married for years. She says to Barb, "Well, you finally get it." That's the way it works: you can't experience something you're not vibrationally "in range" of.

CHAPTER **4**

Conscious Creation

IN order for your life to work the way you want, it is necessary to deliberately create
it through the conscious exercise of your free will choices. If you do not, your
experience will be dictated by the beliefs of others. This is creation by default! For
example, as a child I always believed I was powerless. I never deliberately challenged
this idea, never even inspected it, and so into adulthood I often found myself in dead
end jobs, without much money, and not having a clue what I wanted from life. I didn't
believe I was even worthy of having a good life! I believed my life was lousy because
"that's just the way life is." I realize now that this belief was the cause of my lousy
life, but back then I simply created my life by hanging on to old beliefs I learned in
childhood.

Look at your life like a piano sonata. When playing the piece, you are constantly hitting new notes while old ones die away and the most recognizable notes are the ones
being struck right now. Those listening are mainly responding to what you are playing now, and it is the same with the vibrational signal you send out to the universe.
In other words, life is a constant creation, and whatever you don't like about it can
be changed.

Sometimes I practice piano with a metronome. A metronome is a little electronic
device which flashes a light and ticks at regular intervals. At first using it was mad-
dening, for I became painfully aware of the inexorable passing of time, which caused
me to make mistakes. After a while though, it became my friend and I hardly notice it anymore. The banging of the metronome has ceased and it has been replaced
with a feeling of contact with the now moment. I don't know how to explain it, other
than to say that time disappears and is replaced by a feeling of connection with the
rhythm of the piece, and a feeling of well being. There is a window of now, which at
first corresponded to each beat and grew to encompass the entire time I played the

piece. This is what happens when you get control of your life and begin to consciously create it.

The difference between conscious creation and creation by default can be illustrated by the guy who is at the piano and the guy who is sitting in front of the TV. The guy at the piano may be making some mistakes, but he's expanding his abilities and is in control all the way. Creative energies are flowing through him, and he's really juiced. The guy at the TV is dependent upon the creations of others for his happiness. If the program he is watching is funny he will laugh, but even so he's got to put up with those commercials!

Conscious creation is possible because, as we've said before, the universe's operating system responds to each conscious personality on an individual basis, through the matching of vibration. The effectiveness of this subtle energy phenomenon can range from utterly non-existent (for those who are not mindful) to extremely powerful.

4.1 The Role of Beliefs

THERE is an important corollary to the principle of conscious creation; namely, it is impossible to create beyond the content of your beliefs. Another way of stating this idea is, "If you don't believe in it, it can't happen for you." This sounds fuzzy until you begin to analyze it vibrationally. Vibrations that are too dissimilar either clash or cannot see each other, as we have already seen. It's just simple physics. Another way of stating this idea: if you aren't aware of something, you can't experience it. Now this really sounds obvious, but it is actually quite profound!

The content of your conscious vibration, on the reflexive flow, literally determines what you perceive, for you only have access to those vibrations that are in your range. In other words, if your TV is tuned to the Food Channel, you aren't consciously receiving the signals from ESPN. The signals from ESPN are out there, but at present they are out of your range. This does not mean you can't ever watch ESPN, for to switch channels merely involves a different choice. Things get sticky, however, if you have a belief that says you *have to* watch the Food Channel.

A belief is a set of activated vibrations within your consciousness to which you, and everyone else, responds. A belief is simply a pattern of thought that allows only a limited set of choices, and therefore results in a limited set of actions and responses. A belief is something you constantly recreate, in every moment.

A belief proceeds from a state of being. A state of being is a way of looking at the world; it filters all choices and preferences and determines what is thought, spoken, and acted upon. An example of a state of being is, "I am a realistic person," or, "I am very intelligent," or, "I am a loser," or, "I am lucky." States of being are necessarily expressed in language as "I am" statements, for they are powerful and fundamental choices of how to BE. Thoughts, beliefs, and attitudes about life proceed from states of being. For example, a person who has decided, "I am a religious person" might have the belief that "The Bible is the true word of God." This belief will then generate many thoughts and actions: "In order to attain salvation and enlightenment, I must go to church every Sunday," or "It is my responsibility to volunteer in community organizations and help others," for example.

Because states of being are so fundamentally rooted within a person's consciousness, some people are fond of allowing their beliefs to control their thinking and their action. "I can't stay healthy because my family has a history of illness." "I can't have a successful relationship because my mother was divorced three times." "I will never have enough money because my family has always been poor." Some even go so far as to assign cause to a past life. This is a convenient crutch to lean on, but it usually justifies your present position and ensures that no change is possible. Personally, I'm a great believer in past lives, but not when they are used to bolster self-limiting ideas.

Beliefs have far-reaching consequences. A skeptical person, for example, does not believe in subtle energy phenomena, and probably believes firmly that the origin of consciousness is biological. Such a person would find the ideas presented in this book utterly ludicrous, and he or she will offer many proofs of their absurdity. And for a skeptic, these will be undeniably true, for his life experiences will directly mirror his beliefs. He or she will rendezvous with persons of like mind, and all will be able to conclusively show that the so-called Law of Vibration and Law of Attraction is just new-age nonsense. That's the beauty of the Universal Operating System. Each person draws unto him or her, an exact replica of their state(s) of being, *and it is always true for them in their personal experience.*

Arguments about truth become thorny when one tries to impress one's beliefs on others, for every conscious being has a unique set of preferences and beliefs. That is why I have gone out of my way to insist that the principles in this book must be applied and tested on an individual basis, and cannot be imposed on another from the outside.

Beliefs are funny things, for they are merely our own thoughts, yet we often become a slave to them. At the same time, a belief cannot be, unless it is continuously self-created. This circular cause-effect chain is typical of the logic of consciousness, for consciousness creates and then perceives what it has created. Consciousness is the alpha and the omega, the worm Ouroboros, the question and the answer. A conscious being asks, "What is the meaning of life?" and finds, after a lifetime of searching, that the answer lies within himself or herself. In other words, when discussing consciousness, the answer to the question is the questioner. Our beliefs create the rooms of our personal house of life and they are as ephemeral as mist, yet powerful as corded steel. The dog next door never leaves his yard because he believes his collar will shock him, even though the equipment was deactivated long ago. This kind of psychological conditioning only works because an individual decides that it is so, and acts accordingly.

Beliefs can be freeing or imprisoning, but they are always changeable.

4.2 Regaining Control

How do you gain control of a life that isn't working?

I turned my life around by doing three things:

Figuring out what I wanted.

Keeping my attention on that and ignoring, as best I can, unwanted and upsetting things and in every moment reaching for the thoughts and feelings which make me feel the best.

Taking action only when inspired to do so, and not worrying about "what will happen if..." scenarios.

The first step is crucial. You have to know where you're going, otherwise you're like the guy in the middle of a rainstorm whose windshield is so clouded he can barely see.

In order to figure out what you want, it is helpful to spend 15 minutes or so a day visualizing and imagining your life the way you want it to be. Sometimes you can only come up with something negative, like "I know I don't want this crummy job anymore." But if you can set aside just a few minutes and do this every day, you will soon come to a positive and detailed definition that feels good: "I want a job in a medium sized company, with a salary of _____, working with a team of 5 or 6, in which I can exercise my communication and leadership skills." You want to get to a point where you can feel just what it would be like to be actually living your ideal life. The feeling of what you want is very powerfully molding and amplifying your vibrational signal, and lining it up with what you want. It's fun! The immediate benefit is a feeling of well-being and positive emotion within you. Fortunately, changing your state of being and the way you feel always evokes a matching response from the world at large, so you get rewarded for your inner work.

It is important that before you do this, you get as happy as possible. In other words, do not visualize your life from a state of negative emotion. Negative emotion places you back at the starting gate, for it is a sign of resistance to the goal.

What you want to do is place yourself in an ideal scene and feel yourself there. One of my favorites is placing myself on the shore of Lake Michigan, feeling the wind in my face and the sun on my back and smelling the fresh air as it comes off the water. You want to actually be there and feel yourself there, not observe from the outside. I am beginning to get so good at these visualizations that if I am feeling crummy during the day, I can stop for a few moments and get feeling good again.

This process is very powerful, and is not just positive thinking. One of the greatest geniuses of all time, Nikola Tesla, used creative visualization to design his turbines, engines and generators. He became so good at creative visualization that he did not need drawings of any kind in the design process! He knew every part, how it operated, and how the entire machine would work when assembled. His machines are still studied today for their elegance, power, and efficiency.

Albert Einstein also used creative visualization to develop his theory of relativity. He called these visualizations "thought experiments." Any artist will tell you that a clear picture of what is to be painted, sculpted, etc., is vital to a successful result. If geniuses and artists successfully apply this process, then we can too. We can begin to sculpt our own life as we wish it. I learned this the hard way, by just becoming tired of feeling crummy. I began to look for a better way, to hope that I could be a source point in my life. This led me to look into the Big Picture, to turn my life around, and to write this book detailing my understanding and my progress in life, from a nothing to the dynamic being you see in front of you right now (joke!). There are few things more satisfying than to consciously create a vision for something you want and receive it.

4.3 The Executive

How does creative visualization work for an executive (or a parent) whose effectiveness is dependent upon those below you? It is not possible to control the actions of others, only your own. The process is the same, however. When you get the feeling of where you want to go and the end result, inspiration will come as to how to get there. You might say, "That's a hell of a way to run a business." But creative business people will tell you that inspiration is an important ingredient in success. The job of an executive isn't to micromanage everyone in his or her department; it is to provide a creative environment where all team members can express themselves and utilize their abilities to the greatest extent possible. An executive is a visionary, a vibrational trend-setter. The goal of the executive is not to persuade others to follow his lead, but to lead by example. An executive who does not have his or her own act together cannot possibly exert positive influence over another; for, if you have lived long enough and have been observant enough, you find that people *always* respond to your true state of being, not to your words.

Some executives, when things do not go well, will resort to coercion, fear and punishment. This will work for a while, because people get motivated. However, motivation is a poor substitute for inspiration. Motivation occurs when someone is afraid of consequences, but inspired action comes from free will choices and connection to creative energy. Motivation wears off after a while, because a motivated person is usually somewhere in the range of negative emotion, and when in negative emotion, you're stupider. Companies that use motivational tactics usually have higher employee turnover ratios and things seem to get done only with a lot of sweat and effort. That's because a motivated person always needs a push from behind, and that's a lot of work for an executive. You wind up busier than a one-legged butt-kicker, and that takes a lot out of a person.

It's important, however, to realize that creative visualization is just a tool. Many successful people simply get an idea and follow up on it without a lot of mental gyrations. Nevertheless, the elements of creative visualization are present in every creative process. All successful people have a goal, a vision and a feeling of excitement about the goal, whether or not they consciously practice creative visualization.

4.4 What is The "Guidance System"?

THE emotions are an accurate gauge to the state of your consciousness. The way you feel tells you precisely where you're at vibrationally, relative to any subject. In other words, if you are feeling rotten about your career, you have self-limiting thought (resistance) connected to it, no matter what you would like to think. I used to go through life totally ignoring my emotions and making myself right about my life choices, even though those choices weren't getting me anywhere. The brilliant and inspirational lecturer Esther Hicks calls the emotions the Guidance System, and that is an accurate description, for if we will only consult our feelings about a subject, we will be guided unerringly to our own highest good. It only takes a few seconds to listen.

The equation of the guidance system is: good = good, bad = bad.

Society teaches us that good = bad and bad = good.

In other words, if something feels good then it is probably a bad thing to do, because it is either not productive, or it is illegal, or it is frowned upon by some religion, political group, opinion leader or family member. But if it feels bad, then it is merely an obstacle to overcome, so stop being a baby and just roll up your sleeves and get to work. This is another of those completely screwy, but commonly accepted ideas floating about in the mass consciousness.

Especially for the males in the audience, consulting your feelings can have a bad ring to it. Males of my generation were taught that consulting the emotions is a sign of weakness. We were taught to shut down our emotions and pay no attention to any feeling. We were taught that the ultimate male is the tough guy. But this is a recipe for self-sabotage. If you have ever seen a person who has shut down his emotions and feelings, you will notice that person behaves robotically. There is no joy.

If you are a woman, you may have been taught to ignore your feelings and be logical and reasonable.

In both cases, ignoring feeling is the common denominator. The emotions are your connection to life force energy, so ignoring them is tantamount to a ship trying to navigate without a rudder, and will eventually result in stress and, eventually, illness. But it is a good thing for those who wish to control and manipulate you. Someone who distrusts his or her inner guidance can be swayed by outside influences. That is the story of our society, as we see politicians and mass media influencing the consciousness of so many. But it does not have to be that way. Trusting your feelings is the surest way to live a life of greater joy, for the energy of life that makes up your very being is joyful. And it's intelligent too. In other words, action taken along a path of positive emotion will always result in a positive experience. The only way it can't, is if you begin to worry about what the end result might be. But then, of course, you are no longer feeling positive emotion! Worrying is self-sabotage, like the mountain climber who cuts the rope which supports him.

Your guidance system will respond with positive or negative emotion in response to whatever you are choosing in the moment. So by paying attention to your feelings, you can determine, in a general sense how successfully you are aligning or controlling your energy.

Being aware of your feelings is crucial to the entire creative process. It is vital if you want to create deliberately, and be at cause in your life! Those who decide to shut down their feelings are leaving themselves without a steering wheel. If you put your foot on the gas pedal but had no way to guide your vehicle, you would soon crash into something. So don't listen to anyone who tells you that feelings and emotions are illogical or meaningless.

The guidance system is meant to mean the character of the flow of life force energy through the human energy field. It is a subtle energy phenomenon, but because consciousness itself is subtle, it feels very powerful.

In Chapter 2 we proposed that the HEF (human energy field) is in the form of a torus, that self awareness itself is the recursive or self referencing flow of life force, and that thought directly interfaces with and influences the smooth flow of this infinitely sensitive energy. In its natural or default state, life force energy feels wonderful, because it is the quintessential substance of the universe which proceeds directly from what we can call universal consciousness, or the Creator. It is the carrier wave upon which thought throughout the universe travels. It is what my friend Ed calls the Universal Data Bank. Upon this life giving stream comes the inspiration to create and act. Upon this flow of energy comes the subtle connection and communication with every person and resource you will ever need. It is the medium through which the guidance system operates. It determines the quality of the emotions you feel, and it will let you know instantly when you are on the good foot, or are engaging in self-sabotage. When the human energy field is not blocked or distorted by resistant thought, you feel good; and when it is, you feel an appropriate negative emotion that is a direct reflection of the content of your thought. A simple system, but very powerful!

Paying attention to your guidance system will make it more effective, for you become more and more aware of the subtle nudges and hints from within that, if followed, can result in more effortless action cycles.

4.5 How to Know What You Want

SOMETIMES it is difficult to know what you want, especially if your life has not been going so well for a while. Moreover, some people have a difficult time visualizing anything.

In that case, go through the day looking for things to like. This process only involves observation, not imagination. All you have to do is identify things others have created that please you: A new car that passes by on the road, a nice house, a well-dressed man or woman, a pleasing architectural design, a beautiful garden. The idea is, find something to appreciate! If you do this long enough, consciously, you will have a palette of things to choose from, and it will make visualization much easier.

It's easy to get on automatic pilot, never really being conscious of the environment in the moment. But then we miss some amazing things. Driving to work the other day I saw a big cardinal chirping away. The morning was dull and snowy but the sight of that beautiful splash of red and the sounds he was making made my morning. When you start the day off noticing something positive, that gets you in a good vibe. And then by the Law of Attraction, you are a magnet for good things to come into your experience.

It doesn't matter what you feel good about, if you are in a good vibe, you will rendezvous with good things. In other words, feeling good about anything, no matter how trivial, will bring positive things to you from the environment. You could be feeling good about your golf game, and as a result, write a sales proposal and get approval on it the next morning.

"We really liked the golf metaphors you threw in there," the client tells you. "Yesterday I shot 3 strokes below average and..." At first you thought the golfing metaphors would be inappropriate, for your client seems like a serious guy, but you followed a hunch, threw caution to the wind and put them in anyway, along with a few humorous jokes.

You never know what good things will come about by feeling good. This does not mean that every time you feel good you will make a sale, but it does mean you set yourself up for the result of *something* wanted.

Finding something to appreciate can be very difficult if you are a negative person. I used to be one of the champion pessimists of all time. I was a "glass is half-empty" kind of guy, and even now those old habits of thought are so ingrained that I occasionally find myself slipping back into them. I know from experience that sometimes you just have to force yourself to honestly look around for something to appreciate. The reason for this is, you have been practicing resistive thinking for so long that your eyes and ears always notice the negative stuff. You've got a reflexive flow energy stream going, and a mirroring stream on inflow. Even though you feel lousy most of the time, you are used to it. Well, you got negative by practicing. It took a long time to get there, because being negative is a lot of work! Your very nature is positive, so once you start down the road of finding something, anything, to feel good about, it gets easier very quickly. It is possible to experience, sometimes unexpectedly, rushes of positive energy while just looking around for things to appreciate.

Because the Universal Operating System matches vibration, a conscious being is only aware of that which is already activated vibrationally within his or her consciousness. The more you practice feeling good, the more the environment seems to reflect your good feelings. In other words, looking at a sunset after a long day of work may make you feel irritable, knowing that there are chores to do at home. But the same sunset can evoke a feeling of awe and wonder when you feel great; same sunset, different reaction. A conscious being can always determine the way he or she feels about anything.

4.6 Be Selective When Consciously Creating

SOMETIMES, when noticing things that are wanted, it comes packaged with something undesirable. This tends to turn us off to the wanted thing, but it doesn't have to. For example, my Uncle Harold was very large "souled" (powerful and forceful), but arrogant and obnoxious. Observing Harold, I associated personal power with conceit and egotism. This was an assumption that cost me dearly for many years, for I was reluctant to step into my own personal power. I see now that I could have simply appreciated Harold's powerful aspect and left out the other stuff!

If your boss is an obsessive and irritating workaholic, you need not imitate his behavior when you reach the management level. Just because the successful high school football coach was a jerk, you don't have to do the same when coaching the Little League team (poor kids!). Take the good from your observance of life into your deliberate creative process, and leave out the undesirable stuff.

A proper creative visualization will result in inspiration. You'll feel like getting into action, and the work you do will be fun, and won't seem like work at all! A proper creative visualization is a combination of mind and heart – clarity of thought about what is wanted, and the feeling of what it would be like to have it.

We've been emphasizing creation more as a function of consciousness than action cycles because it is the starting point, but also because our society teaches us that hard work, sweat and effort is the only valid way to reach the goal. However, without a properly oriented state of being, all your hard work may generate little value.

CHAPTER 5

The Law of Allowing (or, the path of least resistance)

THE last principle of the Universal Operating System is called The Law of Allowing. Allowing simply means elimination of resistant thought toward what is wanted. Traditionally, allowing has been called non-resistance, but non-resistance has been distorted to mean that you should eliminate desire. True non-resistance is really enhancement of desire, for a desire funnels life-giving source energy through every part of your being and every cell of your body.

Allowing essentially keeps your attention on the wanted thing, and off of the fact that you don't have it yet! In our vibrational view of the universe, allowing simply means not interfering with the creative process that you have begun using the first three principles. Allowing is not proactive, it is passive. But paradoxically, this passivity is powerful, for it unleashes the creative power within you.

Allowing is a letting-go. Letting go of what? It's the letting go of the idea that what you want cannot happen, of the impossibility of it all, of worry and anxiety and "what if..." scenarios.

"Yeah, yeah, so what," you say. "Every self-help book in the universe says the same thing." Yes, but the difference is, in the vibrational model of the universe, we now have a clear understanding *why* allowing is so important! It is not some fuzzy airhead concept, but a methodology that can result in getting what you want.

I have a website (www.kjmaclean.com) which has been growing larger and larger and I was beginning to experience it as a big pain in the rear end, for a website needs tending and maintenance and it was starting to interfere with my writing. One day I just decided, "To hell with it. I'll just take it down." When I said that, I felt a tremendous release of resistance and I began to laugh. The very next day, so many people came onto the website that it set an all-time record by a huge margin. Was this happenstance or co-incidence? Well, at the time I had not advertised or promoted the site in any way; it was just out there. Somehow, my release of resistant thought concerning it cleaned up my vibe around it, which let the law of "like attracts like" go to work for me.

The idea of releasing resistance within yourself also works in relationships, but sometimes you have to hit rock-bottom before you can truly change your attitude. A woman (name withheld) in one of my Internet groups told an amazing story about the power of allowing. She said that a long time relationship with a friend had soured and for quite a few months, became unbearable. One day she just gave up trying to do anything about it, for it was just too painful, and vowed never to think about her friend again. Two days later, the individual involved called her and wanted to get things back on track, which they were quickly able to do. The point is, a full release of resistant thought can quickly shoot your vibration up the scale, and result in amazing manifestations.

A lessening of resistance can also bring unexpected side benefits. Let's say that Rick has exchanged email addresses with Bill on the airplane (going back to a previous example) and although nothing tangible has yet occurred, Rick is really excited all of the following week. On Friday his boss calls him into the office and out of the blue, gives him a small raise. When he gets home the phone rings; an old friend he hadn't seen in years wants to get together and discuss old times. Rick thinks, "What a remarkable series of happy events!"

These things have logical explanations of course, and we can follow along the sequence of actions in the physical universe and say, "There's no evidence that Rick's feeling of joy is the cause of any of it." Nevertheless, if you do an analysis of your own life, you will find that when you are on a good roll, it is inevitably accompanied by positive emotion, and vice-versa. In other words, you do not feel rotten and experience good things! Your good or bad mood *preceded* the events in the physical universe. The more conscious and aware you are of your own thoughts and feelings, the more obvious this will become. The subtle, vibrational nature of consciousness often obscures the function of the Universal Operating System, but it is always in operation underneath the surface of your life.

Allowing is a state of being. You do not have to do anything to achieve it, and in fact, the more you try the further from it you get. *Feeling good is a matter of being, not doing.* Many people think that if they could only have a lot of money, happiness would be guaranteed. If only the ideal mate would come along, then life could be perfect. If only that new job would come through, it wouldn't be such a struggle to get up in the morning. But these manifestations are a *result* of a state of being; that pot of gold or that perfect relationship cannot come unless you are already in tune with it! In other words, even though we have placed the Law of Allowing last, it really almost has to come first. In every moment each one of us sends out a vibrational signal, to which everything in the universe responds. The key is lowering resistance enough to be able to generate the proper signal, and become aware of the responses. In an electric circuit, for example, too many resistors can cause a lack of power at the business end, or result in overload and burnout, and so it is in life.

Doing (action) is most effective in tandem with a compatible state of being. Trying to resolve a sticky situation solely with more and more action cycles just leads to stress and overwhelm, for it is your current state of being that has brought you to the present difficulty. It often leads to a feeling of desperation: "If I can only get out one more mailing, I'll get the responses I need to stay afloat..." etc. The result of this mailing will inevitably be a direct match to the content of your vibrational signal. This is not an earth-shattering statement, for the content of the mailing mirrors your vibration, which is then transmitted in the physical universe to your target audience. Essentially, it's thought transmission. The only difference between a pure thought transmission and a mailing is that the thought impulses must first be encoded on the physical media (paper, DVD, radio waves, etc.), and it takes time to get the message out. In other words, the actions involved are almost trivial in comparison with the conscious intent of the message.

The mailing may restore your confidence that something good will happen, and the outcome may bring in enough business to keep you going, or it may result in a crash which forces you to seriously change your outlook. Either way, your state of being is eventually mirrored back to you in the physical universe. Proof or disproof of this idea, like everything else in this book, can be ascertained by performing life experiments.

5.1 Allowing is Loving

A LLOWING is loving. True love is complete allowing. It might be said that the Creator of all has so much love for us, that He/She places no restrictions upon us at all. Although man places restrictions on human behavior, a cursory glance around our planet shows the operation of free will everywhere. The behavior of human beings runs the gamut from the most heinous to the most inspired. Acts of murder, torture and depravity exist alongside those of beauty and selflessness. Such a state of affairs only makes sense if the ultimate nature of humans is eternal. Does it make sense to say "When you die, you're dead" in the case of the little baby who dies in a car accident, or the child who is strangled by its psychotic parent? It is grotesque to suggest that there is any point at all to such a truncated existence. It would be cruel indeed to bring forth new life and then snuff it out forever before it ever got a chance to live, would it not? Only if conscious personalities have a non-physical component and continue their existence separate from the body can we make any sense of life on planet earth. In such a scenario, there must be complete freedom to experience life in every conceivable manner, and it must always be possible to begin afresh.

Allowing is difficult enough to do with self, but it is sometimes almost impossible with others. I remember as a child, my father would insist upon "correct" behavior. This always meant behaving in ways that pleased him, not me. He would say, "I'm doing this because I love you," but I don't remember feeling any love! This sort of thing happens over and over in relationships, and especially with parents and children. Really, you cannot be angry, or anxious, or controlling (even in the best sense of ensuring that no harm comes to your loved one) and be loving at the same time. If you can recall times you felt loving towards someone, it was inevitably accompanied by a feeling of expansion, release, joy, and infinite tolerance. In other words, truly loving means loving no matter what the other thinks, says, or does, without conditions attached. As soon as right or wrong enters the picture, there is judgment.

Judgment = resistance, and resistance = negative emotion. Negative emotion is incompatible with the vibration of love.

"Tough love" is not love. Tough love is resistance to someone else's conduct, and the attempt to straighten them out. Usually it is accompanied by the idea that "it's for your own good." However, if you have ever been on the business end of one of these fixer-uppers, you know how uncomfortable it can be.

Sometimes tough love is employed to stop a pattern of self-destructive behavior and can be very effective, but we must not confuse sternness and discipline with love!

Allowing does not mean letting someone get in your face, and smiling like an idiot. If someone is in your face then you have been practicing resistance, not non-resistance! Allowing simply means, do not resist the actions of others. Resisting something just places your attention on it, brings more of it to you, and makes you feel crummy in the process. Allowing can only come from a position of strength.

My friend Mark has an enormously talented brother who refuses to utilize his abilities. Marks brother, Michael, designs furniture (when he's not drunk) and decided to start a business. His designs were immediately accepted and he received many commissions. Unfortunately Mike spends most of his time in bars and "doesn't have time" to fulfill his contractual obligations. As a result, many of his customers asked for refunds and Mike is now broke, with two pending lawsuits against him. This despite the fact that his only employee, a very smart businesswoman, offered to handle all of the accounting, paperwork, and the day-to-day drudgery of the operation. All Mike had to do was get the customers, something he enjoyed doing, and they would split the profits. It was a sweet setup that promised big bucks and success. Michael, however, declined the offer. He told her, "Why should I give you half my business?" then fired her. In order to stave off his creditors, Mike has borrowed a lot of money from his 82-year-old mother, who is not in good health. Mike's family is outraged by his behavior. They have tried cajoling, persuasion, and logic. And when those tactics were ineffective they tried coercion and threats. Nothing has deterred Mike from his downward spiral. Many in the family have given up on Mike, but still experience great upset at his behavior. Mike's brother Tony says, "Let it go. Mike is a screw-up and there's nothing we can do about it." Tony, however, while seemingly tolerant of his brother, continues to feel anger. "How can someone as talented as he is act like that?" Tony often says. These sentiments are echoed by many in the family. His brother Tim says disgustedly, "If I had his ability I'd be a millionaire by now, but what can you do." Tolerance is not true allowance, for in tolerance there is still upset.

My friend Diana works in a division with an incompetent boss. This fellow issues many policy directives and micro-manages everyone in the department. At the weekly meetings, team members used to try to get him to see that the problems in the department stemmed from his inept management style. First politely, then forcefully, then after a while lots of screaming! After a few months of this, they wised up. Now, all team members let the boss say and do whatever he wants, without protest. Then each one simply does whatever he or she pleases. According to Diana, this guy is so useless he does not even notice that what his workers do is exactly the opposite of his directives! But she tells me that peace has been restored to the office. The boss is satisfied with the appearance of managerial responsibility, and the workers enjoy their freedom. Allowance is the key.

5.2 The Creative Process

ALLOWING is very important in the creative process, for self-criticism destroys vibrational purity and leads to negative emotion. Self-criticism chokes off and distorts the flow of creative energy, and makes it impossible for you to maintain the vibrational disposition that keeps you inspired.

The creative process, in order to succeed, must involve something different than the current reality. It is, actually, a revolutionary process; for it demands that you come off the status quo. That is why so many artists and creative people get involved in politics, for their lives are built around a continuous process of building something new and different.

Almost all of us would like to change something in our lives for the better; therefore, all of us are involved in the creative process. However, society has many strictures about creation, because society is not so good at allowing. Just look at the laws that are passed every year regulating behavior!

"Don't rock the boat." "You have to go along to get along." "If it was good enough for your father, it's good enough for you." "The tried and true, that's the best way," Etc. If you have been subjected to this sort of mindset growing up, it is sometimes awfully hard to change anything in your life, for there is a belief that change is fundamentally risky. "If you go out on a limb, you're likely to fall off," is the attitude of many in our society. In our schools, we are all taught the scientific method, which says that if something cannot be observed it is not true. This has led to the idea that unless something has already manifested, it is invalid. But of course, this halts the creative process before it can even get started!

As a result, a lot of people find it almost impossible to take their attention off of their currently manifested reality, so they never get started; or, they give up way too soon.

Say you want a new car. You go to the dealer and find the perfect vehicle, until you see the sticker price. "That's too expensive, I can't afford that." End of the manifestation process. That is how most creations are killed before they have a chance to manifest. Or, you talk about a great idea you have and your friend tells you how unrealistic it is. You go into agreement with him and it's the end of that one as well. Or perhaps you tell your girlfriend that you'd like to learn to play the guitar. She looks at you and says, "Yeah right fumble fingers. You can't even screw in a light bulb without breaking it." You think, "That's right. The truth is, I'm kind of clumsy. Why bother?"

When you understand that the creative process is not the manifestation but the steps along the way, you can then allow yourself the time it takes to follow your creative impulses and achieve your goals, instead of becoming discouraged. This idea is obvious when discussing an artistic project, for one understands that a composition must be built gradually; however, in life we do not consider that the actualization of something wanted is a vibrational composition. In fact, as Esther Hicks says, the creative process is 99% complete before manifestation occurs. That is because although the vibrational matching property of the universe instantly responds to all thought, there is a threshold level necessary for manifestation; just as water will not boil until a sufficient quantity of heat is applied, or a broadcast signal must have enough power before it can be picked up by your radio receiver.

If you want the new car and do not have the money, you must first create the proper vibrational orientation that will lead to an inspired plan of action. The creation of a state of beingness and an action plan is just as much an artistic composition as a beautiful painting or sculpture. A great artist always has a vision and molds the physical creation from that vision, and it is the same with life goals. We are all great *artistes,* many of us have just forgotten that life itself is a dynamically changing, creative expression of self.

As a person in a relationship, you have to lessen your resistance to the goal anyway you can. In a relationship, noticing the good facets of a person's character and paying attention to those will draw them out in your lover. It is often difficult to resist the temptation to "fix" bad habits but remember that whatever you focus on is vibrationally activated within you. And if it's active in you, not only do you feel crummy, the other person will pick up on it. My wife, for example, can sense my disapproval of her immediately, regardless of my words, and that just brings her right down to my level.

Whatever you notice about others *must* be activated within you first; otherwise it would not be visible to you. For example, you are driving along and you see someone cut in front of another guy. "Jerk!" you think, "if everyone was like you the world would be intolerable." In order to criticize the other you must have first activated a negative emotion inside you. First comes the thought of disapproval, which creates the critical feeling, then come the words. Always the thought comes first, then the emotion. Why is this? Because the life force energy flowing through your human energy field is in constant motion. Critical thoughts block or distort this free flowing energy, which causes negative emotion (emotion can be thought of as energy-in-motion).

In our vibrational model of the universe, thoughts interface directly with the human energy field and you always feel the distortion within your own energy field first. You feel the pain you inflict on others, and you feel the love as well. Before you strike another, you must already feel the hatred inside yourself. Some might say that hatred is a good feeling compared to the pain you have inflicted on the other, but if you continue to spend time in the negative vibrational range, you will eventually experience pain and illness yourself. Sometimes in relationships a person needs another to love before he or she can feel love for himself or herself. But the love you feel for the other *must* already be present in you before you can project it! Those things you admire about others are already within you, otherwise you couldn't feel them or recognize them in the other. All of us are far more complete than we acknowledge ourselves to be.

5.3 The Power of Limits and the Creative Process

THE creative process takes time, and that can be frustrating. According to Chick Corea, world famous pianist, you practice until you get a win. This idea can be applied in general living as well.

A positive point of attraction will keep you aligned to the goal, and interested in it. I don't know about you, but when I'm down on myself it seems as if a million bummer thoughts cascade into my heart and mind, and I become more and more discouraged. Trying to sweat and strain through this morass of negative energy, I make little progress, and I wind up associating bummer vibes with what I'm doing.

The idea of stopping at a win is an example of the power of limits. People are uncomfortable with the idea of limitation, associating it with failure, or halting short of the goal; but limitation is built-in to physical existence. Our bodies can only go so long without food and rest, daylight recedes and darkness falls, summer fades into winter, etc. Natural processes are all built upon the idea of limited cycles of action.

If you can feel good about every step you take, no matter how small, paradoxically your progress will accelerate. If you practice for 15 minutes a day to even a small win, you'll go faster than if you practice every day for 2 hours, struggling and wrestling with the material. Of course, when you get a win it encourages you to play more. As long as you keep the idea in your head that it's OK to stop and take a break, you'll move faster, for you will maintain a vibration which is in alignment with your creative process.

No matter what the endeavor, forcing yourself to make the target is counter-productive. Quicker progress is possible taking little steps at a time, so long as they are inspired little steps! It is much easier to get inspired about something you really want than something you do not. Therefore, the alignment of energy to the goal is the single most important step in the creative process.

Furthermore, if you can get off the idea that you have to do the thing perfectly every time, and allow yourself to make mistakes, you will learn much more quickly. Turn bugs into features!

Laughing at mistakes takes you out of self-criticism and allows a positive framework for the creative process. In fact, in order for there to be a creative process at all, there must be access to creative energy, and that is not possible in the presence of self-limiting thought.

The mechanics of the creative process requires knowledge of where you are, as well as knowledge of where you're going. In my piano playing I kept thinking I was supposed to be Vladimir Horowitz right off the bat, so when I made a mistake I was all over myself. Clueing myself into reality, I finally realized I am a tyro, not an expert. My state of being was correctly that of a piano player, but my expectations of performance were too high! Now, I just laugh at my mistakes and I am very satisfied with my progress.

For a detailed explanation of the mechanics of the creative process, see Robert Fritz's book, "The Path of Least Resistance."

The path to creation can be difficult, or joyful. Difficulty only arises when you begin to disallow, and put up resistance to the accomplishment of it. In other words, difficulty has nothing to do with the magnitude of the task, only your orientation toward it (more on this later).

It is the focus on not-having that causes hard work. I found this out the hard way in my piano playing. I had been taking lessons for a year and made little progress. One day I decided to monitor what I was thinking while playing. I soon found I was focusing almost completely on my lack of ability, on my clumsiness in finding the correct keys, and most of all, doubting whether I would ever be able to play at all.

When you have the goal in mind it brings a feeling of joy, and whether you accomplish a lot or a little in any one creative session should not be a concern. It's progress toward the goal that keeps you going!

In my work as a contractor, I set a daily target. Sometimes there is a lot to accomplish, especially if the amount of work has been underestimated; but if I stay in the moment and take the job one step at a time, I remain positive and the stuff always gets done more quickly than I thought. When I am thinking about the totality of the work that remains, progress is slow, the day drags on, and I never make my goal.

Limitation is not limiting at all, but freeing! To understand this, imagine an infinite universe with nothing in it except a perfectly blue sky. You are a hawk, soaring, with total and complete freedom. Where would you go? What would you do? Fly, I guess, but how much fun would that be after a while? There's nothing to fly to, or at. There's nothing to play with; just the unending sameness of total freedom. Now let's introduce some limitation: we divide our universe and put some land and water, cutting the volume of sky in half. How much more interesting did things just get?

In order to have a game, there must be freedom, purposes, and barriers. A football field is precisely 360 feet long and 160 feet wide, and there are more rules in football than you can shake a stick at. But look at all the excitement it generates!

Without limitation there can be no freedom.

This idea is counter-intuitive. If you could have everything you wanted or would ever want right now, there would be little excitement left to life. So, especially when you are beginning the creative process, it is important to relax and let the process unfold. The fun is getting there!

Limitation relies on the idea of allowing. Allowing is the same thing as saying, being in the moment, which is the same thing as saying, going with the flow. There are probably lots of ways to express it, but they all have one common denominator: non-resistance. When you give up trying to frantically make it happen and relax into the moment, troubles disappear. Paradoxically, the more you relax the harder you can go. The best athletes, for example, are those who "make it look easy." The true professional in any field gets the most done in the least amount of time, and hardly even breaks a sweat.

5.4 Everyone is Sovereign in Their Own Experience

IT is tempting to look at the world and wish others would shape up. If only our obnoxious sister would stop whining about her problems, family get-togethers would be a lot more pleasant. If our stupid boss would stop giving orders and listen once in a while, the office would run smoothly and everyone would be happier. Funny, when you talk to sister and the boss, they say the exact opposite. "Joe is a control freak and he's always butting in," sister says. The boss thinks, "Joe is a good employee but he never seems to be able to follow simple directives. He's always going off on his own." The point is, trying to get others to do what you want is like herding cats, it's very stressful. People just seem to be stubborn, and do not want to listen to reason! Even the most irrational person will argue, stubbornly, for the correctness of his or her behavior.

Apparently, the desire for freedom is built-in to consciousness itself; attempting to buck that current is impossible. Of course, you can coerce people using violence and get them to go along for a while; but soon people rebel. The rise and fall of empires is largely the attempt of some to gain power (or financial gain) over others, but it never lasts. Freedom, represented by the Law of Free Will, always reigns supreme because it is an inherent property of consciousness.

If it is impossible to control the actions of others, is it possible to be truly sovereign? The Universal Operating System guarantees that you have control over your personal experiences. It does *not* grant you direction over the experiences of others! This is a very difficult concept to understand, for it is thought that the actions of others (cross-flow) must inevitably spill over into your life. However, a pure vibration of peace, for example, guarantees that no violence can ever come to you. A pure vibration of health will lead inevitably to health, etc. Because we are all in this together, immersed and commingling upon the surface of this crowded planet, it would seem inevitable that observation of the activities and manifestations of others must lead to vibrational corruption, of the importation of viruses into our personal operating systems. Well, it all depends on how conscious you are, how aware of yourself you are, how determined you are to direct your life. That is always a personal decision; however, a purely held state of being is the most powerful weapon you have in your arsenal of sovereignty. Even though we are raised on the idea of self-limitation, within each one of us is a kernel of connection to true self. The more you practice feeling good, the more conscious you become, the more aware you become of your status as a divine being. The better you feel, the more powerful you are, the more you discover about yourself.

The road to enlightenment and personal power is the road of joy, not the road of data. It took me 50 years of searching to discover that, and now I am passing it along to you.

As we talked about before, you can practice feeling good. Enlightenment is not some esoteric, difficult thing. The common denominator of all enlightened people is a simple feeling of joy. Even a blockhead like our friend Thorpe can feel joy! Happiness has nothing whatsoever to do with your IQ. Sometimes we lose sight of this fact in our zeal for personal growth. Simply put, the more joy you feel, the more enlightened you are.

5.5   It Is Not Possible to Create for Another

IT is not possible to create for another; therefore, you cannot help another if he or she does not want to be helped. This can be agonizing, especially if those around you are in difficulty. There is a doctrine on our planet that service to others is a requirement for right conduct. In other words, there are those who say it is our *duty* to help others less fortunate. This idea is divinely inspired, but unfortunately, it violates the inviolable sovereignty of consciousness. It is certainly desirable and admirable to uplift and inspire others, but you do not get any black marks on your chart if you don't. That is because the idea of karma, or original sin, does not make sense in a universe where consciousness is eternal, and, in its native state, a pure positive potential.

Personally, some of the most enlightened people I have seen are those who have devoted their lives to helping others, for such selflessness comes first from a powerful, personal connection to source energy, and a desire to share the love. This is service in the intended manner. Some have given this idea a little fillip, however, and used it as a club to beat others over the head. If you have ever been "helped" by such a well-meaning but misdirected individual, you know how irritating it can be!

Ultimately we must allow others to experience life as they choose. Each and every human being is a powerful orchestrator of his or her experience. Universal law supports every decision that is made, by every conscious being in the universe. So after you have given your all, it is time to let go. In other words, if your help has not been successful, then it is time to release your feeling of responsibility. Sometimes you just have to allow the actions of others not because it is good for them, but because it is good for you! There is no sense in stressing out, for that does not improve the other. Feeling bad does not enable another to feel good. If you feel bad, there is just one more person in the world feeling rotten, and that situation leads to an overall decrease in the planetary vibration. The world needs as many people as possible carrying high vibrations! (The equation is: you feeling good + others feeling rotten > you feeling rotten + others feeling rotten.)

The only way to help another feel better is by feeling better yourself. In other words, in order to raise emotional level you must be at a higher frequency (emotion), otherwise, there will be no energy potential, and nothing will happen.

In a battery, the positive pole has a dearth of electrons and the negative pole has a surplus. When a load is connected to the battery, the voltage potential between the two poles allows electrons to flow, lighting the lamp.

It is the same with emotions.

The light flows into the dark, effortlessly illuminating it. A higher vibration has the capability of moving a lower vibration toward it. The problem is, in order to be real to someone you have to be in the same emotional range, and that may involve going down the Emotional Scale to reach him or her. Have you ever felt miserable and had some happy person tell you to cheer up? I always wanted to smack somebody who did that, and there is a perfectly good reason for it: a vibrational clash. The frequencies of the emotion of misery and the emotion of cheerfulness do not mesh. A cheerful person who wants to help a suffering person must deliberately lower his or her level in order to be real and then bring the person up with them. That is why practitioners and counselors sometimes find themselves drained at the end of the day. However, it is possible to raise another's level without losing your connection *if* you understand that positive emotion is not a scarce resource. In our examples above, the gas flows into the bedroom from the bathroom and the temperature of the two rooms equalizes; and the battery eventually dies. It is different with emotions, however, because there is not somewhere a universal vat of joy that needs replenishing. It is not possible to take more than your fair share!

Well-being is in infinite supply. Therefore, it is possible to counsel another from a position high on the scale of emotion, while remaining real to the client. The best counselors are always those who establish a positive vibrational potential, allowing the client to move upward to them. No matter what the situation, allowing yourself to feel good is vitally important. The point is, helpful people should have an understanding of the emotional/vibrational scale (see Table 2.1) before proceeding. Later on in the book we will give a detailed example using the Emotional Scale to lift another from a lower to a higher emotion.

5.6   Failed Help

THERE isn't anything more frustrating than seeing so very clearly how a person is messing themselves up, offering constructive help and assisting in the most loving manner, but seeing no results.

Failed help is often crushing to self esteem. "I should have done better"…"If only I had said it differently"…"I should have known"…"If only I had done more"…. We have all had such experiences, and very often, they stay with us.

If you have done your best and have still failed, it's OK. You haven't really failed because every person has at his or her core a source of beautiful and positive energy that can never die.

It is neither possible nor desirable to change another's state of being without their consent, for by doing so you violate their free will and their integrity.

When you look at the world emphasizing the primacy of consciousness, your fellow human beings become transformed into powerful beings with complete sovereignty and power over their lives. I have a lot more tolerance and understanding of people since adopting this frame of reference and, most important, it just happens to be true!

5.7   Feeling Good Is Always Appropriate

It was said previously that the better you feel, the more intelligent you are, and the more enlightened as well. However, the idea that a person should feel good all the time is objectionable to some.

Society tells us that there are certain times when you are required to feel rotten. Like at funerals, or during times of tragedy, or when your friend feels horrible. If you don't tune into the bad vibes (sympathize), you are considered heartless and unhelpful. But wouldn't the world be a better place if people felt safe to feel good all the time? That does not mean smiling and joking in the midst of tragedy, but it does mean quietly staying in a high vibration. Shortly after the 9/11 incident I recovered my balance and began to feel the joy of life again. I walked into a toy store and bought my wife a Christmas present, a beautiful baroque glass and wood display case. I was in a great mood. I said something like, "Well the Christmas season will be here soon and there will be lots of people buying toys." One of the clerks looked at me like I was crazy and said, "How can people buy toys after what happened in New York?" I didn't know what to say, really. Her remark to me was disapproving, as if I had no business being happy when so many were sad. I knew that saying anything would be taken the wrong way, so I just walked out. At the time, it never occurred to me that feeling good could be interpreted as a bad thing, but afterwards it was clear to me that their reaction was perfectly natural. I was the vibrationally clashing cheerful guy, totally out of place. If I had been more observant, I would have noticed the long faces as I entered the place.

However, I have found a simple solution to this problem: quiet affinity. Quiet affinity means that you become less demonstrative physically, but you do not compromise your emotional state. (I learned this from watching some world-class piano players like Bill Evans, Vladimir Horowitz, and Chick Corea. These guys perform at an incredibly high emotional level and the music is uplifting, inspiring, orgasmic almost, but their bodies are quiet. The music comes out of their hands effortlessly and at such a high level that it's impossible for me to be still listening to it, yet they sit there, perfectly calm. I imagine the musician being a channel for a huge vortex of creative energy, yet able to perfectly control it.) The point is that when you find yourself in a situation that demands you lower your emotional level, don't do it! Use quiet affinity, maintain your vibe, and watch what happens. I think you will be pleasantly surprised.

Many people will disagree. They will say "If you are a good friend, you will be there for me when I need you." What usually happens, however, is your friend comes over and begins to recount her troubles. She wants sympathy; which means, she wants you to match her vibration. However, if you sympathize, you prevent your friend from going up the emotional scale, for now there are two powerful vibrations resonating to the lower emotion.

It is a truism, as Esther Hicks says, that you cannot feel sad enough to make others happy. My solution is to try to see to the positive core of my friend, and ignore the resistant thought which comes forth, making only positive and uplifting suggestions. The fundamental nature of consciousness is positive, so when you only acknowledge the positive, you are being completely truthful.

It is not crazy to feel good, ever, no matter what the circumstances.

However, you may be one of those who believe that there is a time to feel good and a time to get serious and be realistic about life. You may be one of those who believe that life is hard and then you die, and you only go around once and that life is experienced in a world of uncaring universal forces and that you just have to make the best of it. But if you have ever been connected purely to life force energy, even for an instant, you realize in the deepest reaches of your being that this feeling is who you really are. You understand with complete certainty that positive and uplifting feelings are intimate to your being.

The most powerful universal force, by many orders of magnitude, is well-being. If that is hard for you to believe then take a walk and just observe the world. Observe other life forms. Observe the trees, plants, animals. Look at the rocks, the mountains, the rivers and the oceans. Notice how beautifully and elegantly each exists within itself, and its relation to the whole. If you just open your eyes and observe your world for a long enough time, you will have a mind-blowing realization about the nature of reality. You will come to realize the overwhelmingly beautiful character of life, and of existence. You will never again be able to listen to the news, and its negativity, without laughing out loud. I mean that. The energy of well-being will flood through you so strongly that the negative statements of others will seem like great good humor.

5.8   Creating Your Personal Reality

You can become so good at determining your emotional level in a positive way, and allowing others to act without judgment, that almost nothing anyone says or does can affect you negatively. This does not mean that you merely tolerate the actions of others, rather see them for what they are; misguided. When you tolerate another you may feel sorry for them, or be irritated at their stupidity, but decide not to stop their activities. But this doesn't do much good, because you still feel lousy. Tolerance still involves a degree of resistance and often results in suppressing your emotions.

When it's time for Joe to visit Uncle Harold, he knows he will be subjected to home movies and obnoxious boasting about Harold's golf game, probably followed by some fictional and embellished stories about "the old days." The best Joe may be able to do is refrain from pulling all his hair out, but this tolerance is not very comforting.

Joe cannot change the irritating behavior of Harold, but it is possible for Joe to determine the alignment of his own vibration. And the way to do that is with a shift in perspective. The next time Joe is forced to see Harold (at Thanksgiving dinner), he decides to regard him as a headstrong child. Doing so makes Joe laugh, for he realizes that Harold *does* act like a child! Joe realizes that Harold's antics are just a demand for attention. For Joe this is astonishing because he has been brought up to regard older people as wiser than he.

Joe begins to compare Harold to a lovable puppy, who also craves attention. By the time he leaves, Joe can honestly tell the old codger that he's never had such a great time. Harold looks at Joe as if he has just gone bonkers, for Harold is not used to people laughing at him. He is used to provoking people and getting a rise out of them. However, Joe has turned the tables on Harold, not by insulting or demeaning him, but by a shift in his own perspective. Joe has transformed his family obligation from a time of irritation to one of great good humor. And the really cool thing is, Joe's positive experience had nothing to do with Harold, for he was just as annoying as always to everyone else.

True freedom is experiencing positive feelings at all times, no matter what the conditions. This statement is the opposite of traditional teachings. For example, Goethe said, "None are more hopelessly enslaved than those who falsely believe they are free." In other words, you can't be free if political or economic conditions seem to indicate otherwise. However, even if there is a policeman on every corner, you have the choice to feel enslaved, or to wave hello. When you are consistently feeling positive emotion, you become more intelligent, which leads inexorably to a higher state of consciousness and a greater appreciation of self. With this vibrational orientation, your environment must improve to match your new signal. In this way you change the world, using the vibrational matching property of the universe. In other words, no matter how lowly the place from which you start, practicing the simple act of raising your emotional level will inevitably lead you to a better situation.

This is clearly mastering physical experience on a very high level, but really, it isn't so hard to do. It just requires a commitment to feeling good. In order to feel good you have to want to feel good! Sounds stupid, but if you ask yourself "Would I rather feel good or pay attention to reality?" most of the time we prefer to think and act within our comfort zone, even if that comfort zone is not so comfortable.

True allowing always feels good, because it's a letting go of resistant thought. If it's possible to do this with an annoying person like Harold, it might even be possible with an irritating boss or co-worker, or even with a teenage daughter! Of course, when you get yourself into a state where you are allowing as a natural part of your life, you don't meet up with any more annoying people, and the people you live with magically exhibit improved behavior. That is the beauty of the Universal Operating System. When you do a little work on altering your perspective, you are rewarded for it. Remember, a change on the reflexive flow must lead to a change on the other flows. Without a change on the reflexive flow, there can be no change in your personal circumstances.

5.9   How Do You Allow?

ARE you the kind of person that wants to be in control? That is understandable, for part of deliberate creating is consciously defining and creating your life. However, there is a subtle but important distinction between the need to be in control, and conscious, mindful creation; the former proceeds from a feeling of insecurity and the latter from a feeling of power and confidence.

As soon as you really work at allowing, you are not allowing any more.

Paradoxically, the more powerful you are, the less you are working at it. The less you work, the more relaxed you are and the easier it gets. The easier it gets, the more you get done. Allowing, or non-resistance, is about maintaining a state of being which sustains a vibrational orientation, creating positive emotion within, leading to more effective action cycles, and matching you up with the people and resources necessary to accomplish your goals.

Complete non-resistance to something leads to complete freedom from it. The time to apply this principle, however, is *before* you find yourself in the path of that fast-moving car.

5.10   What is Resistance?

R ESISTANCE is a pushing-against; an offering of thought in opposition to some-thing you have observed or experienced. Because thought interfaces directly with the human energy field, resistant thought will cause a descent on the Emotional Scale. For example, you see a dead dog on the road and you may feel sad. You observe a person getting hassled on the street and you feel angry. All of these feelings are self-generated energy patterns, caused not by the event itself, but by your resistance to the experience.

The range of negative emotion you feel consists of various degrees of resistance to experi-ence. Pure allowance (complete non-resistance) of all experience would not generate any negative emotion.

In other words, there is nothing intrinsic to what is observed, (even a polluted lake, for example) which must generate a critical or negative response. It is always our choice (reflexive flow) about how we wish to experience the event. Mostly we have 'pre-packaged' choices, taught to us by the society we live in, and to which we have been exposed so often that we have bought into them.[17] So when we see that guy getting hassled, we are predisposed to be angry with the aggressor. Since most of us are not aware of the operation of the Law of Attraction, we see the antagonist unfairly attacking the victim, when it is really a co-incident event, an interaction of matching vibration.

In our wrong-way-forward society, our opinions and emotional states are established almost solely from what we observe, instead of the other way around! We allow phys-ical manifestations to dictate the way we feel, failing to properly utilize the naturally causative principle of conscious choice, and failing to understand that thought pre-cedes emotion.

---

[17] Advertisers and propagandists know that the repetition of something may lead to its acceptance. The Army's Psychological Operations Field Manual No. 33-1 suggests that "an idea or position is re-peated in an attempt to elicit an almost automatic response from the audience or to reinforce an au-dience's opinion or attitude. This technique is extremely valid and useful because the human being is basically a creature of habit and develops skills and values by repetition (like walking, talking, code of ethics, etc.). An idea or position may be repeated many times in one message or in many messages. The intent is the same in both instances, namely, to elicit an immediate response or to reinforce an opinion or attitude."

In this unnecessary backwards scenario, something is observed that results in a knee-jerk opinion or reaction, which is most often criticism, judgment, anger, etc., setting up an internal vibration of resistance. If this continues long enough, stress is the result, or perhaps anxiety, or that sinking feeling in the pit of your stomach. Whatever it is, it will feel uncomfortable.

The idea of non-resistance has been demolished in our society because there is no understanding of universal principles. It is thought that practicing non-resistance means getting constantly run over, but nothing can be further from the truth. Non-resistance establishes a vibrational proclivity, an activated vibration which draws to you wanted experiences and, like the radio tuner, automatically eliminates unwanted experiences.

In this society (United States) at the time of this writing, it is thought that protecting yourself from the dangerous thing will lead to safety. However, this is exactly the opposite of what happens!

5.11 Protection From Something Unwanted

ONE night while watching the news, a local reporter says that crime is up 53% in the city. Your wife looks at you and says, "We've got kids to think about." So you go out and buy an alarm system to protect yourself and your family.

There are now two ways it can go.

(1) The guys from the alarm company come to install the system, and they are very pleasant, answering all of your questions and allaying all fears. Their technology is up-to-date and the hardware is very impressive. That takes your attention off being broken into. You cease to focus on that vibration, deactivating it. You feel safe and are now drawing to you experiences of safety.

(2) Or, the alarm system is installed but the next night on the news, a burglary right in your neighborhood is reported. Or perhaps the installers were rude, or the system was not as elaborate as you had hoped. That gets you concerned once more about robbery. Now, even though you have a perfectly good alarm system, you are still focusing on the fear of being robbed. If there is someone out there looking to enter houses unlawfully, you will be resonating quite nicely to that person.

In the first case you say, "Installing that alarm system was great! I'm going to recommend that company to everyone." For you, it is the presence of all that hardware which secures your safety, and that is what you tell your friends, but in actuality, it is your focus on safety that is causing your experiences of safety. The alarm system is irrelevant.

You might say, "What's the difference? If the alarm system makes you feel safe, then go for it." Certainly there is no harm in having an alarm system, but we must not confuse cause and effect. It may be that every time you pass the control box you feel a warm fuzzy feeling of security. That feeling is the best guarantor of your continued safety, regardless of the presence of the alarm system.

In the second case there is a break-in, even though the guy is eventually caught. In both cases, there was an alarm system, but in only one case was there a robbery. The senior datum is where you are focusing your attention. Stated more precisely: It is always and only your offering of vibration which determines your experience.

One of my former clients is the son of a holocaust survivor. For him an alarm system is utterly essential, even though he lives in a neighborhood that has not experienced criminal activity in years. The alarm system has gone off several times however, all of them accidental. Once a contractor set it off, another time, his son forgot his house key and entered through a window, another time movers triggered it. Each time this fellow had a panic attack. The alarm system is really an albatross for, due to the location of the house, there is no way police or security companies could prevent a determined burglar. Nevertheless, without the system my client would feel completely helpless and vulnerable, for he has tied his state of being to an assemblage of electronic components. Paradoxically, he is a slave to the alarm system, but its presence is so soothing it allows him to feel safe.

Protection is a concept rooted in fear-of-something, and only serves to get you resonating along with the thing you are attempting to protect yourself from. It is unnecessary and if carried far enough, self-defeating. People who meditate or do metaphysical work often feel the need to protect themselves from harmful energies or beings. But it is this feeling that attracts unwanted things in the first place. In business, it is standard procedure to install security systems; but your best security policy is your own inner feeling of well-being.

Unwanted things will come into your life gradually, because the universe is fundamentally vibrational. It is not possible, in other words, for a person who has never vibrationally activated "car accident," to suddenly get into a car accident. There are over 40,000 automobile fatalities every year, but that is a statistic, a report about how others have misaligned their personal energies.

In order to get a manifestation, there has to have been conscious attention to something for quite a while, a long-standing habit of thought which has set up an activated vibration to which others can respond, or a sudden, extremely powerful vibrational orientation. Usually the latter happens after observing or hearing something shocking.

The universe we live in has been described by science as probabilistic. The Heisenberg Uncertainty Principle says that it is not possible to precisely determine the behavior of the subatomic particles that constitute the objects in our physical universe, and that idea has been carried forward along with the development of the mathematics of probability and statistics. Unfortunately, this has led to a mindset that life is fundamentally unpredictable as well, when nothing could be further from the truth.

It is only your continued resistance to things you don't like that causes you to experience more of them. When you first notice something unwanted, allow it! Let the energy of it pass through you. Notice it, say, "I see that and I don't like it. That's OK." If you continue to pay attention to it, you will begin to resonate to it more and more strongly. Allow what you don't like to help decide what you do like. Then focus on that! If you see a mugging on crossflow, for example, that is an indication you are perilously close to a personal manifestation on inflow, and it would be a good thing for you to clean up your vibrational orientation. When attention is taken off A and placed on B, you begin to resonate to B and the vibration of A dies away. This is the only way to de-activate the vibration of something unwanted within your being.

We have seen how resistance leads to discomfort, but earlier we also said that non-resistance leads to freedom. How does this work?

First of all, freedom is a feeling and it doesn't have anything to do with environmental conditions. You could be in jail and feel free. I met a guy once who had an enlightening experience while in prison for robbery; he told me that at first, being confined was so crushing that it forced him to completely re-evaluate his life and his beliefs. At one point in this process he had a personal awakening, and made a determined decision to stay out of trouble from that point on. He was so excited about what he'd discovered that he spent the rest of his term trying to teach his fellow prisoners. I should look that guy up and get him to write a book!

Freedom is personal. It is not possible to guarantee freedom for anyone but yourself, because there are billions of people on earth all acting with free will.

That brings us to the Universal Operating System and its relation to group dynamics.

CHAPTER 6

Group Dynamics and Sovereignty

6.1 Overview

NONE of us live in a vacuum. If the federal government decides to inflate the dollar, for example, we are all affected. And what about global pollution? It doesn't look like we're going to get rid of fossil fuels anytime soon. How does the vibrational universe concept work with group and national dynamics?

The short answer may seem objectionable: In a free will universe, all conduct is sanctioned. Polluters have just as much right to their activities as those who stand for clean air and water (if you don't think this is true, I invite you to try and stop them). The medium answer is that we are all in this together. Ninety-nine percent of the people interested in clean air use polluting fossil fuels, for they are by necessity connected to the grid. Their vibration is just as much a part of the species consciousness as the greedy capitalist who doesn't give a crap. The long answer is that well-being is the dominant vibration in the universe, by so many orders of magnitude that humanity's contribution isn't even a pimple on a pickle. I have read all the conspiracy theories and the "we almost destroyed the planet" scenarios, but here we still are.

Attention to things like pollution, nuclear war, overpopulation, resource depletion, etc. just maintains the vibration of them, and makes manifestation of them more likely. However, such things cannot come into existence unless, as a species, we all contribute. The point is, a vibration of well-being will not support them.

The conditions that exist on earth today are a combination of every individual's vibrational makeup, but attempts to change unwanted behavior simply contribute to the unwanted activities. My friend Craig found this out the hard way. He went to Israel with a group of activists in an attempt to promote peace in the Arab-Israeli conflict. His description of the fighting and their futile attempts to prevent it was both disheartening and enlightening.

So what's the solution for those who want to improve conditions? It is exclusive focus on and creation of what is wanted, and an utter refusal to acknowledge what is not wanted.

We live on a planet full of life forms trying to make the best of it, trying to make life as happy as possible for themselves. We call it the biological instinct for survival, but that is a crude way to describe it. Every life form is always reaching for well being, for its own personal connection to life force energy. The Law of Attraction is managing the whole thing, and vibrationally there is always balance. As a species, human beings have just settled for balance at a lower level of well being, but it doesn't have to be that way.

Group dynamics stem from a combination of individual vibrations and their matching responses. A group response is always the sum of many individuals thinking alike. For example, the Japanese attack on Pearl Harbor in 1941 generated national anger and led to the United States' entry into World War II. When the World Trade Center went down, the reaction was much the same. When numbers of people believe and act similarly, a powerful vibration is set up which can entrain others; nevertheless, such vibrational tendency of thought is not an irresistible force. There were many people during the Second World War, and recently, who were not in favor of the actions taken by our government, even though the current of popular opinion was very strong indeed. All beings have the power to remove themselves from the "group think" by simply exercising their freedom to choose differently.

Many people approach group issues from the outside in, instead of the inside out.

After a series of employee confrontations, the corporate board issues instructions to all employees for greater tolerance, all the while fighting amongst themselves! We have all done it, for it is so much easier to demand that others change their conduct than it is to alter our own. However, in order to alter group dynamics it is necessary to first get your own act together, moving outward to cooperatively include others. A person who attempts to alter the behavior of others without fixing himself up first is called a hypocrite, with good reason! Such a person is doomed to failure in his interaction with others, for his vibration is incompatible with the result he is seeking. People react more powerfully to your state of being and your vibrational signal than they do to your words. There is a saying that recognizes this understanding of group forces: "One [heart/mind] at a time."

In signal processing, which includes radio and TV broadcasting, musical sampling, and the analysis of brainwaves and heartbeat, it is possible to separate a complex waveform into sine waves of different frequencies that sum to the original waveform. Mathematically these techniques come from the work of the French mathematician J. Fourier, whose ideas resulted in a mathematical analysis called the Fourier transform.

Mathematical transformations are applied to signals to obtain further information that is not readily available in the raw signal. A Fourier transform can identify and distinguish the frequency and respective amplitudes of each sine wave that makes up the whole.

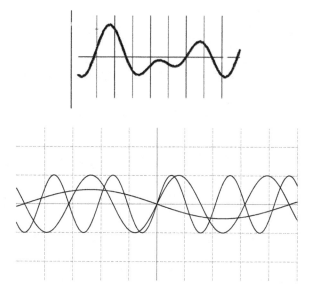

Figure 6.1: Waveform on the top can be decomposed into three waveforms

The signal on the top is a combination of the signals on the bottom. A Fourier transform can take the signal on the top and discover the individual signals that compose it.

A practical application of this concept can be found from the examination of the grooves on a vinyl phonograph record using a magnifying glass, or a microscope. The recording of an entire symphony may be captured and recorded vibrationally. The orchestra's many component sounds make a single complex wave pattern that is etched on the vinyl, and used to move the loudspeaker via the cartridge pickup. Despite its apparent complexity, the wave can be analyzed mathematically and shown to be a composite of each of the various waves that were produced by the instruments playing at that time.

What this suggests, in our vibrational model of the universe, is that *a group vibration is composed of different frequencies and strengths but is always a sum of individual signals*. In group dynamics, the predominant characteristic of a vibration (like a fad, fashion, popular belief, etc.) is just the interaction of individual vibrational signals. When enough people lose interest, their vibrational signal drops out of the mix and the fad dies off. Even though a group vibration has a tendency to entrain individual ones, every person is always in control of the vibrational orientation of his or her consciousness.

An example from my neighborhood illustrates the group dynamic perfectly. I live in an agricultural/residentially-zoned township. Two years ago, a non-resident who owned three acres of land on the corner of our subdivision negotiated an agreement to sell his land to the County Road Commission. In apparent violation of township zoning ordinances, the CRC intended to put in a gigantic road commission yard complete with heavy machinery and huge piles of salt, asphalt and other toxic substances. Well, the uproar from the community was loud and vehement. There were three meetings with the township board, the first two of which were filled with a lot of angry protests, and the board tabled. the proposal each time. I could see in the faces of even the board members who were inclined to support us, a turning away from our position. Finally, the neighborhood got organized, money was raised to investigate our legal options, and a former employee of the state Department of Environmental Quality eventually found a law forbidding such a proposal. It was brought to the attention of the township board at the third meeting and the proposal was defeated. It was fascinating for me to watch as more and more people changed their vibe from resistance to the government, to the creation of something positive, and how this was reflected in the outcome.

6.2 Group Dynamics – Non Resistance and Politics

Does the Constitution really guarantee liberty? Or is the influence of the Constitution just a reflection of the nation's collective consciousness? Recent political events in the United States seem to suggest the latter. If you follow politics at all you know that laws cannot guarantee protection, for they are just statements written on a piece of paper or lodged in a computer. There are so many examples of people violating laws and getting away with it that we won't even go there. The Law of Free Will, the Law of Vibration, and the Law of Attraction will always find ways around man- made laws, for these fundamental principles interface directly with consciousness.

Is it possible to fight for freedom, or to protect it with coercion or violence? Fighting for liberty/freedom is a theme that is especially prevalent in the belief system of the United States. Implicit in this belief, however, is the assumption that others will challenge our freedom, that there will always be a source of evil attempting to surmount the good. Here, we as a nation, offer a vibration, creating the conditions for a matching response; a self-fulfilling prophecy.

Growing up, I was told by parents, teachers and in civics classes that we must always be on guard to protect our liberties. "From whom? From those who would seek to destroy us, was the response. "Who are they?" I asked. "Communists," was the usual reply. Yet communism collapsed in Eastern Europe and in the former Soviet Union all by itself. "No it didn't!" some will say. "It was our diligence in fighting communism all over the globe which led to its demise." Well, I respectfully disagree. What you resist persists. Paying attention to something feeds it more power. Communism is just a way of organizing societies, nothing more. It started out with a bunch of intellectuals, and was attractive to those who favored a socialist, egalitarian way of living. Back in the day, however, there were philosophical differences between those who favored a socialist orientation and those who favored a capitalist orientation. A big vibrational energy clash ensued, hardening opinions and feeding energy to the conflict like two fire hoses hitting each other, making a big mess and eventually creating a 'cold war.' (The cold war was cold because the existence of nuclear weapons made a real war impossible.) Communism was a molehill that was made into a mountain, like the bar fight that spilled out into the parking lot. Soon passersby joined the fray, the police were called, and a full-scale riot broke out with millions of dollars in property damage. The way to prevent the riot is to ignore the bar fight! "Turn the other cheek."

Energetically speaking, when there is a power source, it beckons. The vibration can be positive, like the idea of freedom; or negative, like gawkers on the highway slowing down at an accident scene. An energy source reaches out, inviting others to come. It creates an energy potential. Physics tells us that a potential creates movement. The release of potential energy is called kinetic energy and in our universe energy is conserved, so the kinetic energy at the end of a reaction will be equal to the potential energy at the beginning. In other words, the amount of movement generated by any potential is proportional to the strength of the potential.

If you believe you have to fight for freedom, you are going to fight; it's as simple as that. The degree of conflict will be proportional to the strength of your belief, as others react in opposition. For some people, fighting is good stuff, but the vast majority of us would prefer to be left in peace. I guarantee you that if no one resonated to fighting in any way, there would never be another war, for that vibration could not take hold.

The point is that fighting, and peace and freedom, are vibrational opposites, and cannot coexist.

If you are fighting something you are a slave to it.

Upon examination, the idea of "fighting for peace and freedom" is ludicrous. No matter where you are born, freedom is your birthright, for you are a sovereign, independent consciousness, an aspect of the Divine. Personal freedom cannot be guaranteed or established by the actions of another, or by a document.

6.3 Non-Resistance and the Armed Forces

Pᴇᴏᴘʟᴇ object to the concept of non-resistance, especially in a political context. There are some who think, for example, that the armed forces protect a country from attack and guarantee the freedom of all of its citizens, and that non-resistance is a cowardly attempt to duck the responsibilities of a good citizen. But this is just another of those uninspected "truths" which are floating around in mass consciousness.

The armed forces exist to fight. They are an exact vibrational match to others who also wish to fight, and to those who are resisting fighting, war, and conflict. (The energy stream of resistance is building a wall, and the energy of the warrior is to knock down the wall.) This resistance to war can take many forms, but it always resides on the lower levels of the Emotional Scale (fear, anger, hatred, etc.).

Their little play is acted out upon whatever stage is chosen by them, and their actions only affect those who are resonating to the vibrations of conflict. And indeed, most of us in this society have been raised in an environment of war (cold or otherwise), and if we watch the news every night, it is very likely that almost all of us have activated somewhere within us, support for, or fear of, conflict. Those who resonate purely to the vibrations of peace, harmony and love will never find themselves involved in a war, unless it is their conscious choice to become so involved (like James Twyman, the peace guy). This is something most people find impossible to believe, but it is entirely consistent with universal law. Nevertheless, we say here with absolute certainty that the Law of Vibration and the Law of Attraction are inviolate and infallible and will always work in your favor if you focus positively. You cannot be a victim of conflict, if you do not resonate to conflict.

The armed forces protect no one, for it is impossible to protect anyone from anything, as we have already seen. If you are a warrior, then you love fighting and the military is a perfect career, for you then associate with other warriors and you can have a grand time. Blood and guts! But don't make the mistake of thinking you are protecting anyone else. Vibrationally speaking, as a warrior you add your individual contribution to the overall vibe of fighting and war. For a true warrior fighting is a release, but to the rest of us, war is a very imprisoning activity.

The idea that the armed forces protect the citizens of a nation from attack is, however, a great justification for their existence. You could not think of a better reason to promote military activities! It is actually a very clever way of psychologically training people to resonate to war and conflict. If you have followed me so far, however, you understand that fighting those who wish to promote or fight wars is pointless. Vibrationally speaking, you engage the other on his own ground! You become that which you hate, and find yourself part of the problem instead of the solution. Eventually, you learn the hard way that attempting to change the activities of others places you squarely in opposition to the Law of Free Will. Actions stem from beliefs, and although you may physically conquer, it is impossible to ensure a change in thought. Objecting to unwanted things feeds energy to them. Thus, love is the only way to deal with hate.[18]

There may be many objections to this. "OK, what about WW II? If morons like you had their way, we'd be speaking German right now and living in a dictatorship." Well, resistance to Hitler (or fear, same thing) allowed him to grow in power. In Germany, much discontent and agitation existed from the grossly unfair terms imposed on that country (in the minds of many Germans) by the allies after WW I, and the hyperinflation of the Weimar government threatened to wipe out what was left of the middle classes.

Hitler grew powerful internationally because of an enormous amount of resistance. Hitler started out as a little punk who grew more influential, not because people ignored him, but because they did not ignore him. Historical evidence shows that some of Hitler's funding came from sources outside Germany. Somebody who wants to fight needs another to push back. A vibration of conflict needs a matching vibration in order for it to take root. The martial art known as Aikido operates upon this principle, essentially refusing to resist the fighter and by using his own energy against him. Every time you resist something, you feed it power.

Many people think this is nutty. "If we didn't fight Hitler he would have walked all over us." People like to point out examples in history where peace-loving people were massacred by invading barbarians. The lesson, they claim, is that negative forces, if ignored, can overwhelm entire societies. But this is not how it works. We do not live in a universe where beings in it are powerless. There are no victims. The belief in negative forces is a massive distortion that mankind has placed into the species mass consciousness. It sets up a self-fulfilling idiocy in which a powerful vibration is offered, and eventually matched.

It may seem nutty to say that if people outside Germany placed their attention on well-being instead of resisting Hitler, that he would not have attacked them. However, the universe responds to individuals, even though it seems that groups of people are randomly affected. The only way every one of a group of people could be affected by the same event is if all of them thought alike. Mankind as a species has a tendency to want to agree. This is a divine impulse born from inner knowledge of love and

---

[18] A truly loving person never encounters hatred. That is an inevitable conclusion from the vibrational universe concept. There are, however, unacceptable religious consequences (for some) that proceed directly from its acceptance, and which are beyond the scope of this book.

connection to all things, but it gets people into trouble when the agreement is on something uncomfortable! That is why mass media is so effective, for it gets people thinking and agreeing on the same thing. It allows those who control the media to inculcate ideas into the minds of people on a massive scale.

Group dynamics are always a function of individual dynamics. Every individual conscious being in this universe is guaranteed to have complete freedom of choice, and the universe is designed to always respond to those choices, no matter what others are doing. I don't care how many history books or political commentaries you have read. All individuals are guaranteed by the laws of the universe to be sovereign regarding their own experiences. If this seems hard to believe, I invite you to test it for yourself.

People don't believe in their own power because the history of planet earth for the past several thousand years seems to be one of inevitable disaster. The thought stream of conflict and war is very powerfully activated in the human mass consciousness. We are raised from birth immersed in the idea that in order to be secure, it is necessary to protect yourself from the bad guys. However, no one ever bothers to actually look at history. The history of this planet is mind-numbingly predictable: find something you don't like, try to get others to change their behavior to suit you, if they don't do what you say start a fight. Or, look at something you don't like, become afraid that it will come into your experience, and try to protect yourself from it. Just like Joe Doakes and Cecil Aldershot, those who want to fight and those who protect themselves are perfectly matched vibrationally. This nonsense has been going on for millennia, stupidly, over and over and over and over.

You cannot protect yourself from anything. The attempt to protect yourself from something unwanted draws it to you. It's a simple application of the Law of Vibration and the Law of Attraction.

When the battles are fought, a person with a vibration of peace will not be present. He or she will be at a dinner party, or somewhere out of harm's way. A person who is tuned to well-being has far greater probability of being somewhere that war is not, and well-being is. That is because the ratio of well-being to disaster is overwhelmingly in favor of well-being.

History texts and news media proclaim "country A is at war," implying that every person in the country is affected by the war and supports it, and that war is present over every square mile. But of course that is not true. Go back to WWII and look at where battles were fought and bombs were dropped. Even during the height of the destruction of Germany, only a small area of the country was involved in conflict at any one time.

"Country A is at war" means that a relative handful of people in the government of country A have declared war on the government of country B. Now, goes the mantra from mass consciousness, it is the patriotic duty of every citizen to get behind their government and support the troops, thus entraining the vibration of the populace to war. An analysis of how this happens and how entire populations get involved is beyond the scope of this book, but it would make an interesting political study.

In the physical sciences, resonant entrainment of oscillating systems is a well-understood principle. If you hit a tuning fork which produces a frequency of 440 cycles per second (an A note) and put it in close proximity to another 440 Hz tuning fork, the second tuning fork will begin to sympathetically oscillate, or resonate. The first tuning fork is said to have entrained the second. The physics of entrainment apply to biosystems as well, especially brain wave entrainment.

In other words, the idea of patriotism sets the citizenry up to resonate to the vibration of fighting and war. The more powerful vibration has a tendency to entrain individual ones. However, knowledge is a powerful thing. Once you step into your power you can't ever be fooled again. No one can BS you, propagandize you, trick or coerce you. You become immune to harm.

In this book, we have extended the meme concept mentioned in an earlier chapter and the entrainment concept above to consciousness itself, and have postulated a thought/vibrational interaction based upon the influence of a universal field of subtle energy. The validity of such an approach only becomes apparent when you begin to think and act from such an orientation. Then the value of it becomes obvious, for it places you always at cause-point in your life.

In our vibrational model of the universe, vibrational proximity is more important than nearness in time and space. In my rural neighborhood, there are a dozen houses close to mine, but there is little interaction. I have much more in common with some of my Internet friends who live hundreds of miles away. A salesman may approach you with a sales pitch, but he has no hope of success unless he is vibrationally aligned with you. In fact, vibrational incompatibility results in physical separation. I remember, several years ago in my negative phase of life, I showed up at a group meditation for world harmony and peace. There were a dozen people present, and after a few of my cynical comments, some guy looked me in the eye said politely but firmly, "You don't seem to be catching the spirit of this. Perhaps you shouldn't participate." Everyone turned to me in silent agreement, and I felt like a puppy caught crapping on the carpet. I slunk out of there with my tail between my legs, embarrassed, my negative contributions powerfully rejected. Vibrationally, I was incompatible and could not comfortably occupy the same space.

It's not my purpose to bad-mouth the armed forces. As I said earlier, warrior types love to fight and the military is a perfect expression for their desire to mix it up.

The rest of us just have to wise up and stop trying to "fix" them. The Joe Doakes' of the world are not going to go away, because their decisions are fully supported by universal law. There is nothing wrong with someone who disagrees with you, or acts differently than you. He or she is just different, and contributes their valuable note to the overall symphony of life.

"Yes, but the military kills innocent citizens and wreaks destruction," you say. It does. But I invite you to stop them! You will quickly find out what an impossible task it is, but you will probably learn a lot about the principles of the Universal Operating System in the process.

If you do not want war, then paradoxically you must allow all war.

By that is meant, you must not resist or push against those who believe in war. If you do, then in your worry, fear, or anger, even if it is only for others, you will begin to resonate to the vibration of war and contribute to it. This is the impossible principle so many wise ones have tried to explain to the bulk of humanity for millennia. Stated more generally, non-resistance to the vibration of X is the only way to guarantee that you will never become involved with X.

The implications are enormous, for it means that you cannot prevent another from becoming involved in harmful activities! Each being is sovereign and has control over his or her vibrational platform of attraction.

What is the solution, then, for those who wish to prevent war? It is to focus exclusively on peace, to BE peace, as my friend Craig would say. To focus on peace and network with others who are also of like mind and begin to spread the vibrations of peace around the world. The more people who pick up on these vibrations, the less chance of war, for those who might be drawn into conflict, in their fear of it, will be placing their vibration in an attitude of peace instead.

The best way to influence others is by setting an example. Help, in the form of persuasion, coercion, reward and punishment, will eventually fail. By living your truth you become a beacon for all who observe you. You walk the walk, and not just talk the talk.

It is very easy to talk the talk. It is very understandable to want others to change their behavior, because if you don't like "A," it is obvious that if you can eliminate "A" from your environment, you can be happy. But going down that road is a long, hard trek, for you must constantly monitor your environment, vigilantly ensuring that those who disagree with you behave themselves. Unfortunately, you usually end up morphing more and more into what you dislike. As Walt Kelley, the late writer of the old "Pogo" comic strip once said, "We have met the enemy, and he is us."

Those who want war are very good at spreading the vibrations of war, fear, and anxiety. The news is almost completely about negative events. The other day I heard about a conflict in India, a bomb blast somewhere in Asia, and the threat of nuclear proliferation somewhere in the Middle East. What this has to do with people in the US of A, is a mystery to me. I guess those who promote these things do so with the attitude that it is better to be aware than ignorant. But is it better to be aware of negative things or ignore them? If one ignores negative truths, then one never resonates to them, and so is safe from them.

This is precisely the opposite of what we are taught. "If you ignore something it will hit you in the face. Try standing in front of a moving car and ignoring it." However, one merely needs to ask, "Why are you standing in front of the car?" "What prior decisions have you made that placed you in front of the car?" People who deliberately stand in front of moving cars do so because they want to die. When one resonates to the idea of death, many avenues lead to that result. If one never pays attention to death, one never finds himself standing in front of a moving car. All life scenarios lead back to the decisions of consciousness. It's not rocket science, just common sense.

You might say, "You're nuts. If someone drops an atomic weapon on your city, you are going to get snuffed. And the radiation effects can spread for hundreds of miles. Ignore that!" The Universal Operating System is designed to interface directly with consciousness, so if you are resonating to well being, you cannot possibly experience disaster. The laws of the universe are powerful and infallible and you are always guaranteed to be in a good position, as long as your vibrational signal is in a good position. You just have to get a grip on your thoughts and feelings. In order to do that, find things to feel good about! Feeling good is your best protection against the bad stuff.

Atom bombs dropping on your city can only occur if there is a massive, overwhelming shift in that city's vibrational orientation. One of the purposes of this book is to point out the inherently positive nature of consciousness, and thus prevent such a shift. You just have to understand how powerful and pervasive well-being is. That can only happen if people open their eyes and actually look around. Many of us look, but do not see. We live our lives as automatons, failing to mindfully and consciously create the belief systems that can change our lives.

The principles stated here cannot be proven intellectually or scientifically, nor can they be proven broadly to groups of people. The vibrational universe concept must be applied and experienced for yourself, on an individual basis.

A philosophy that places a conscious being always at cause-point is not for everyone! For some, it will simply be too difficult; for others, incomprehensible. However, if you have made it this far, dear reader, then you understand that such a philosophy can be inspiring and uplifting, for it reminds you that you are inherently a powerful being, a sovereign, eternal, divine consciousness that has incarnated on earth to experience joy and well-being. Such a philosophy resonates deeply with every person on this planet, even those who choose to deny the most fundamental truth about themselves.

Let's say, for the sake of argument, that mankind in his insanity is capable of blowing up his societies and wrecks the earth, killing all life upon it (don't worry, it'll never happen). What is the result? All consciousness returns to its non-physical, expanded state, and resumes a full connection to joy and well-being. The dirty little secret of death and life is that all outcomes, no matter how terrible from a physical perspective, are positive. Mankind has such an unwarranted fear of death that any scenario which leads to death is immediately pronounced dreadful. It is of course impossible to empirically prove that death is a positive experience, but those who believe that consciousness is ultimately non-physical in nature will have the last laugh. The proof will come to every single individual on earth, during the "death" process. Meanwhile, as Andy DuFresne says to Red in the box office hit 'The Shawshank Redemption,' "Get busy livin' or get busy dyin.'"

6.4 More on Group Dynamics

A GAIN, what appears to be a group or a national or a global problem is just agreement in thought between many individuals. And the solution to these problems is only possible by addressing individuals. In a universe of free will, that's the only way it can be.

Take pollution, for example. Most people will say that big corporations and utilities cause pollution, but these only exist because of demand from each and every one of us. If one looks at the local coal burning power plant vibrationally, it can be seen as the locus, or gathering point, of thousands of requesting energy streams. Just as the local food market would quickly go out of business if its customers did not support it, so too would the power plant. "Yes, but we can always find another market," you say, "but finding another energy source to power our homes is impossible." True, but why are there no other sources of power? Because they have not been asked for! The type of and number of food markets in any area is directly proportional to the demand for them, and so too for energy sources. Humanity has simply accepted fossil fuels and pollution and has not, en-masse, asked for alternative sources of energy.

Anything that exists in the physical universe is a reflection of that which is being created vibrationally. A building is constructed from a set of blueprints that come directly from the consciousness of the architect. The power plant with all of its features and characteristics is a perfect mirror of the consciousness of those who use it.

"The power plant was built and is maintained by XYZ Energy, not some fuzzy vibration," you say. "And I am utterly dependent on it." Well, that is what everyone else in your city thinks as well, and that is why the thing exists in the form that it exists. Of course XYZ built and maintains the power plant, but it could never exist unless there was conscious acceptance of it. In order for conditions in the physical universe (no matter how established) to change, first there must be a change in consciousness, for the animating principle is the impetus behind everything that exists, and precisely determines the characteristics of that existence.

It is often irritating to reformers when it is understood that in order to effectively change group dynamics, one must proceed "one heart/mind at a time." That is why people band together to pass laws compelling others to toe the line, because it is easier to coerce masses of people than it is to educate them. "Might makes right," as the saying goes. But such tactics always fail, for they are in violation of universal principles.

If one is opposed to the polluting power plant one may organize a group and force it to clean up its act. This necessitates the installation of expensive new equipment, which increases the price of the service, making energy even more costly and scarce. The solution to a problem, whether on a group level or individually, will always mirror the predominantly activated vibration. In other words, a consciousness of scarcity generates solutions that involve more scarcity! This is how self-similar solutions to problems continually recur.

On a happier note, one might begin to investigate alternative ways to generate electricity in your home. And who knows where that will lead? That is the wonder of the creative process! New technologies and methodologies cannot come forth unless there is first an asking, and then follow-up. If there is no demand, there can be no impetus to fill that demand. Vibrationally speaking, a desire or a demand creates an inflowing energy stream, which wants to be satisfied. This is a fundamental economic idea that is firmly based on universal principles.

Once a thing has been established in the physical universe, the tendency is to observe it and continue to validate its existence. In other words, if something is observable, as individuals we think that it deserves our attention. This keeps it ingrained in the culture and its existence becomes unquestioned, even if it no longer serves us. For example, there is, at the time of this writing, a debate in country A about the current structure of the intelligence community. A proposal is advanced which will dismantle the current configuration and create an intelligence czar along with a powerful new agency. When the debate begins, it is presented in the following format: "Should we go to the new system or keep the old one as it is?" Many critiques of the old system are brought forward and wonderful new arguments for the new are offered. However, no one thinks to ask the question: "Is an intelligence operation necessary or even desirable?" In 1947 an intelligence agency was formally created in country A, and since that time the national politics of country A have become dependent upon an institution which was created to simply gather information, and has now morphed into an ever growing "black" and secret shadow government. Threats to country A naturally appear more and more frequently from around the world as the intelligence establishment grows larger and larger, requiring the military presence of country A in more and more nations.

The formula goes, as X (fill in the blank) appears more and more dangerous, it causes more resistance to X in country A and leads to actions against X, which causes retaliation from X which requires more action against X...all in the name of protecting its citizens from X. A self-fulfilling idiocy.

The deputy national security advisor of country A offers the following rationale for the new system: "These reforms are designed to help better secure our nation and improve our ability to bring our enemies to account." (Source: the *New York Times*). What's wrong with this picture? The two most important concepts in the above statement are "secure" and "enemies." It is internally self-conflicting and the fallacy of it is self-evident.

Let's say you want to promote "B," but "B" goes against the interest of the majority. You set up organizations to further "B" and you encourage opposition to it as well. The latter seems stupid until you look at it vibrationally, for now all attention is on "B." Even if those who oppose "B" actually want "C," their attention can be effectively co-opted to "B."

It doesn't matter whether there is agreement or disagreement on "B"! As long as the attention of all parties is focused on "B," it will continue to grow larger in the consciousness and in the life experience of all concerned. As the saying goes, "All pub is good pub." Humanity as a species is childishly easy to manipulate!

For example, let us consider fossil fuels again. Those who promote the use of fossil fuels also encourage conservation, which continues the focus on fossil fuels and promotes the currently activated vibration of scarcity. The obvious solution to polluting and scarce fossil fuels is the encouragement of cleaner, more efficient sources of energy. However, this is a no-no. One merely has to trace the amount of money spent on energy to confirm this. In some circles in country A, the Department of Energy is known as the Department of Fossil Fuels, and for good reason.

Mankind as a species seems to operate on the equation, "In order to get B we have to first eliminate A." We inculcate our children with the idea that if something is unwanted, it must be fought. When a highway construction worker was killed a few years ago, my state passed a law mandating "Injure/Kill a Worker $7500 Fine or 15 years in Jail" signs posted at all construction sites. Now, every driver who passes the site has injuring and killing highway workers activated in his consciousness just before he reaches the work area! "But we have to DO something to protect highway workers" is the response. Very well, but perhaps we can think of something a little more intelligent!

Vibrationally speaking, there are no accidents. The worker who died and the driver who killed him participated in a co-incident event. At first glance this idea may seem absurd, but the more you work with the principles outlined in this book, the more control you will have over your life and the more sense it will make. It appears to be a false concept because we observe what happens to others and assume that we are vulnerable as well, but it is impossible to get inside another's head and know what has been vibrationally activated within him or her.

Posting signs, passing laws and making people aware of the bad stuff is ineffective because it attempts to prevent individual co-incident events using a "one size fits all" approach. The broadness of such an approach renders it useless; it's like trying to kill a gnat with a shotgun.

The same applies to disease prevention. "Awareness of X (fill in the blank with the illness of your choice) is the key to prevention," it is said. Well, this just gets you worrying about the condition, and resonating to it. The best "disease prevention" is a complete and exclusive focus on HEALTH.

The above principles apply both individually, and on group and national scales. History books tell us that WW II ended because the valiant forces of freedom defeated the evil Axis powers; but vibrationally speaking this is not true. The war ended because there was simply no longer a desire for it. When the predominantly activated vibration in the affected countries changed from "war" to "peace," peace prevailed. When history is written, we only hear about the decisions of governments and policy makers, but this is just the tip of the vibrational iceberg. All governments and government policies are a reflection of the consciousness of the people. Individually, in groups, nationally and globally, war, peace, prosperity, illness, and poverty are all created conditions and are physical reflections of the vibrational orientation of ALL of the people. Always and at all times, mankind has control over the conditions that exist within his societies.

Cultural traditions and religion have served to continue old patterns of thought in the species consciousness over the millennia, dictating sameness of belief and action. As a result, the pressure to conform has been strong in almost all cultures on our planet. Mankind believes that group forces are more powerful than individuals; therefore, when a group grows strong individuals almost automatically fall into line, consciously disempowering themselves. If our ancestors hated the Walla-Balla tribe, then we have to hate them too.

Politically, our species is fond of hierarchical structures. In democratic societies, we elect representatives who pass laws telling us what to do, and in dictatorships we allow a small clique to enforce their own dictates. Either way you slice it, mankind seems to enjoy giving up individual power to groups, who then order us about. Way back in 1941, Erich Fromm outlined the psychological reasons for this behavior in his seminal book, *Escape From Freedom.*

Free will and individual self-awareness are not only quintessential properties of consciousness, but fundamental characteristics of incarnated beings. In other words, human beings are, by definition, consciousness associated with physical containers and are necessarily separate personalities. Although I believe that we are always connected to each other through a universe-wide field of subtle energy, the physical experience is designed to be individualistic. In this framework, the exercise of personal power and personal self-awareness is the only way to personal enhancement. Excessive reliance upon others in group situations (e.g., "safety in numbers") diminishes personal power and lowers self-confidence and individual integrity. Furthermore, anything that lowers self-awareness is not only harmful individually, but also lowers the strength and integrity of the group. As the old saying goes, "A chain is only as strong as its weakest link."

In short, denial of self is not only the underlying cause of irrational personal behavior, but also group and species behavior.

As a species, mankind approaches life in an inverted fashion, focusing on unwanted aspects. Imagine, for example, a huge buffet, filled with foods of every possible description from every culture on earth. There is enough variety so that every conceivable preference can be satisfied. Instead of happily choosing and tasting, however, people begin to argue over the appropriateness of many of the items. "What is this? Blood soup? Revolting!" "No more revolting than haggis!" "Better than Yorkshire pudding!" Soon vegetarians are quarreling with meat eaters, and the whole thing turns into a food fight.

Now imagine a planet where there existed so many creative people and so many divergent interests that the smorgasbord of choice ranges from torture and sadism to beautiful works of art, and apply the same concept. Now you have the reality of planet earth! All activities are automatically islanded by the operation of the Law of Vibration and the Law of like attracts like into separate groups. It's your choice to join or pass by what you decide to give your attention to.

It's time for our species to wake up and smell the coffee. For millennia we have been repeating the same mindless patterns of thought and actions over and over and over again. Mankind has been enamored of negative truths, instead of positive ones, and so we have continued to create and recreate in a self-similar fashion, over and over and over again. Poverty, illness, and war have been the lot of mankind, but it doesn't have to be that way.

Once again: If you want something, focus your attention and your activities exclusively upon it. If you don't want something, don't be a dork and try to fix it. Positively work to create what is wanted, instead of trying to eliminate what is unwanted.

When you try to fix that which is not wanted, you are stepping on the toes of those who *do* want it. In this world of incredible variety there will always be things that displease you, which others like. So what? Try to avoid the impulse to get everyone to think and act like you. You are an incredibly valuable and vital being, but so is everyone else. Even when they do stuff that you don't like.

It's just a matter of choosing differently. You don't have to change the world to get a world you like. The UOS guarantees that you can live any way you want, *if* you are smart enough to just keep your attention focused on the life you want. There are millions of people out there who think similarly to you, even though there are many more millions who don't. You can attract people of like mind to you, and positive life situations, as long as you do not try to renovate those who disagree with you. When you try to fix other people you are butting heads with the First Principle and the Law of Free Will. There just ain't no way of defeating these fundamental universal principles, and it's not necessary.

The concept of choosing things you like and ignoring the stuff you don't like is what the Law of Allowing is all about. It is just a common-sense application of the idea of non-resistance. In this book, we take non-resistance from the arena of metaphysics and religion and place it firmly in the arena of day-to-day living. Non-resistance is not esoteric or difficult! All that is required is to choose/create what you want and relax about the other items in the buffet. If you don't like Brussels sprouts, help yourself to some beef and leave those yucky little devils to someone else

6.5 True Non-Resistance Comes From a Position of Strength

ALLOWING and non-resistance mean total freedom. For example, would you say that a guy who is packing a weapon and knows how to use it is free, or a guy who is unarmed but joyful? A lot of people would choose the former. But truly, the answer is the latter. A person who is truly joyful cannot match up with a gun-wielding criminal. A guy who is ready to defend himself will likely have to, because that is where his attention is focused.

Applying the Law of Allowing is only possible from a position of power and strength. The guy who is packing is angry, or afraid. He is low on the emotional scale, in the area of negative emotion. That is why he feels the need to protect himself. He is disconnected from his true nature, which is a connection to life force energy and a feeling of well-being. This energy is the strongest and most powerful energy in the universe; it is what creates and maintains the universe. Think of the power that it takes to keep the planets in orbit around the sun. That is strength on an unimaginable scale! The guy who is joyful is connected to this energy. He is unafraid, and therefore, truly free.

Freedom is a positive thing, a connection to and an orientation toward joy. Freedom is not a protecting from danger. This sort of "freedom" is a trap, for one is now focused upon danger, and drawing it to you. It is born from an orientation of weakness. The famous speech by Franklin Delano Roosevelt, about freedom from want, and freedom from hunger, was either a misguided attempt at inspiration, or a deliberate attempt to focus attention upon the bad stuff.

Freedom cannot be guaranteed by a Constitution, or a law, or a gun. True freedom is the ability to be joyful, no matter what the conditions are around you. And when you are joyful, the environment around you becomes joyful as well.

So in concluding this section, we say that allowing and non-resistance are positive and empowering concepts, coming from an orientation of strength, while resistance, fighting, and protection are negative and come from an orientation of weakness.

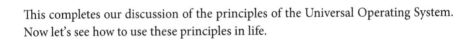

This completes our discussion of the principles of the Universal Operating System. Now let's see how to use these principles in life.

6.6 The Sovereign

WHAT is the orientation of a being who fully understands the Universal Operating System? It is one of complete sovereignty. When a person has consciously and deliberately used these laws and experienced the positive changes within, and seen the desired manifestations in the physical universe, there can no longer be any doubt about his or her ability to accomplish anything that is desired. The concept of sovereign is one that has been lost by this society, with our mass produced, consumer based economy and its highly regulated and organized system of government. Everyone is expected to "obey the law" (man made laws, that is) and respond immediately and humbly to any authority figure, but this is opposite to the orientation of a fully empowered being, to the spirit of the law itself, and to the spirit of our beloved Constitution and the great men and women who created it.

In law, a sovereign is defined as

- "one who possesses supreme authority..." *Funk and Wagnall's Dictionary.*

- "Supreme in power, rank or authority." "Independent of all others." *Webster's Collegiate Dictionary.*

- "Self-governing, independent." *American Heritage Dictionary.*

In law, a sovereign is a conscious, flesh and blood human being. It is understood in law that one always has a free-will choice to engage in any activity, and that a human being is responsible for his or her own choices and actions. In other words, if a policeman stops you and asks you to roll down your window and you do, you have given your free-will consent to engage in a contract with the policeman, which usually results in getting a traffic ticket! Of course one could argue that there are sanctions for not participating, but that is legally irrelevant. The law recognizes that if a person is placed under duress, no contract of any sort can be legally binding. In law, a flesh and blood human being is always recognized as having free-will choice, in all matters relating to his or her life. Furthermore, ignorance of the law is not recognized, no matter how convoluted and voluminous it is. Sovereignty is a fundamental concept that is firmly embodied in legal discourse.

When one is approached by an "authority" figure, many times one meekly condescends to give out any information that is requested, even though one has a free-will choice and legal right not to do so. This behavior has been drummed into us since birth, first by our parents, then by our teachers. By the time many of us reach adulthood, we have either learned to meekly submit, or rebel. Rebelling is almost the same as submitting, for both actions involve habitual responses and are really a disconnect from self. Both actions are not mindful, and come from a feeling of vulnerability.

Someone who is confident and secure doesn't feel the need to fight or push back. He or she simply follows his or her path without a lot of fuss and bother. Rebelling is often taken from the attitude, "I'll show them." On the emotional scale it resides somewhere around anger. And as we all know, an angry person is angry because he or she feels a loss of freedom or control! Submission is even lower on the scale, for submission is a giving-up of personal power; an acknowledgement and a bowing to a superior force. Many of us experience this as children, and in school. Submission and rebellion are learned responses because it is not natural to feel vulnerable! We have simply been taught of the necessity to obey authority. However, this paradigm is a distortion of the inherent nature of consciousness itself, which know itself as powerful, joyful, and utterly free!

6.6.1 Mass Consciousness

Books, radio, TV, movies, newspapers, etc. often originate and maintain estab-lished ideas and memes into the culture. If you consciously watch TV for a few hours and carefully note what is said, you will be amazed at some of the stuff you hear. You are in a passive, accepting state in front of the tube, and foreign thoughts and beliefs can become part of your personal belief system, un-inspected.

We're not talking about fads and fashions which tend to spread rapidly and then die out, but long standing patterns of thought which have survived generation after gen-eration in the consciousness of our species. This collection of beliefs is referred to as 'mass consciousness.' Some of the major themes of planet earth are scarcity, con-flict, competition, follow-the-leader, injustice and victimization. All of these con-cepts transcend cultures.

Below were some of the beliefs I picked up along my life trail:

- "You have to work hard for everything you get." (Dad)
- "You can't always have it your own way." (Grandma)
- "You have to be tough to survive in this world." (Gym teacher)
- "There's only so much to go around." (Economics textbook)
- "Nobody out there cares about you. It's a dog-eat-dog world." (Dad)
- "You can't fight city hall." (Grandpa)
- "Once you die, you're dead." (Older classmate)
- "Politicians are corrupt." (Teacher)

There are probably hundreds of beliefs like this floating about, most of them negative, and many of them completely irrational.

The content of news programs are almost exclusively about these ideas. Of course, one can say that the news just reports actual events, but it is instructive to compare that litany of negativity to your own life. Almost everyone reading this will find that the latest robbery, murder, bomb blast, deadly fire or fraud has no resemblance to their own experiences. It is a well known fact of the news business that well-being does not sell. It doesn't sell because it is so common place! An accurate one hour newscast would have 59 minutes and 59 seconds worth of "boring" well being and 1 second of bad stuff. Go outside right now and look around. Observe your environment, including nature. If you see any muggings, bombs, or murders, write me an email. I don't expect to see too many!

Watch TV consciously for a couple of hours and you will probably find at least a dozen. Commercials, especially, place people in self limiting situations which then require a response that includes buying some product. Hair loss commercials show bald guys rejected by women, until they get some hair. Body products attempt to get women to believe that using them somehow increases self-esteem. And of course the endless drug commercials that show sick people needing immediate help from the latest (and unavoidable) germ or disease. The message is: The bad stuff is inevitable and it is only a matter of time before you get it.

It's not a big conspiracy, just a proclivity to emphasize the negative in order to reach the positive. It's the age-old human idea that in order to reach B, you have to first fight and overcome A. This orientation places a conscious being at result point instead of at source point, and in a vibrational orientation which gets people attracting the very thing that is unwanted. That in turn keeps the unwanted condition vibrationally active, which means you need more of the product...hey, maybe it is a conspiracy!

The only true aberration is denial of self, for it sets up a state of being which denies your natural birthright of well-being.

Like a bacterial culture placed into a growth medium, negative and self-limiting memes seem to flourish in our species consciousness, and have done so for a long time. Thought is a component of mass consciousness. If thought is vibrational and has any persistence at all, then a sea of thought surrounds us all. If you consider that there are over 7 billion human beings on earth, there are billions of thoughts inserted every day into the species consciousness. If the ratio of human thought is more negative than positive, perhaps this ocean of ideas provides a vibrational proclivity toward limitation.

The point is, many people go through their day without ever consciously originating a thought. Instead of consciously directing their own lives, they are buffeted about by the ideas of others all day long, or stuck in old beliefs that have never been thoroughly examined. And therefore they are very easy to manipulate; through mass media, friends, bosses, authority figures, opinion leaders, etc. It's perfectly understandable, but self-limitation does not have to be a way of life.

6.6.2 Characteristics of a Sovereign

A Sovereign is one who consciously generates his or her own thought, and who can recognize the difference between his or her conscious thought and one from mass consciousness. A sovereign's actions are then always consciously self-directed.

In Eastern tradition, this is called being mindful. When one is a sovereign, one has conscious control of his or her destiny. When one is a robot, mindlessly following the thought stream of mass consciousness, one's life is dictated by default, or in reaction to the decisions and actions of others.

A Sovereign understands that in order to accomplish something, one must have a vision and align one's energies to that vision. Action that is performed is then along the path of least resistance. In this scenario, BEING controls ACTION.

Most people are confused by the relationship between being and doing. The effectiveness of action is dependent solely upon the degree of evolution of thought upon the subject. For example, a chef in a 5 star restaurant can throw together a wonderful meal in a few minutes, because his sophistication of thought, brought about by attention to the subject of food, is highly advanced. The same amount of action taken by a novice would not get him anywhere.

Have you ever seen a person who is working hard? A lot of the time there is a lot of sweating and cussing, but very little is getting done! Their state of being is not one that allows the job to be performed with ease and grace. I remember a cabinet installer at one of my jobs. This guy was there just to collect a check and his state of being was one of "lets get the job over with." I heard him say a number of times, "I got to get out of here." Well, after a lot of frenzied activity, and a series of screw-ups in which he had to take down a couple of the cabinets and start all over, he finally got done. A job that should have taken a couple of hours lasted all day, the guy was pissed the whole time, and he worked ten times as hard as he had to.

Action follows thought. Being is senior to doing. Clarity of thought determines the success or failure of any venture.

This concept is very important, for there is always a split-second free will choice made for every situation in life, even if it is something as trivial as what to have for breakfast, or making that left turn into the parking lot at work. The life of a physical being is a continuing series of free-will choices.

This may seem incorrect, because so many of the decisions we make every day seem to be already defined for us. We cannot decide to take a week off and go sailing, otherwise our job is in jeopardy. And if the mortgage isn't paid, we will wind up with our fannies on the street! That is how the mantra goes from mass consciousness, anyway. But there is always another choice that can be made. If one gets fired from one's job, there is another job out there. If you are a Sovereign, you know this because you have been making conscious decisions for a long time. However, if you are new to the concept of Sovereign, there may be doubts. The only way to find out is to try it. Begin making conscious decisions and see how it feels. Don't just slide off into the old thought pattern or old routine. Take a careful look at your life and see where you would like it to be better, then, as one with 'supreme authority', begin making self-generated and mindful decisions in more and more areas of your life, and watch what happens.

6.6.3 The Subconscious

THE idea of the Sovereign becomes somewhat difficult to understand, given some of the ideas that are floating around in the human psyche. One of these ideas is the "subconscious mind." This idea, all by itself, is responsible for so many abandoning their natural position at cause-point and becoming a slave to the group mind. When many people think of the subconscious mind, they think of a compartment of their consciousness that is hidden from them. This leads to the idea that at any time, the conscious mind can be controlled from the subconscious.[19] This is sometimes used as an explanation for inexplicable behavior, or for failure.

The subconscious mind does not exist. There is not anywhere a part of your consciousness that is inaccessible to you. What passes for the subconscious mind are usually habitual patterns of thought and belief, and sometimes, thoughts that impinge on you from mass consciousness, brought to you by the Law of Attraction, based upon your current emotional state.

Even if we grant the existence of a subconscious mind, by definition it has very little power. Only vibrations that are consciously activated have power. Conscious thought is analogous to the struck piano key, subconscious thought to the vibrations of previous notes that are dying away. The powerful vibration always swallows the weaker one, so decisions made in the present moment are always more powerful than past decisions. Subconscious thought is, by definition, so subtle that it is beneath your awareness. If it's below your awareness, you're not aware of it. And if you're not aware of it, how can it affect you? The answer is, it cannot *unless* you make a conscious decision, in the present moment, to act upon it. Therefore, all thought which leads to action is conscious thought.

Defense lawyers sometimes use the "subconscious" in an attempt to explain away the reprehensible actions of their clients, and some use it to argue for their limitations. It's easy to see that once a vibration is established, the Law of Vibration and the Law of Attraction go to work bringing more and more of it to you, so at first there is vibrational inertia to overcome. That's why, at first, it is sometimes difficult to change an old belief or pattern of behavior. However, we have seen that the decision right

---

[19] See the article "Mysteries of the Mind: Your unconscious is making your everyday decisions" (*U.S. News and World Report*, 2/28/05). The article states that thoughts and actions are controlled by neurons firing in particular parts of the brain. This inverted idea is prevalent throughout our scientific and medical establishment, and leads to the idea that human beings are mere biological automatons.

NOW is more powerful than past decisions, so all you have to do is begin and it will get easier and easier. Each and every human being is a powerful, conscious creator of his or her state of being, and of his or her experience.

In order to see that the subconscious mind is a phantom, perform the following life experiment. The next time you get happy, check to see if you notice an unconscious or subconscious aspect. There will be none, of course. The reason there is no sub-conscious component at this time is because you are vibrationally far apart from detrimental or irrational thoughts. You will find that a "subconscious" component only exists when you are in the negative emotional range. But how do you get into the range of negative emotion? Through conscious decision-making. Once you begin to experiment with yourself in this way, you will begin to realize more and more how powerful you are regarding your personal mental and emotional state.

The subconscious mind was popularized by Sigmund Freud who, in order to explain neurotic and irrational behavior, developed the idea that consciousness is layered into unconscious, preconscious, and conscious. Because neurotic behavior has no rational explanation, it made sense to Freud that some psychic events must percolate below the surface of the mind; then, like a cancer, explode into conscious awareness. For some reason this idea has found wide acceptance, but vibrationally, it makes no sense at all. Only something that is given conscious attention can get bigger. The pot that sits on low heat will never boil, only when the dial is turned up can enough energy be imparted to the mixture! In other words, things do not happen all by themselves.

A vibration will fade away unless more energy is fed to it, or it is entrained by another vibration. But the entrained vibration is already in close proximity to the source of entrainment; and that cannot happen unless there is already a conscious orienta-tion towards it.[20] No matter how far back you take arguments which place you at effect-point, you always return to source point: consciousness itself! The answer to the question is the question: Geometrically, a circle representing the eternal nature of self-awareness.

As you become more and more sovereign, such explanations and justifications for unwanted thought and action become unnecessary, and are discarded like an old pair of crutches.

---

[20] A classic argument in ethics has a train full of people heading toward a fork in the tracks. On one fork there is a person standing who does not have enough time to move out of the way. The other fork leads to a damaged area of track, which will cause the train to overturn. You have the switching mechanism in your hands and have to make a split-second decision: Do you kill the individual or overturn the train? The overturned train MAY lead to many deaths, but it might not.

Such arguments are disingenuous, for they do not account for prior, free-will decisions from a previ-ously established vibrational orientation. Ultimately such scenarios revolve around the horror of death; itself an impossibility for an eternal being.

Belief in the idea of the subconscious mind is disempowering. Belief in any disempowering idea detracts from the Sovereign concept and being the supreme commander of your life. Therefore, do not think or participate in any thoughts, beliefs, or actions that do not lead toward a feeling of your own empowerment. This is fool-proof. If you do not feel empowered by something, then it is not right for you. Period. A Sovereign never questions this, rather knows it consciously. The acts of a Sovereign are based upon what feels good to him or her, and he or she ignores the opinions of others if these do not align with the goal. This is how some people become known as mavericks. Very often, however, it is the maverick who comes up with the brilliant new idea or invention that benefits the whole.

- A Sovereign is in control of his or her thoughts, his or her life, his or her destiny.

- A robot is a slave to his or her own self limiting beliefs, and those from mass consciousness.

- A Sovereign is able to recognize self-generated thought, and distinguish between it and the thoughts and beliefs in mass consciousness. A Sovereign is able to consciously direct his or her thoughts and attention in a positive direction. A Sovereign knows that each and every event in his or her life is created by Self, and is a reflection of Self.

- A Sovereign does not pay attention to what others say, unless it feels like a great idea, in which case he or she makes it her own and begins to consciously create with it.

- A Sovereign makes conscious, free-will decisions in every moment. A Sovereign is aware that he or she is consciousness, the source point, the supreme commander of his or her own life.

- A Sovereign realizes that the decisions and actions of others need not have any effect on him; because he knows that the universe responds uniquely to his own vibrational signal.

- A Sovereign has practiced conscious creation and living; it is not just a nice sounding theory. He or she has demonstrated to himself the ability to positively direct his life so many times that it is no longer in question.

- A Sovereign NEVER believes in anything that does not advance his or her feeling of empowerment and connection. This is the same thing as saying, a Sovereign does not believe in anything that does not truly make him or her feel good. A Sovereign consciously searches out thoughts and activities which are pleasing and life giving.

Successful people, no matter what area of endeavor, regard the above statements as self-evident.

All it takes to become a Sovereign is a little conscious attention each day to become aware of what you are thinking and feeling. It does not have to take years of effort. It's fun! Diligence is not required. Whenever you think about it, try to become more conscious in the moment about what you are thinking and feeling. You do not have to study with a guru, or attend seminars, or wear crystals, or meditate, or any of that stuff. By practicing conscious awareness one may gradually and easily become a Sovereign, progressively assume the directorship of one's life, and even attain higher states of awareness. The Universal Operating System is always behind you, supporting your efforts to be sovereign, because it is designed to mirror back to you the content of every decision you make.

6.7   Right and Wrong

THE concept of right and wrong has inspired philosophers for millennia. It has found its way into laws, cultures and religions throughout the world.

In Eastern religions, there is the concept of Right Action leading to a state of internal harmony. In Western religions, we are told that good works will lead us to heaven and doing evil will lead us to hell.

Surely killing someone against his or her will would be a wrong thing to do, and helping another would be considered right? In France a law was even passed making it a crime to walk away from an injured or helpless person without assisting.

Wrong could be defined this way: that which is opposed or directly contradictory to one's own vibration.

Right is: that which is in agreement with one's vibration.

We use the term "vibration" because it denotes the entirety of a person's thoughts, beliefs, and attitudes about anything.

Right and wrong are, by these definitions, concepts that proceed from one's own personal viewpoint.

The questions is, is there a universal concept of right and wrong, as philosophers and religions have tried to assert?

Almost all schools of thought agree that the Creator is unconditionally loving.[21] If the Creator loves us unconditionally, it means the Creator loves us no matter what

---

[21] Here we assume that the Creator is a being separate from the rest of us, as in traditional Western religious teachings. Personally, I believe that consciousness is universal and individual personalities are aspects of a universal consciousness.

we do. If this were not true, then the Creator would say, "I love you when you do THIS, but if you do THAT I will not love you as much." "If you murder someone I will not love you as much as if you help someone." That leads the Creator to the slippery slope of judgment. If you take a knife and injure someone, but don't kill him, does the Creator love you more than if he died? Or maybe it's your intention that matters. After all, the Creator is omniscient, so the Creator knows everything. If your intention was to kill, then you would be censured even if your victim did not die. We can see where this is leading. It's some sort of graduated scale of love based on "good" or "bad" action. But we already agree that the Creator is all-loving, so there cannot be a favored mode of conduct (or thought) in the eyes of God. If there is no favored mode of thought and conduct, then all thought and action must be permitted. Therefore, it would seem there can be no universal standard of thought or conduct, only personal ones. Observation of affairs on planet earth today confirms this! We see the most horrible acts of cruelty and also the most loving acts of kindness and beauty.

The unconditional love of God translates to unconditional allowing of all thought and action. Here we have once more come back to the Law of Free Will.

If all thought and action are allowed, then there is no "right" way or "wrong" way. There cannot be any universal judgment of thought or action, otherwise there are conditions placed on thought and action.

If there are no conditions placed on thought and action, then there is no right or wrong!

Right and wrong must then be a human concept, not a universal one.

"That is all fine and theoretical," you say, "but what about when someone puts a gun to *your* head?" The answer to that lies in the operation of the Law of Attraction (which we have already discussed at length).

Briefly, if you have a strong enough fear of someone killing you, you may vibrationally attract a killer. This does not make the killer wrong, or you right. The action of a killer finding a victim is simply vibrational matching, via the Law of Vibration and the Law of Attraction. The Creator permits us to experience anything we would like. If you are fearful of being killed, you are focusing there and so sending that message to every-thing in the universe; by your decision to focus on it you have given permission for a co-incident event with another (or others). So if you live your life joyfully, there is no possibility of meeting up with a killer, because both of these vibrations are opposed.

Let's distinguish between rightness, wrongness, and efficiency. An engineer might construct a bridge that collapses; in that case we say that it was wrongly constructed;

meaning that the beings who built it did not have a correct understanding of their subject. Fortunately, scientists and engineers have developed rules that tell us how to work with matter and energy in the best possible way.

By "right and wrong," I mean in relation to universal principles. One might say, "The engineer who built the bridge was ethically wrong, for he cut corners. He is responsible for the deaths of those who were on the bridge when it collapsed." Let's say a jury felt the same way and the engineer is convicted of voluntary manslaughter and spends the next 30 years in jail.

However, we do not send the engineer to jail because he has caused pain to the friends and family of those who died; we do not send him to jail because he has created a big mess which requires a lot of time and money to clean up. We say, "You're in jail because you have terminated the existence of innocent people."

But what if death does not really exist? That has been the premise of this book from the outset, for we have claimed that consciousness is eternal, and that death is just a transition from a state of awareness associated with a physical body, to a state of awareness without the physical body. If we look at what happened from a broader perspective, the situation looks much different.

The people who died immediately transition out of their bodies and return to Source. Bodies die, consciousness never dies. Like the little cat who steps out of the cat door into a much grander and broader world than the house she has known, so too does consciousness return to its greater, non-physical perspective; death is an instantaneous re-connection to pure, positive life force energy. In the execution of criminals, society thinks it is snuffing out an evil force, when in fact we are doing the criminal a favor! The punishment that is meted out is a return to joy.

Relatives of the murdered being watch as the murderer is strapped into the electric chair, eagerly waiting for vengeance. But after it is over, there is no real satisfaction, for deep down within every conscious being is the knowledge of his or her true self, his or her connection to the divine, and everyone else's as well. Everyone knows, deep down, that a physical being is consciousness having a temporary physical experience.

"If death is so great," you might say, "then how come so many people die in pain and agony? If that murderer is so divine, why did he scream and cry in the electric chair?" Well, notwithstanding the fact that the process is incredibly painful, we are on safe ground when we say that the fear of death is the single biggest fear in the consciousness of humanity. Our entire society revolves around the removal of risk; from day one our parents tell us not to go out in the cold without our coats (because we might get sick, and that might lead to you know what), and attempt to guide us in innumerable ways out of the path of danger. The underlying reason is because danger might lead to death, and death means you are gone forever. That indeed is something too horrible to contemplate!

However, if death really is a return to joy, then it must be resistance to the death experience which causes pain and agony, not the transition process itself. The physical life experience is a circle with birth and death at the same point, so all actions in the physical universe must ultimately lead to a right outcome! Our engineer might deserve to be in jail, but he is there for all the wrong reasons.

The human population of planet earth is over 7 billion at this writing. If we assume the average life span is 65 years (some people live to 100, but others die young), then every 65 years, we have a completely new planetary population! If we divide 7 billion by 65, there are about 108 million deaths and births every year. That is an astonishing figure, is it not? It's 295,000 every day, 12,300 every hour, and over 3 every second. If we include plants and animals, the figure is even more staggering.

The point is, death is happening everywhere, all the time. We make a big deal out of death, but it is, in fact, astonishingly commonplace. "New" beings are coming in, and "old" beings are leaving all the time. Consciousness is constantly recycling itself on our planet, entering and leaving physical bodies. If you ask yourself the question, "Who or what is managing the entry and exit of consciousness on planet earth?" it leads to some mind -blowing realizations.

Part III – APPLYING THE UNIVERSAL OPERATING SYSTEM TO LIFE

CHAPTER 7

Using the Universal Operating System in Life

7.1   Understanding the Emotional Scale

Behind all emotions are thoughts. If you are experiencing negative emotion, you have some thought or belief that is causing it. However, it is very difficult to think your way out of feeling rotten. It is much easier (at least for me) to try to connect with a more positive feeling.

When trying to help yourself or a friend to feel better, you have to be aware of how you're going to be feeling when you step up or down the scale. Failure to do so can make you think you are on the wrong track, and can save you a lot of hurt feelings when trying to counsel another.

This scale, from top to bottom, is a measure of increasing life force energy (see reprise on following page).

As an example let's take Barb and Jill, who had planned to go out for lunch. Barb is apathetic about her life, and calls Jill up to cancel their appointment. She's moping around at home and Jill says "I'll be right over." Let's say that Jill has a good knowledge of the emotional/vibrational scale.

Sam and Rick, our friends from the last chapter, are in the same situation. Sam calls Rick and tells him he can't play golf that afternoon, and Rick, who hasn't got a clue about the scale of emotions, comes over to get his friend out of his funk.

7.2   Barb and Jill

(The full conversation from Chapter 2)

"What's wrong Barb?" says Jill.

"Oh, I just don't care anymore," Barb says apathetically.

Jill is just about to fire off an angry comment about Thorpe, (Barb's former boyfriend) but she realizes that apathy is very low down on the scale and doesn't want to overwhelm her friend, so she says gently, "It's Thorpe isn't it?"

Emotion	Attitude
Apathy	"I give up."
Grief	
Propitiation	"I'll do anything to make it up to you!"
Sympathy	"I feel your pain."
Fear	
Anxiety	
Hidden Hostility	He's smiling in your face and stabbing you in the back. Says one thing and does another.
Callousness	"Tough for you. Just do it."
Anger	Out of control, lashing out at the world.
Antagonism	"Hey! Come over here and let me kick your butt!" Feistiness.
Boredom/ Complacency	Yawn
Conservatism	"Things are fine just the way they are"
Interest	"Hey that's cool!"
Enthusiasm	"Wow! Let's do that again!"
Exhilaration	"I feel fantastic!!!!!"
Serenity/bliss	Complete connection to Source, or God force, or life-force energy. This is the feeling consciousness has in its native, non-physical state.

Table 7.1: Scale of Emotions, repeated

Suddenly Barb bursts into tears, an activity that used to really piss Thorpe off. "Damn woman," he'd think, "what's wrong with her now?" But Jill knows that grief is the next harmonic of vibration up on the scale of emotions, so to her Barb's reaction is perfectly logical. Barb is wailing on about Thorpe and how lonely and rejected she feels. Jill is a good counselor, and even though she thinks to herself, "You're a whole lot better off without that loser honey," she says nothing and lets Barb vent. She knows that although being around grief is uncomfortable, matching Barb's vibration would result in failure, for two vibrations of grief would just reinforce the other, sticking both women right in it. Jill knows that only by maintaining a high emotional level can she be of any use to Barb at all.

After several minutes Barb is cried out and looks up at her friend. Jill recognizes that Barb is poised at an emotional brink; and that a word or gesture from her can send her friend up the scale, or downward again. She also knows that people can hit an emotion and pass by it very quickly on the way up or down, so she's not sure exactly where Barb is going next, but she knows it's going to be some version of negative emotion, and is prepared for it.

Jill says, "You had some good times together, didn't you?" hoping to bring Barb up a little. She doesn't say, "Still feeling sad about Thorpe?" because that might stick Barb back in grief.

Barb says, sympathetically, and a little defensively, "Yeah we did! I remember the time we went to the putt-putt golf course and he put his arms around me…"

Jill let's Barb go on a bit, because she recognizes the emotion of sympathy, which is a little bit up from grief.

After a time Jill suggests, "Maybe you'll meet somebody else."

A look of anxiety comes over Barb's face and she says, "Do you really think I can? All the guys I'm attracted to treat me like sh-t."

Jill immediately recognizes the vibration of fear, and understands that it is a step up. "Yes I think you can," she says. "You're such a great person."

Barb says fearfully, "I don't think so. Thorpe didn't think so anyway. Maybe I'm doomed to be lonely forever."

Jill puts a little anger in her voice and says, "Remember how he cussed you out at the amusement park when you didn't want to go on the rollercoaster?" That was a little reach by Jill, because anger is the next major harmonic on the scale, but it could backfire and put Barb right back into grief. Even if it does, Jill knows it's not a problem, for it just means Barb needs to cry a little more and fully release it. Barb's face is a study in emotion as she goes up to anger, down to grief and up to fear again.

But Jill's statement hit home, because Jill knows something about Barb's life and how her friend thinks.

Barb remembers many more incidents almost as bad, and her face hardens. "That bastard," she says.

Jill is secretly thrilled, for her regard for Thorpe is like a gooey mess on the kitchen floor, but she keeps her opinions to herself and recognizes Barb has reached no-sympathy, and that if she's successful, the dam will burst. Jill hates anger but she steels herself for it anyway, knowing it's the next harmonic. After probing around a bit on that subject, Barb starts screaming. "Did I ever tell you what he said to me after I made dinner for him???@!@!!" etc. This goes on for a while as Barb recounts all the times Thorpe was mean to her. Jill is holding it together in the face of Barb's anger, even when her friend picks up a glass of water and hurls it against the wall. Jill knows that even if the session ended right now, a lot of progress has been made, for anger is a big step up from apathy.

After a while Barb calms down and begins to tease herself about Thorpe. "Maybe I should go over to his house and put a dent in his truck." All of a sudden she bursts out laughing, realizing that Thorpe liked his new truck, and paid a lot more attention to it, than he ever did to her.

Barb says, "Why did I ever hook up with that guy?"

Jill smiles and says, "I don't know sweetheart, but I do know that there are plenty of guys out there a lot better than him."

Barb says, "There better be!"

She's feeling a lot better now and Jill suggests they go out and get something to eat. Barb is eager to talk some more to her friend and agrees. Jill hopes to get her up to at least interest on the subject of the opposite sex.

7.3 Rick and Sam

THE conversation with Rick and Sam would probably be a lot shorter. Rick walks in and sees his friend apathetic, and knows it's all about the new company he wants to start, and his job. But Rick has heard that story over and over and he's tired of it. He's got a beer in one hand and his keys in the other and says. "C'mon Sam, let's go. We're gonna be late."

"Eff it," Sam says apathetically. "I'm not going."

Rick says angrily, "Get out of it, you woman! Are you going to sit around here all day and cry?"

"Eff you Rick!" Sam says.

"C'mon, let's go," says Rick, rattling his keys. Since Sam is a guy, and guys aren't supposed to cry, (although that's exactly what Sam feels like doing) he has to make a quick decision. Sam decides, hell, why not play some golf, it doesn't matter anyway. So they both go out and Sam plays like crap. He's not very interested in the game, thinking about his crummy job and how desperately he wants to change his life, but he just doesn't know how.

"You played like shit Sam," Rick crows after the round. "Got you by 13 strokes."

"Yeah whatever," Sam says.

"C'mon, let's go to the clubhouse and get a few beers," Rick suggests cheerfully.

"Sure."

We leave Rick and Sam here. At this point, Sam is still stuck in apathy, because he hasn't really changed his thinking or his focus. For a brief moment Rick angered him, but it didn't last.

The point is, you can use the Emotional Scale to bootstrap yourself, or another, up the emotional ladder.

Someone in apathy who begins to cry is making a step UP. Mostly what happens, a person begins to cry and says, "Oh what's the use! I still feel like crap" and gives up. Giving up is the same as apathy. So you are right back where you started.

When you are fearful and make a step forward, you get angry. Society does not like angry people; the authorities like to put such in jail. In school, angry kids are drugged to make them conform. This puts them lower on the scale, in apathy mostly. The fact is, an apathetic person is easier to control and easier to get along with, but an apathetic student is a dumb student. Intelligence increases as you move up the scale, for the cognitive function decreases in the range of lower emotions. Therefore, drugging children in a learning environment is counter-productive.

Why is anger more positive than fear or grief? Because an angry person is more animated. The animating principle is consciousness. In general, the more animated a person is, the more conscious he or she is.

(This is not a hard and fast rule. If you read the books of the great masters (Swami Muktananda, for example) you'll see that these wise ones were completely conscious yet able to totally control their life force energy. The same goes for great artists and athletes. They demonstrate a feeling of total power, serenity, and joy all at the same time).

When you are in anger and take a step up, you might feel antagonistic. An angry person is spewing, he's out of control. An antagonistic person is more directed, more under control. He is resisting much less and feeling a little better. And he's more rational.

Why is boredom higher than antagonism? Because there is less resistance. Boredom is a higher harmonic of apathy and a lower harmonic of serenity, antagonism is a higher harmonic of anger, and a lower harmonic of exhilaration. Emotions are just vibrations, and they have higher and lower frequencies, just like waveforms.

Of course, the emotions on this scale will feel more comfortable to different kinds of people. For example, I knew a guy who much preferred antagonism to boredom or conservatism. Once you get out of the deep negative emotions it's just a matter of where you feel most comfortable.

7.4   Enabling the Intellect

I'VE found that when I'm feeling rotten, I'm a lot dumber than when I'm feeling good. The negative emotion obscures and dulls my intellect, so I cannot think straight. When this happens, I cannot think of a solution to a problem, even if it's an emergency. Last summer, my email program crashed. I had two very important business related emails that needed immediate responses, and was unable to reply! I was in a panic. So I reached for a feeling of "problem solved" and imagined my email working fine again. It seemed pretty ridiculous intellectually, because I felt I was asking for a magic solution. Nevertheless, I kept at it and after working myself into a fine rage and venting my anger at the crummy software, a solution suddenly popped into my head: "What about that old email program you have lying around on the D drive?" I fired it up and all was well again.

Sometimes, in order to enable the intellect, you have to deal with the emotions first. It seems illogical, but I've found that the intellect functions better when I'm clear-minded, and I can't be clear minded when I'm at the lower end of the emotional scale.

7.5   Fate vs. Free Will

IF a person finds himself facing an illness (or any unpleasant situation), one may simply say, "Well, you are resonating to it so you attracted it."

This sort of explanation is irritating to say the least, besides being unhelpful, but it also sounds suspiciously like the guiding hand of Fate, for one can look at the world and say EVERYTHING that occurs simply IS, because it's meant to be that way.

There is a crucial difference, however, in a philosophy based upon fate, and a one that postulates consciousness always at cause-point. In our philosophy, there are no outside forces determining your destiny, even though it sometimes seems that way!

7.6 Focusing

THE idea of fate is indirectly supported by the scientific method, which has dominated the consciousness of the general public, especially since the end of WW II. Science teaches us that only what is observable is valid; therefore, we are conditioned to believe that what-already-is, is unalterable truth.

To further complicate matters, to say "that which exists is meant to be," is true.

But it's only true because the decisions and actions of conscious beings made it that way.

We often accept the established things of this world as universal facts of life, when they are really continual creations. For example, I accept the fact that if I am hungry I can drive down to the local supermarket. Supermarkets have been around almost my entire life so I don't question their existence, but in my grandfather's world they did not exist. One can simply say, "Supermarkets were fated to occur because of the increase in population density" but the fact remains that someone had to create the idea of a supermarket, then actually put it into the physical universe. In fact, every supermarket in the world is being continuously created, and without continued attention to the idea of "supermarkets" they would all disappear.

Anything that exists in the physical universe is being constantly created by one or more conscious beings. This leads us to another obvious, but very important conclusion:

When the focus of consciousness is no longer present upon a thing, that thing (including a life form) will disintegrate.

A city becomes a ghost town when its inhabitants leave.

A car that sits unattended in the backyard eventually corrodes and falls apart.

A flower wilts when it no longer has the nutrients to survive, or when the consciousness connected with it decides to depart. A human body disassociates when the consciousness associated with it no longer creates the human energy field that sustains it.

It is the focusing of consciousness that begins and sustains the creative process. Hoping and wishing, in the absence of a clear vision, will not create the vibrational conditions that lead to manifestation. The answer to the question of "I don't know what I want!" is therefore, "Find something to focus on." An undirected vibration will lead to an undirected life.

7.7 The Creative Process

How is anything created?

First, a conscious being somewhere has an idea.

What is an idea? An idea is a thought about something. It's a tiny bit of focus or attention to a subject. However, lots of times when we have ideas they do not go any further:

"I want to invent an anti-gravity machine." For me, this is a wonderful idea but I am pretty sure I'm not going to be successful, so I cease to give more attention to it. Therefore, my thoughts concerning the subject of "anti-gravity machine" are relatively small in number, vague and unfocused. I haven't "gotten my act together" upon this subject.

The guy who invented the compact disc (CD), however, had an idea and followed up on it. By that I mean, he gave it more attention. He looked at how lots of information could be coded into a very small space and proceeded in steps to evolve his ideas: first comes the polishing of the glass plate, then the coating of photoresist (a chemical that hardens when exposed to light), then the information is written into the photoresist, then a negative of the information is created...etc.

Any creative process begins with an idea, then more ideas coagulate around it in some kind of sensible geometric arrangement. Now there exists what I call a thought prototype, or TP. A TP is an evolving thought form about something. It is an actual collection of energy, for in our vibrational model, every thought has a tiny bit of virtual mass. I call it a prototype because it might or might not work in the physical universe, but the energy associated with thought is just as real as the stuff on your workbench, or on your painting palette! A thought form is a buildup of energy brought about by a focusing of consciousness in a particular area, which can then be mirrored into the physical universe.

Without the focusing or attention of consciousness, nothing can ever be brought into physical existence, because every single thing in the universe was preceded by thought; as my father used to say to us kids, "That broken window just didn't happen."

As the TP gets more and more sophisticated, a completed Thought Form is created which acts as a design template for the object in the physical universe. As long as the completed thought template exists and is accessible, one may continue to construct and maintain the physical object with which it is associated.

These mental templates are crucial, for even if a physical blueprint exists for an object, it cannot be utilized without the corresponding thought template. Example: Most of my computer programs. Even though I have a written record of each one, after a time I cannot figure out how they work. I have several with minor bugs, including a halfway decent Mandelbrot/Julia Set generator, but I have lost the thought templates connected to them, so the programs are worthless, for I cannot debug them. This is how technology gets lost. Another example:

Figure 7.1: A Sumerian Tablet

One may have a physical blueprint, but without the corresponding thought template to give it meaning, the blueprint may be useless.

Every step of the creative process is first and foremost an evolvement of thought, and everything we see in the physical universe has a unique template of thought connected to it. That is how a competent psychic can "read your energy," or contact an object and tell you its history.

7.8 Back to Fate

"Fate" is just attention to something for a long enough time. Often we go through life oblivious to the focus we are giving to a subject, or we simply get into a habit of thinking or believing a certain way.

For example, every time Joe changes jobs he gets a domineering and micro-managing boss. Joe would prefer a job where he has freedom to breathe, but he is so focused on NOT GETTING ANOTHER CRUMMY BOSS that he continuously attracts one.

We have already gone over the reasons for this so we won't repeat it here, but if you ask Joe how he keeps getting the same sort of boss he might tell you it's fate. And he'd be right – Joe is fated to attract the same situations (self-similar situations, fractally speaking) as long as he continues to focus in the same way. Joe is iterating his life from the same set of initial conditions.

But the point is that the First Principle and the Law of Free Will guarantee that Joe has, in every moment, the choice to change his focus of attention! And when he does so, magic happens, or coincidence; a happy accident maybe.

The label assigned is irrelevant; Joe's life will change when he changes his focus. Therefore, fate is just continued focus on something until it is brought into your life experience. A philosophy based on fate and one based on free will are both operating from the Law of Free Will, it is just that a person who believes in fate never makes a decision to change his focus!

In order to experience this, you have to test it out for yourself.

7.9   Risk

"You shouldn't quit your job and start your own business. It's too risky."

"If you smoke cigarettes you are risking your health."

"Selling anything on the internet is a recipe for failure."

Statements like this are made every day by well-intentioned persons, and sometimes we say similar things to ourselves. Although there may be a lot of truth to them, there are also lots of examples that go the other way.

So what is risk, exactly?

In my contracting work I sometimes get into unusual situations. One day I was 25 feet in the air working on some molding at the top of a house. I had to position my ladder awkwardly in order to avoid a decorative stone pool and fountain underneath. I was feeling a little vulnerable, even though I have been that high before. I thought to myself "I could get killed doing this. I'll just tell Ed I can't do it."

Halfway down the ladder I changed my mind, for I had had a realization.

I had been working away for half an hour before without any problem. Now all of a sudden it was too risky. What changed?

I told myself "Before, your ladder was well placed. Now it isn't and you might fall."

But that wasn't true at all. That was just the story I was telling myself.

What had changed was my alignment of energy to the task at hand. For some reason I had made the decision that I did not want to do the work, then I found reasons to support that decision.

My realization came after I reviewed why I was up there in the first place.

It was a pleasant autumn day, and the house itself was a historic old brownstone in a great neighborhood. I liked the people I was working for as well. As I looked around the property at the beautifully designed and well-tended gardens and landscaping, I began to rediscover my purpose.

I raced up the ladder and completed the rest of the work in less than an hour, even though there were two more difficult ladder placements.

Risk is simply the misalignment of thoughts, beliefs and feelings toward a goal.

If something is risky, then either you do not have a clear idea of how to proceed, or you have not fully committed to the activity.

When putting together some credit card software for my web site, I had a number of product choices. I could get a credit card terminal and deal with the local bank, or choose from one of several internet software packages. Being a neophyte, I considered that ALL of the choices were risky. What if the software didn't work? How was I going to get help from some faceless company I'd never dealt with before? What if the bank was uncooperative? (I've had some experiences along that line.) What if I got a lot of fraudulent orders? What if nobody wanted my stuff? After wallowing around in that for a while I finally decided to just apply the things I'm always preaching to others.

I made up my mind on one of the Internet products and aligned my energies to that. I told myself that this software looked good and it could do the job. Mostly I contemplated why I wanted the software in the first place: Because I wanted to offer products to my readers. Because I wanted to enhance the website. Because it was an expansion of my reach to the world at large. Because I wanted to inspire and help others. And mostly because the general idea felt fantastic! All of a sudden the risk evaporated.

Did the riskiness of the operation change? I was still dealing with the same uncertainties. But it *felt* like the risk was gone and I've learned to trust those good feelings.

An objective observer, however, would determine that statistically I was no better off than before. "Just another guy using the internet to hawk products," he might say.

The only change was my conscious decision to go ahead, and to focus on the desired result. But that was enough.

Risk is often present when you go into action before you are ready. Sometimes this happens because you have a goal you want so much to reach that you just don't feel like waiting around, and so you plunge in. This often works because once you dive in it's either sink or swim. You have to align your energies or you drown.

But often it just leads to a lot of hard work and struggle as you desperately try to make things go right.

So I define risk this way: your degree of uncertainty as to the outcome.

Notice this definition has nothing to do with the amount of money or resources you presently have. It has nothing to do with your present reality, or the 'dangers' others may describe to you.

How can you lessen or eliminate risk?

The traditional way is to get the resources and the environment lined up around you before you begin. "Know before you go," as the saying goes. That is certainly one way to go about it. But what you're really doing here is aligning your energy toward your desire. Looking at all of that stuff gives you a feeling that it is OK to proceed.

However, you can be confident without ever gathering two pennies to scrape together. It is possible for anyone to change in a positive direction no matter what the present reality.

Many of us have been taught that if the observable reality does not at least somewhat resemble the goal, then we are at risk of failure.

"You want to start an Internet business in this economy? You're crazy right? Don't you know that dot-coms are going bust all over the place?"

Well maybe that is true. However, if it is true that the physics of the universe responds to each conscious being on an individual basis (and I believe it does, based on my experiences) then all that is required is self-alignment.

This is a very powerful and, some might say, reckless statement.

"You're just encouraging people to go out on a limb and you are doing them a disservice."

What I'm encouraging is a little less focus on the 'risk' and a little more focus on the visualization of the end product and the reasons for undertaking the activity in the first place. There is a very good reason for this.

All doing is preceded by inspiration. This inspiration could be something very minor, like "it sure would be nice if those dishes were done." Or it could be something huge like "wouldn't it be nice if the people of the world could find a way to live in peace." The point is, concentrate more on that inspiration, and less on the reasons your project might not come off.

(I'm not saying, go blindly forward without lining up the resources and support you feel you need to get started. I am saying that if you focus on that beautiful and powerful kernel of inspiration you can't go wrong. I don't care what anyone says.)

Inspiration comes from a desire. A desire is just a decision to align with life force energy. Life force energy is who we are, fundamentally. Life force energy ultimately composes all matter and energy in the universe. Consciousness itself could be said to be life force energy. This physical reality is cocooned within a universal field of life force energy. This is the medium upon which all vibration travels, and so when we align with it, our signal to the universe is pure and we allow ourselves to meet up with the persons and resources we need, *even if we start off with nothing.*

"Yes, but it's harder to start with nothing."

Is it?

But it might be more rewarding! It's just that most people don't think you can be successful if the current reality is at zero.

Human beings have confused cause and effect. Cause is consciousness. The result of the decisions of consciousness is the physically manifested reality.

In order to get the ball rolling you have to start somewhere. It makes absolutely no difference if you start from scratch or if you're Rupert Darbyshire Bentley III and have a million dollars at your disposal. The success of your operation will depend mainly on how you align yourself to it. Rupert Bentley may start with a million and be able to set up his music business right away, but if Rupert does not have strong, clear and positive feelings about his venture, he is not aligned to success. Whereas Downtown Freddie Brown may have a killer rap that just won't quit. Freddie may find himself as rich as Rupert one day, if that is his desire. The manifestation of that desire is dependent only upon Freddie, not on the state of the economy, the disbelief of others, or anything else.

Rupert is probably used to the idea of success because he has been raised rich. Rupert's reality reflects the success he has been born into, but that reality was in place before Rupert was born. In other words, Rupert has done nothing to create the prosperity around him, so his vibration may or may not be oriented toward success. A person may have the money to set up a business, but the success of that business is not dependent upon the money. It is dependent upon the people, resources, and design of the operation and that is always a direct reflection of the person in charge.

Guys like Freddie are told so often by parents, teachers, peers and society that their chances are very few, and then they begin to believe it. "You have nothing," they will say, "and you are severely handicapped because of the circumstances of your birth. Get used to a life of scarcity right now." This idea then becomes their platform of attraction. "Statistics show that only 1.5% of inner city residents will ever start a successful business…" blah, blah, blah.

The amazing thing is that Freddie has an equal chance as Rupert of being successful. Universal law applies equally to everyone.

Risk is proportionate to your misalignment of energy toward the goal.

If there is perfect alignment, there is no risk, for things just open up smoothly for you at every step along the way. Freddie may have to attract a lot more resources, but that's just a few extra links on the vibrational chain.

I'm finding that out with my writing career. I started at zero, and I mean absolute zero. Five years ago I had the desire to write down some of my experiences. Gradually I found myself working less and writing more, and having a lot of fun with it. I write when I'm inspired, not because I feel I should. Now I've got a website up and four manuscripts. I have an Internet shopping cart to make it easier for people to read what I have to say, and to promote my work.

It has taken me a long time to get to this point but it sure has been fun to do something just for the fun of it regardless of the outcome. Like Freddie, I don't have a lot of present-time-reality resources, but I know it doesn't matter! My success is guaranteed if I just keep my vibe in high gear.

Some people might say I am a fool for paying good money to print books people might never buy. Some might say I'm a double fool for paying even more money to set up shop on the internet. But it feels good, so I'm gonna do it. One thing I'm sure of: there's no risk involved!

So how do you eliminate risk?

By staying confident and maintaining your vision. If this is accompanied by a feeling of well-being, things will begin to line up for you.

How do you stay confident if you don't know whether you will succeed? By paying attention to the inspiration which was the launching of all of your activities. By staying in contact with the good feelings that made you want to reach your goal in the first place. These feelings are the ultimate guarantor of success, for they are always associated with having already achieved the goal. This is the same thing as saying, "matching up vibrationally with your desire." The Law of like attracts like guarantees that if your signal is a match to that of your goal, manifestation will result.

The other day I was thinking about how to get a lot of CD's made in case there were a lot of orders. The very next day my brother-in-law Victor tells me about an acquaintance who has a professional CD duplicating machine that he's not using. This guy was going to start a big project but it never came off. So Victor is going to see about buying the thing for me (at a discount!). I found this to be astonishing. In the first place, I had no idea how to even duplicate CD's, other than shoving them in a CD writer. I didn't research CD writing, nor did I investigate products and compare prices, nor did I talk to Victor. The thing has basically shown up in my lap, just like magic, in less than 24 hours.

You might say, "Yeah but what if this thing is a piece of junk? How do you know you've got the best product for your needs? How can you know it's the very best deal you can get?" These are all questions the intellect must ask, because it cannot feel the vibration connected to the undertaking. But I can just feel that it's the right thing for me. That feeling is priceless. It's worth more than a dozen professional analyses and hundreds of hours of research. And if the thing turns out not to be the perfect fit, so what? If I can create a window of opportunity for something like that in 24 hours, it will be a piece of cake to create another one. That's what it feels like anyway.

Risk occurs when you overreach your feeling of alignment with the goal.

Risk has little to do with the available resources.

Have you ever seen or read about a person who plowed ahead almost recklessly yet still achieved success? We often hear that such people were just lucky. "Jackie caught a few big breaks. YOU can't count on that." But you can, because those big breaks were simply windows of opportunity that opened *because* of Jackie's vibrational signal.

The senior datum in any manifestation is the attitude of a conscious being. That is something we have emphasized over and over in this book. The decisions (thoughts) of consciousness are all vibrational in nature. Every time you make a choice or think a thought you send out a little pulse from your human energy field, just like the stone that falls into the pond. This vibration travels along the universal medium from one end of the earth to another. When you have a feeling or a belief about something you generate a constant vibration which travels the universal pathways, interlacing with signals which resemble it, and avoiding those that don't. A signal which is constantly broadcast will eventually attract another (object, person, or situation) like it and a co-incidence will result.

Why did the "reckless" person succeed?

Because he lined himself up with a vibration of success, and was smart enough to follow those inspirational nudges he or she received at the appropriate times.

What appears reckless, or lucky, to an observer may simply be a personal vibrational alignment to the goal.

When the lucky or reckless person is asked how and why he or she succeeded, very often they will not be able to give a precise answer. Because the intellect cannot understand a series of what appears to be coincidences, it assigns the end result to good luck.

In the vibrational universe concept, manifestation is a result of a matching of signals.

So any manifestation you receive is never luck, or chance.

All manifestation is the last link in a chain that begins with and is maintained by your thoughts, beliefs, and choices. A manifestation is an important event, for it means that you have been paying attention to something for a long enough time for it to come into your life.

What most people consider as risk is actually a comparison of the present reality with the desired reality, but it's really an energetic gap between a desire and a belief. A belief of inadequacy to the task itself creates the conditions that result in failure, and in the feeling of risk. It generates more reasons to consider failure and looks to the manifested reality in support of these limitations. The belief then composes the dominant vibration in your signal to the universe at large.

Freddie says: "I have a great rap but how am I going to promote it? Oh what's the use of even trying?" Because people like to feel that their decisions are appropriate, Freddie will now look around at his current reality for confirmation. And he will find lots of "facts" to support his new decision.

However, once you understand that risk is self created, you can change your orientation from one of uncertainty to one of confidence.

To the degree that you understand the powerful role of consciousness in the creative process, the risks on your road to manifestation will lessen.

7.10 Judgment

To judge someone has been considered a pejorative act since biblical times; we have all heard the saying, "Judge not, lest ye be judged."

Judgment is considered a bad thing because the object of that judgment is often offended or hurt.

One Sunday morning obese Aunt Hilda wears a low cut, brightly colored dress to church. Cap, the usher, says "For God's sake old woman, tone it down will you? Nobody wants to look at your ugly body." Cap determines that such a dress is inappropriate and might offend the sensibilities of others; just as, say, he would expect people at a church service to remain quiet and attentive.

Judgment stems from the comparison of actions with regard to an agreed upon code of conduct. That code of conduct is different in different cultures of course, so it is really impossible to say that any conduct is right or wrong from a universal standpoint.

For example, one might say that to take another's life is a universal wrong; yet, in a culture of warriors, such may be considered a badge of honor. To die well, to count coup over an enemy's body, were all highly regarded principles in some of our own native American cultures, demonstrating the idea that free will choices determine the appropriateness of any action.

Let's take a look at the statement, "Judge not, lest ye be judged."

It has been interpreted to mean, "If you say nasty things about someone, they'll probably say nasty things about you." But there is, I think, a deeper meaning behind it.

What happens when Cap judges Hilda?

Mainly, he first has to look inside himself and find something negative.

Why would Aunt Hilda be hurt or offended by Cap's statement?

Because she looks inside herself and finds something negative. More accurately, Aunt Hilda, in the present moment, *decides* that there is something inappropriate about herself.

But why would she do this?

When Hilda got up on Sunday morning she felt awfully good; the sun was shining, she had a good rest, she was looking forward to the church dinner and talking with her friends and, as a special treat, she was going to have a talk with that nice pastor who was thinking of displaying some of her art work in the church foyer.

So that morning, Hilda was feeling expansive and joyful; she gazed in her closet and saw the bright yellow print dress she'd been longing to wear since the cold gray day last winter when it caught her eye in the clothing store. "Oh, why not!" she says. "Let's put it on today and shine our light out into the world!"

When Cap makes his judgmental comment as Hilda walks into church, he thinks he is making a statement about Hilda, but in fact he is making a statement only about the state of his own consciousness. Cap's comment is merely a reflection of Cap's point of awareness and has little or nothing to do with Hilda!

How can this be? Isn't it obvious that Hilda is wearing a dress that could be considered by many to be in bad taste?

Well, let's look at it from Hilda's point of view.

As she walks past Cap just outside the church doors, Hilda is feeling wonderful about herself. For the first time in a long time she is walking comfortably and she loves the feel and look of the dress. When Cap makes his insensitive remark, Hilda has two choices: (1) to continue in a state of connection with herself, feeling good, or (2) to decide that Cap's statement is hurtful.

There is NO reason whatsoever for Hilda to do (2), except that the meme "When someone says something mean to you, you have to react in kind" is powerfully established within the consciousness of all present. Therefore, the expected behavior is that Hilda flushes, becomes sad and cries; or perhaps, Hilda gets angry and whacks Cap over the head with her cherry-wood walking stick.

This expectation creates a powerful vibration within the space of consciousness of all present. Hilda is immersed in that space and, along with Cap, is in fact the center of attention for a split second as all await Hilda's reaction.

All understand implicitly, even if not consciously, that the Law of Free Will and the Law of Vibration are in effect; all present understand that Hilda has complete control over her response, for only Hilda can make the decision within herself whether to respond as in (1) or (2).

The Law of Attraction is the next to come into play, for whatever is Hilda's response will draw forth matching responses from those around her.

Let's say Hilda does the expected: she caves in, begins to cry and drops her cherished walking stick to the ground. Now all in the vicinity respond according to the vibration which Hilda had brought forth: some angrily criticize Cap, others put their arms around Hilda, comforting her, some angrily go to the pastor and demand the removal of such an insensitive usher; the responses will be varied because the Law of Free Will is always in effect.

The point is, the responses of the others to Hilda are entirely generated from Hilda's free will decisions, not Cap's.

This may seem absurd until we think about what happens if Hilda does (1) instead of (2).

Cap says: "For God's sake old woman, tone it down will you? Nobody wants to look at your ugly body."

Hilda, feeling wonderful about herself, smiles and says cheerfully, "That's OK Cap, you probably didn't get your coffee this morning," and without a backward glance, seats herself in her accustomed pew.

What are the responses of the others in this case?

Irritation at Cap, perhaps even downright hostility; but toward Hilda, people smile, chuckle to themselves and say, "My, Hilda is in a good mood this morning!"

The others respond in this way because they were poised vibrationally upon a teeter-totter, and Hilda's vibrational signal, thrown into the mix, determines whether it swings one way or the other, *with regard to Hilda.*

It is possible that the emotional level of the group will be largely undisturbed by Cap's comment, for Hilda has reminded everyone how grouchy Cap is early in the morning when he doesn't have at least two cups of coffee in him, and all understand that on Sunday mornings Cap's wife, encouraging him to "better himself," browbeats him to volunteer at the church.

Hilda's attitude and her insightful understanding of Cap's situation not only promote a cheerful vibrational outcome for her, but may also prompt some of the group entering the church to feel a little sympathy for Cap.

Of course, the exact outcome of the response to Cap will be determined by the precise content of Cap's vibrational offering to the group, but Hilda's cheerful response may bring Cap up the Emotional Scale to the point where the group's response to him is positive as well, and everyone simply laughs the whole thing off. In other words, Hilda gets to determine not only the outcome for her, but may also affect a positive outcome for all in the group! This is the power of consciousness, aligned with the laws of the universe to bring about positive change in the world. And all from a simple, conscious decision to stay centered in her own power.

A judgment is really a statement of the attitudes of the speaker and has little to do with the person spoken to.

The statement "Judge not, lest ye be judged," really means, "Judge not, lest ye influence yourself to feel precisely as you have intended the object of your judgment."

All action follows thought. Thought precedes action. The negative feeling of judgment must always exist within you first, before it is projected to the world at large.

Negative judgment may or may not hurt another, but it will always hurt you.

CHAPTER 8

A New Perspective on Life

IN previous chapters we have described a human being as a powerful spiritual being who has come to earth to have a temporary physical experience. We have discovered the power of consciousness and the power of thought. We understand that in a universe which has been designed for well-being, that is possible to consciously create the conditions of your life. In this chapter we tale a new look at life from this fresh and empowering point of view.

Is it better to be serious about life, or have a good time?
Is it frivolous to do something purely for the enjoyment of it?

8.1 En-Joy

IF I could summarize all of my knowledge from 53 years of life experience, and all of my investigations into the Big Picture, it would be just one word: en-joy. All of science and mathematics, art, business, sports, relationships, any aspect of life, can be boiled down to this word.

The only reason anyone ever attempts anything is the idea that it would feel good to do it. This applies even to those who appear to be acting irrationally. If you could get inside the skin of such a person, you would find that their actions are taken from the conviction that it is the best possible path. En-joy applies even to the most abstruse logician, working in the area of pure Mind, attempting to divorce himself from all feeling and bias. Because underneath all of that attempted purity of observation and reasoning, is the beauty and en-joyment of what is created.

Why do you go into a relationship? Because of the good feelings it can evoke within you. Why start a new business or invest in the stock market? To make money, probably, but why do you want more money? To en-joy the benefits it can bring. No matter where you begin, life itself boils down to the attempt to reach for well-being, in whatever form that takes.

I write en-joy, to emphasize the creative nature of enjoyment. En-joy is often used in the passive sense; that is, if something is observed that is pleasing, then it is OK to feel good. But if something unwanted is observed, we'll feel bad. This experience of enjoyment is conditional; dependent upon observation of the creations of others.

To en-joy something is to place joy into it. It is an active, creative concept, not a passive, dependent one.

Nothing that is observed by you has the slightest power to affect you in any way, unless you decide that it does. This means that anything that happens to you can be en-joyed.

If you are observing something you dislike, that bad feeling does not arise in you because of some inherent property of the object itself. Any good or bad feeling arises in you because of your consideration or judgment or interpretation of what is observed. It is all within you. You are creating and interpreting your own experience. It is hard to understate the importance of this concept!

Most people would say "there are just some things in life that are revolting, and others that are beautiful." That may be true, but is it worth feeling crummy about the bad stuff? If you had your choice, would you want to feel good all the time, or do you regard this concept as a little bit nutty? How important is it for you to feel good? How you answer these questions will determine how much joy and happiness you allow yourself to experience.

In this society, many people would say that en-joying is only possible under certain circumstances, like on a vacation, or at a party. The rest of the time you have to be 'serious' and put your nose to the grindstone. But the alternative to feeling good is some form of negative emotion. Is it any wonder then that the history of our planet is what it is? It would seem rational and reasonable that a person would want to feel good all the time, because that is what every life form is striving for.

"Why are you so cheerful?"

"There's a lot for me to be happy about."

"Are you crazy? We're at work!"

You are not supposed to be joyful at work. Work is something you do to pay the bills. Save your fun for after. As you become more and more conscious, you will be able to recognize lots of strange ideas floating around in society, just like this one. Eventually you get to where you can find amusement in them.

If someone dies, mass consciousness says you must not en-joy. The thought stream connected with death is so powerful that when one of our loved ones dies we immediately feel horrible. We don't think about the fact that grandma made her transition out of the body and into complete re-connection with source. If you were to have a party for grandma and celebrate her life, instead of a funeral, society would condemn you. "Don't you have any respect for the dead?" they might say.

Respect for the dead? What does that mean? There is no death! I guess if you look at people as pieces of meat, if you consider that when the body dies grandma's consciousness is snuffed out forever, then it makes a sort of sense. You would want to have respect for a person who came to earth, lived once, and is now gone forever.

But this idea is ridiculous, of course. Consciousness is eternal. You can never die.

All beings have the choice to experience anything in life joyfully, or not. Experiencing positive emotion is OK, ALL the time. As a sovereign being, it is your right and your choice to feel any way at all about anything in life. Go ahead and try it, you'll like it! Realize that those who criticize you for feeling good are themselves choosing to feel rotten. While this is certainly their right, it is nutty. The old saying "misery loves company" is certainly true; it is just not necessary.

A definition of crazy might be: choosing to feel bad when you have the opportunity to feel good. Feeling good does not mean that you have to run around laughing all the time. Feeling good can be done privately, within yourself, so as not to offend all of those who are busy cutting themselves off from well-being! In short, en-joying life is possible *no matter what the circumstances*. It simply requires a little more emphasis on wanting to feel good and a little less emphasis on the importance of "reality."

In our results-oriented culture, the statement above reeks of illogic, for we have been taught that the worth of something is established only by whether we succeed or fail. Critics, for example, declare a musical composition a "failure" because it did not catch on, or because it did not agree with the critic's musical tastes. But if the artist who fashioned it had a wonderful time doing so, then maybe the three joyful months that were spent in its creation were worthwhile after all.

Objectivity and impartiality are valued very highly in our society. But this places us in a mindset of detached observation, waiting to make value judgments only by the result of our efforts. We become so attached to the outcome that we forget to have fun along the way.

8.2 Joy vs. Selfishness

Is it possible or even desirable to be joyful if it unfavorably affects others? Can "following your bliss," as Joseph Campbell says, lead to selfishness? Here's an example based on a true experience:

Suppose cousin Karl decides to quit his well-paying job and invest his life savings in a restaurant. Karl is bored with his job, even though he makes a good bit of coin. He wants to do something new and exciting. Karl has absolutely no experience in the restaurant business. It is clear to you that his ideas and visions for the restaurant will never work out and that his enthusiasm will never overcome his bad business sense. It's also clear to you that Karl has always been the type to launch into something quickly, then get discouraged when immediate results are not forthcoming. You wonder how he ever got to be good at anything! In short, you can see that Karl's restaurant idea is a recipe for disaster.

Yet for Karl, the whole idea is a big adventure that he plunges into with eagerness. His enthusiasm and hard (but joyful) work manages to overcome his abysmal business decisions, and the restaurant stays afloat. You look at Karl and cannot figure out why he would trade a job which provided plenty of free time and money, to one in which he works seven days a week and barely breaks even.

The answer is en-joyment. Karl loves being his own boss. He loves interacting with his customers. He loves the idea of providing great food and good atmosphere to enjoy it in. In fact, the restaurant has been his secret dream, a dream about which he has never told a single soul and one that he had previously never had the guts to pursue. For Karl, working seven days a week isn't work at all, but fun. It makes no sense to you, and it even seems wrong to you, for Karl has no time for his family anymore. He spends literally every waking hour at his restaurant. You can see that his marriage is going down the tubes. But when Karl is in his restaurant he is happy, happier than he has ever been in his life.

Are Karl's actions wrong? Would it have been better for him to stay in his boring job and keep his marriage intact? Karl has three kids after all, what is to become of them? Is it right for Karl to change his life so that he is happy all of the time in his new work, even though others may seem to be adversely affected?

Well, if Karl is happy, he will want to continue to do those things that make him happy. Are we to tell Karl he must sell his restaurant and find some other, more profitable work so that he can spend more time with his family? That may make the rest of us feel good, but what about Karl? Is it Karl's responsibility to make his family happy? Is it even possible for Karl to secure the happiness of others?

A committee of Karl's friends and relatives, observing his "reckless" conduct, is determined to straighten him out. They put pressure on Karl and browbeat him until he sells his restaurant and returns to his old job. But Karl is now miserable. He does not want to be at his old job (or any other job), he wants to be in his restaurant. His work ethic suffers and he begins to lose the confidence of his employers and his co-workers. Karl comes home every night and complains to the wife and kids. He begins to resent having a family altogether, but the family wishes Karl would just stop whining and act responsibly.

"You took a marriage vow Karl," his wife says. "You're not a little boy anymore. It's time to be a man and a father to your children." To make a long story short, Karl and his wife divorce and he loses his job. Meanwhile, all of those interested in Karl's welfare are criticizing him for being selfish and wrecking his family. Now we have a situation where no restaurant exists, his company is worse off, his family is worse off, Karl is worse off, and all of those who convinced Karl to "do the right thing" are upset.

The above scenario is unnecessary. We know from our study of the UOS that if Karl remains truly happy, then eventually, all of the difficulties in his life will disappear. The situation with his family will work itself out, for a vibration of happiness must attract only more happiness to it. That is guaranteed by the Law of Vibration and the Law of Attraction.

Karl could have taken the kids to his restaurant after school, maybe even have given them jobs. His wife might have found something interesting about Karl's new profession as well; after all, in any marriage there are usually many areas of mutual interest. The situation fell apart because all those involved began to resonate to unhappiness, and so it is not surprising that an unhappy result was forthcoming. Karl's mistake was not being true to himself, not continuing to listen to his inner voice of inspiration and joy!

Can you think of a life situation in which someone who is truly joyful met an unhappy ending? (I don't mean death, because death is the ultimate happy ending – a return to Source.) It's something worth thinking about, for when you become more and more conscious within your life, and become an astute observer of others, you will find that like attracts like is the governing principle.

Personally, I have learned the hard way that to ignore my inner voice is to go down the path to misery. I have learned that when one trusts oneself and looks inward for answers, those answers are always the ones that lead to joy. I have learned that it is not possible to harm another when in a true vibration of joy.

I have learned that, ultimately, it is not about the goal, it's about the journey. It's about the fun you have along the way. The enjoyment of something is the only justification necessary for doing it. That's the answer that has made my life a lot simpler and more fun.

I have finally learned that it's not my job to "fix" other people, no matter how harmful their actions may seem. I have finally realized that people will do what they wish, regardless of my objections, and that it is futile for me to try and stop them. Besides, there are over 7 billion of them! How is it possible to make sure all 7 billion are doing the right things? I have realized that it's not my job to deny others their freedom to be, do or have anything

Every person is en-joying life as much as they are able, and I am now satisfied to allow them to do so. Besides, it's a lot more fun for me, and a lot less work. I no longer have to go around observing and pointing out to myself the flaws in the behavior of others, and thinking up ways of making them better. That way of living caused me so much anger and anxiety that I just had to give it up.

Of course, there are many, many people throughout the world who joyfully go about the business of trying to mold the world into a better place for them to live in. My hat is off to them – as long as they are having fun. It isn't possible to do harm when you're truly having fun, because the actions taken are all from an attitude of light-heartedness. It's when the goal starts mattering more than the enjoyment that problems result. In that scenario, all of us are now expected to follow the rules laid down by the fixer-uppers! Now we have conflict, and even war. When we get off the path of en-joyment, we create problems for ourselves and others.

En-joyment is not a passive, dependent activity, but a conscious choice to place joy into everything we observe, and do. Conscious attention to en-joyment results in the choice to create and experience without judgment or criticism.

8.3 Happiness vs. Joy

WHAT is the difference between happiness and joy? They are both positive and desirable feelings, and it could be said, who cares? If you are feeling good, that is all that matters.

There is a subtle but important distinction between the two, however, which can help a person consciously make himself or herself feel better.

Happiness is observing or doing something in the physical universe that you really like. Joy is connecting with the source of life that is within you.

Happiness is fleeting. Joy can be continuous. Happiness is dependent upon something or someone outside of yourself. Joy is self-enabling and comes from within.

The distinction between happiness and joy is especially important in relationships, for many of us look to our partners to fill in the missing pieces in our psychological and emotional makeup. Unfortunately, this requires the other to always act in certain ways, in order that we may continue to feel happy. But what happens when the other decides that it is far easier to live life for him or herself, and becomes less attentive to our needs? Eventually, we lose the ability to control our own mental and emotional direction, and feel a loss of self-confidence and personal integrity.

When you observe or do something that makes you feel happy, the positive emotion you feel is really just a lowering of your resistance to life. It is an allowance of your own life force, without restriction. For instance, you go on vacation to a really nice place that always makes you feel good. You release all of your worries and cares, and just have a good time. If you could do that in your daily life, there would be no need to go on vacation. "Yes," you say, "but I really like what I do on vacation, and I don't like my job that much. And when I'm on vacation, I don't have to worry about finances, or my mother's failing health, or any of the things that make life unpleasant." However, this is backwards! It's the worry about A, B, and C that keeps A, B, and C in your life in precisely the same form. Unless you begin to consciously change your vibe, you never become aware of this. Unless you begin to use the power of consciousness, you never understand that it is possible to deliberately change conditions in your experience for the better.

"OK," you might say, "but what if your life is really messed up? You can't just wish it all away."

Well, here's how it works: if you believe that the only way to be happy is to observe things you like, then you are trapped. You can never get out of the rut, because you are continuing to create your life from the non-optimum conditions that are being observed. Your vibe never changes! Observe it, resonate to it, get more of it, observe it, resonate to it, get more of it, etc.

As children we cry and our needs get met, but this teaches us wrong-end-forwards for life. A vibration of grief will attract things that make you cry! There is just no getting around it: if you want the conditions of your life to be good, you have to start feeling good.

You just have to develop a habit of lowering your resistance to life. Realize that your basic nature is positive, not negative. It is really hard to change if you believe that you are basically unworthy, and the universe is a cold and uncaring place. But it's not! If you just work with the principles of the Universal Operating System for a little while, you can demonstrate this to yourself. Books, lectures, and words don't teach. Your personal experience is the only true way to learn.

You have to practice feeling good. Seems weird to say it, but it's true. Just practice feeling what it would be like to have everything you want. Most of us practice just the opposite every day. We practice worrying about all of the things that we observe and do not like about our lives, and the world around us. We do this because we think it is necessary to make contingency plans, should trouble overtake us. We look around at others and say, "If it could happen to them, it could happen to me." Although this is reasonable in the absence of an understanding of universal principles, it is just another self-fulfilling idiocy, a maintenance of the vibrational proclivity that brings the unwanted thing into our experience. Mostly we worry because we've made a habit of it. But bad habits can be turned into good habits! The law of like attracts like reinforces whatever habits you have. That is why it is often so hard to change. The more positive you are, the more you will rendezvous with positive people and situations, and vice-versa. So if you've gotten yourself into the trap of negative thinking, you must start envisioning your life the way you want it. That's the long and the short of it.

8.4 How to Stay Positive in a Negative World

DOES observation of reality determine our feelings? We have discussed this before but it bears repetition.

Most people would answer this question with a resounding yes! "Of course," they will say, "would you rather see a polluted river or a clear, sparkling one? Would you rather have someone screaming in your face, or telling you what a nice guy you are? Would you rather look at a beautiful sculpture or a pile of garbage?"

A pile of stinking garbage is guaranteed to cause a negative reaction, isn't it?

While it's true that it is much easier to feel good when looking at something wonderful, the determination of what is pleasurable is only a judgment, or a choice, of consciousness.

For example, one hot summer day I was stuck in the middle of the busiest intersection in town, in a car with no air conditioning. A mass of concrete and metal assailed my eyes. The air smelled like automobile exhaust, and the traffic wasn't moving. Yet I felt wonderful. There was no reason for it! For some reason, I didn't notice any of the "bad" stuff. Instead of seeing a traffic jam, I saw a community of people. Instead of lamenting the press of cars around me, I began noticing the makes, models, and colors I liked. Instead of seeing a mass of concrete, I marveled at the well-paved road.

The next day, I found myself in the very same place, but this time all I could see was the negative. Same place, same observations, but my orientation was completely different.

The pile of garbage has both positive and negative aspects. One could look at it and say, "Think of all the pleasure enjoyed by those who used these things." This statement would be considered nutty by most of us, but that is only because most of us have been taught that logic and reason should supersede the way we feel. "It is illogical to look upon that stinking mess in a positive fashion, for it is now clearly a hazard. And it doesn't smell very good either." Indeed, these things are true. But when you let logic, or the beliefs and attitudes of others, affect your state of being, you are no longer in charge of the way you feel. In this case, logic is used to argue for a lower emotion, which is itself illogical!

The crew that removes the garbage may undertake their task lightheartedly or sullenly. "Won't the street look better after this junk is removed?" might be one attitude. "Gawd, this job sucks" might be more common. But if you were a garbage man, would you feel better at the end of a day's work with the former mind-set or the latter? If two haulers give you a bid for the junk you've just cleaned out of your basement, which one would you hire, prices being comparable? I don't know about you, but I'll take the cheerful one. In my experience, cheerful people are more conscientious than grumps. A sloppy vibration leads to sloppy work.

The point is, there is nothing inherent in the objects, people, or activities you observe that is pejorative.

"Yes," you say, "but when the boss is screaming at me it doesn't feel good."

This is totally understandable!

But there's nothing in a screaming boss that will, like some natural law, cause you to feel bad. The screaming boss feels bad because you have a thought, or a belief, or a mental computation that says something like "The boss is screaming at me because he is unhappy with me, so I must have screwed up. That means there is something wrong with me."

There is nothing wrong with you. There has never been anything wrong with you. You merely have a belief that says, "I must determine my feelings about my environment, and about myself, from what other people think or say about me, or from what I observe."

The only aberration is denial of self.

"Yes, but I screwed up," you say. "I should have shipped that order yesterday, but I forgot."

That may be so, but does that have to mean you feel bad about yourself?

"It means I was incompetent," you say. "The client is really upset and now the boss looks like an idiot. I am a trusted employee and I let the team down."

Again, that is a self-generated value judgment, a denial of self. You're pasting a story about yourself over a sequence of actions in space/time. Energetically, you are allowing what occurs on all other flows to determine your opinion of yourself on the reflexive flow, when it is really what you decide on the reflexive flow that determines what you experience on the other flows! You are going against the laws of the universe when you do this, and you will have to pay for it, because you are reinforcing a vibration that will lead inevitably to more of the same incompetent actions.

"But I'm responsible as shipping manager to ensure that orders go out on time, especially important ones."

True again, but what does that have to do with your personal value?

"It means I'm not as good as I think I am."

Another conscious, self-limiting decision. If you do this enough times it turns into a belief, and then an ingrained habit of thought. Now you have a "hot button" that can be pushed by others, or triggered by the environment. You have essentially turned yourself into a robot in this area!

Have you ever had someone criticize you, but felt so great that his or her criticisms just seemed funny? Most of us have probably experienced this at least once in our lives. This is simply observation without judgment. In our previous example, it is what Hilda did when Cap criticized her. Instead of reacting robotically, Hilda stayed connected.

If you find yourself constantly encountering unpleasant people and situations, realize that you have a habit of thought and belief that is continually causing self-similar, co-incident manifestations. Such a realization is over half the battle, for now you can begin to change the way you feel.

If the boss is in your face, even if it's for something you messed up, you can simply say to yourself, "I'll do better next time." In this society it is almost required that you beat yourself up if you make a mistake, but this is irrational. "Pete didn't feel any remorse for his action," the supervisor says. "He doesn't care about his job." Huh? Where did that evaluation come from? The computation is, "Pete should feel crummy about his action so that he will do better next time." Let's see…feeling rotten about something will lead to more positive actions. Clearly this is bonkers, but it is quite in line with the equation of mankind, bad = good. Fortunately, Pete knows that he cares a lot about his job and his performance, and so nothing bad can happen to him *as long as he maintains that attitude.* In fact, the more confident and happy Pete remains, the better employee he will be. The correct equation is, good = good.

When you feel wonderful, there is nothing that can get you down. That wonderful feeling is something intrinsic to your very being, and can be experienced at will. The key is to understand that what occurs on the reflexive flow is always the beginning of any outflow to the universe, and the last filter in from the universe. Any signal that is transmitted or received, in other words, is directly under your control.

We are just taught the opposite. The dogmas of science teach us that one determines the truth or falsity of something only by the observation of it. This is fine for a scientific experiment that studies the behavior of matter and energy, but it is all wrong for consciousness in its interaction with the universe. Consciousness created the universe in order to experience in it. The world will change around you, IF you change the decisions you make about it. Change your signal to the universe, and your life will change to match.

That prejudicial judgment, bias, or belief you have is something you're creating right now, and it's something that, with just a little conscious attention, you can stop right now. And when you stop, you will feel relief. I guarantee it. If it can work for a klutz like me, it can certainly work for a genius like you!

8.5   Integrity

ONE is able to maintain a positive attitude despite environmental conditions by realizing that something observed is just something that is observed. It is always possible to make an independent assessment, as we did earlier with the pile of garbage. In other words, it is always possible to assume a state of being independent of what is observed, for that is an inherent ability of consciousness. The reason we do not is because others think it is stupid.

"What a moron," Joe Doakes says to Cecil Aldershot when Cecil voices his positive opinion about the garbage pile. "Airhead! That putrid stuff is disgusting, and if you can't see that, you're a jerk!" It is easy to become swayed by such strongly held opinions, because you think, "Wow! If someone feels that strongly about something, it must be true." Your vibration tends to become entrained by the more powerful one. Here is where the conscious exercise of free will is important. Cecil thinks, "If I don't say I feel crummy, Joe might even kick my butt." Well, it is always up to you what you think. Cecil might say, "Yeah, that sucks," satisfying Joe, but really staying positive. Joe Doakes would snort at this solution, saying that it lacks integrity. But Joe does not understand the meaning of integrity.

Integrity is not necessarily telling the truth about what-is. Integrity is not a product of the intellect. Integrity means wholeness. (People who insist that you always tell the truth are people who want to control you. This philosophy is prevalent in the military, for obvious reasons.) Integrity is always accompanied by positive emotion, for when you feel joy, you feel whole. Anything that brings about negative emotion is a violation of personal integrity, because it leads to less wholeness. Therefore, telling the truth about something is harmful *if* it makes you feel rotten.

"Yes, but Cecil is lying about how he really feels," Joe might say, if he knew what Cecil's true feelings are. "He's just a little wimp and I really feel like punching his lights out." Cecil might think, "Who cares what Joe Doakes thinks? I care more about how *I* feel. And it makes me feel better to make Joe feel better." In other words, how you feel is far more important than telling the truth about matter and energy (or about anything). Some may argue with this philosophy, calling it cowardly, but it is never cowardly to feel good. Integrity demands that you stay as high on the emotional/vibrational scale, regardless of what others think and regardless of the prevailing societal mores. That takes courage! It is impossible to go wrong by reaching for a more positive feeling, for the universe will respond positively as well.

What I try to do is simply go through life paying attention to how I feel. If I feel myself getting upset, I just stop to BE for a few seconds and change my crummy thought to a positive one. It doesn't have to take more than a couple of seconds. Don't monitor yourself, that will just drive you crazy! Live normally, and when you become aware of something that bothers you, take a few moments to BE yourself, in the moment. After you practice this for a while, it gets easier and easier.

I can't describe how powerful this is. Don't make a process out of it. If you do, you will become a slave to it!

Every time you do this, you become a little more conscious, a little more self-aware. Bit by bit you become a little more of who you really are, every day. It's fun!

8.6 Connecting With Source

WHEN attempting to describe the subtle energy of life force, we really don't have words for it. I said above that "you become a little more of who you really are every day," but that's pretty vague. It's vague because we're talking about something that is essentially virtual, unobservable, and immeasurable, and there is, as yet, no terminology. Like consciousness itself, it's a quality, not a quantity and therefore, difficult to pin down. We can only see the effects of life force energy (brain waves, for example) but not directly quantify it from the outside.

There is, however, no difficulty in experiencing life force energy from the inside out, from inside your own skin. It's a personal, intimate experience of you with you.

A true connection of you with you produces the most exquisite feeling of joy and well being. In other words, how you feel inside your own skin is dependent only on what you do with your own life force on the reflexive flow. The new-age generality "you create your own reality," is completely true with regard to how you feel within your own skin, and the UOS guarantees that inflow, outflow, and crossflow will gradually mirror back to you what is happening within yourself. That is what is meant by "connect with life force energy."

It's easy to say "connect with the life force energy within you and you will be joyful" but how do you do that? Well, it's more a matter of not doing, because if you removed all resistant thought, you would feel wonderful all the time. People find this impossible to believe, because it doesn't seem reasonable to say, based on the observation of others, that the inherent condition for life is positive. However, we only say this because we have been taught to pay attention to what others say and do, and because we devote too much of our attention to the bad stuff. The bad stuff is so unusual, it sells! But it sells only because it's shocking. And it's only shocking because we all instinctively understand that well-being is the default. And so we often gravitate toward the negative, but assign it the wrong importance. It's like going into a pristinely beautiful forest and noticing the one tree that has been blasted by lightning.

How do you remove resistant and habitual patterns of thought that are no longer serving you? Here is a simple process that works for me: relax, and reach for a positive feeling. That's all it takes. You don't need a guru or a crystal or a therapist. You don't need to meditate, although meditating is doing this exact process, in a quiet place. But you don't even need a quiet place. I do it all the time, while working, writing, working out, etc. It's habit forming in a good way! And I have to tell you that this simple procedure, reaching for a good feeling, has led me to the most profound realizations about myself, which I am going to detail in the next book. It has led me on a journey to my true self that has been the most exciting adventure I have ever undertaken. It is a very simple, but very powerful activity.

If you do this enough you can convince yourself of your inherently positive nature. And the great thing is that IT'S TRUE. You ARE a joyful and loving being to the very core of you. When you get this, it's an indescribable feeling of beauty and joy. You really, really understand that there is nothing to worry about. You feel connected to life. You feel uplifted. You feel that your life can only go in a positive direction. Once you truly understand that you are, fundamentally, a being of joy, you are like a freight train going 100 miles an hour. No one can stop you, no one can hurt you, and in fact, your life becomes filled more and more with people and things that are a match to your new understanding of yourself. That's the Law of Attraction going to work for you.

Once you begin this process of seeking joy, your success is inevitable. It's inevitable because the nature of consciousness itself is joyful. Joy is within you. Happiness is fleeting; happiness is dependent upon observing something outside yourself that is pleasing. But you are always pleasing to you, unless you are engaging in the self-sabotaging process of self-denial.

8.7 Trust Yourself, You Are God

THERE is no "right way" to connect with your source, your inner self. Don't get bogged down in the process, or the way someone else is doing it. Trust yourself; there isn't anyone who knows more about you, than you. That old saying about others being better able to know who you are is a lot of bull. "I know you better than you know yourself." "You are an open book to me." "Don't kid yourself; what you're doing is wrong." Etc. All of these statements are someone else's interpretation of your vibrational signal, seen through the colored lenses of their personal perspective.

Never give away your power to someone else. By that is meant, do not ever allow another to direct the course of your life, assuming that you are incapable of doing so. Trust and follow your inner guidance, which is infallible, and will always direct you to the path of least resistance and the most joy. Every single human being on earth is an aspect of universal consciousness, and has within a deep, powerful well of joy and complete knowledge of self. Once you feel this energy within you, even if for a little while, you can never doubt your fundamentally positive nature ever again. The feeling of YOU is so wonderful it will change your life.

8.8 Control Equals Weakness

IF you need others to do your bidding in order to be happy, then you'd better roll up your sleeves and get to work! It's going to be a long, hard road. This is the road politicians, authority figures, and dictators take. As long as everyone is agreeing with them and behaving properly, the authority is happy, but step out of line, and watch out! It is thought by such types that power is the ability to control others, but really, this kind of power is based in fear and insecurity; for the dictator, in order to be happy, must look around and see everyone marching in lockstep. He is incapable of connecting to the joy within himself; for if he was able to do so, he would feel no need to dominate or control others. The "power is control over others" idea is not strength, but weakness, for a connection to self on the reflexive flow brings a feeling of power and confidence. That rush of joy or love that we occasionally feel is unresisted life force energy, and there is nothing in the universe more awesome or powerful than that. The power of a dictator or politician is puny in comparison. When others refuse to go along anymore with his ideas, he is finished; like a balloon that is punctured, his world collapses about him and he becomes an empty, shriveled shell. Or he winds up like Benito Mussolini with his head bashed in, or Nicolae Ceaucescu in front of a firing squad.

I used to be a control freak in my own life. If something good happened and I did not script it, it was dismissed. "Just luck," I would tell myself contemptuously. "It doesn't count." Duh!

The happy accidents you receive are an indication of your alignment with source, and luck is simply the co-incident matching of vibration. Here I was, going against the physics of the universe, and I wondered why it was so hard to get anywhere! Sometimes I look back at my life and am amazed at the dumb ideas I had.

In my contracting business I never meet up anymore with negative people. My clients are uniformly wonderful, and I get along famously with all of them. This situation is statistically incorrect. In a random sampling of clients, I should encounter a few grumps, at least! For me, it is just one more reason to believe in the vibrational universe concept.

Joy comes from within. It's not something complicated; it is a state of being. There are no processes, blueprints, mantras, or procedures necessary to gain it. Joy is NOT doing, and it comes as an inherent and quintessential property of your consciousness. Joy is not an achieving or attaining, it's simply an allowing of your native beingness. With an attitude of joy, you are in consort with source energy, the energy of the universe. You are going with the flow. You are in a state of grace. When you feel good, you feel God, and the universe reflects your joy back unto you, with every person you meet. Joy is a continuous state of happiness, a continuing state of positive emotion. Happiness is a fleeting thing, brought about by observing something pleasing.

All of us have the ability to create happiness from within. All it takes is a little practice, by finding excuses to be happy, even if it is only for a few seconds at a time. Those few seconds can then stretch out to encompass your whole life.

8.9 Passion

PASSION is the strongest indicator of desire.

Passion occurs when you draw life force energy through you very powerfully, without resistance. On planet earth, passion is often associated with destructive activities, i.e., "crimes of passion." But of course, this is just another earthly inversion of a divine impulse, and involves resistance to something. All desires, no matter how "twisted," have positive roots, because consciousness itself is a pure positive creative potential, and inherently joyful.

Passion is often criticized because it is "undisciplined": it is viewed as an overly emotional state which can be dangerous because the intellect is short-circuited. However, true passion combines both intellect and feeling. Because it is very high on the scale of emotions, and intelligence is proportional to how good you feel, true passion is something very desirable! A truly passionate person is harnessing a ton of life force energy, and can sometimes seem overwhelming to those lower on the scale of vibration/emotion. But that is no reason to avoid that wonderful, powerful feeling!

What are you passionate about?

Are you living your passion, or just dreaming about it?

How do you find something to get passionate about?

Have you ever felt passion?

If you don't know the answers to these questions, continue reading!

Why is it that during most of our early years we are rarely, if ever, consulted about what we want to do in life? The socialization process (school) stuffs heads full of data and memes that encourage a person to "get an education" so he or she can "find a good job" or "get ahead." Now that's a pretty mundane existence!

I think passion is discouraged simply because it is such a high vibration/emotion relative to the society at large, and there is genuine fear that a passionate person is a dangerous person. There is concern that our society would be turned upside down if people were allowed to find their own way without direction from the authorities. I have noticed, however, that when I'm really passionate about something I get very creative. I'm quietly engrossed in my own creative process, not loud or obnoxious or destructive.

A sane society would encourage people to do what makes them feel good, but a fearful one insists upon regulated and standardized behavior. It seems that passing standardized tests is the *raison d'être* of our system of education. However, the attempt to structure behavior goes against the Law of Free Will, and the inherent creative nature of consciousness itself. That's why all hierarchical political systems eventually crumble.

In order to find your passion you just have to FEEL what really excites you and go with it. You have to be willing to share your life with others, even if it's embarrassing sometimes! You have to not care what others think, even if they disagree.

Someone who disagrees with you doesn't make you wrong, or the other misguided. It just means points of view are being expressed. I've also learned that when someone gets personally insulting, that person is giving you a report about THEM. The truly great creators in any field are fearless and confident, unafraid to state their opinions even when those opinions are way out of the mainstream.

When you are passionate about something you are totally centered within your own life force and you feel good about your creative expression regardless of the response.

Making yourself wrong about ANYTHING is counter-productive, even if your thoughts or actions are out of the mainstream. You will notice that when you feel good about yourself you can do anything you want and have it accepted by others. That is what all successful and famous creators have discovered – that when you are totally, completely being YOU, there is a deep connection with others who come in contact with you.

What is that connection?

Contact with the inner divine essence that is the common denominator of consciousness itself, the unifying, directing and animating principle of the universe. When you link with your own life force energy, you connect yourself with all life everywhere. And that is a wonderful feeling.

Passion is felt when you discover the beautiful you inside of you.

Others can see it and feel it as well. That's why setting an example is the hardest but most effective way to change the world. One at a time, all those who come into contact with you are enriched, not because you are some guru or saint, or because you're above it all, but simply because you remind others of who they are. A balanced, passionate person can evoke that feeling in others, and in himself or herself. You don't need any training or education; in fact, anyone can do it by just deciding to.

Sometimes you are nowhere near your passion, but that's no reason not to try again tomorrow, or an hour from now, or in the next minute, or maybe even right now!

Just focusing on fun can be deep and rewarding. All it takes is finding something to have fun about. And anyone can do that.

Passion essentially involves the focusing of your attention on something you like. The more you do this, the more ideas occur to you. It doesn't matter how much time you spend on it. If you work and have kids, you may only be able to find half an hour in the day to devote to your passion. But that is fine because half an hour every day will soon strengthen your vibration in that area more and more. You will find it easier and easier to find that half hour, and you will notice that the half hour gradually becomes a little longer.

The more time you spend on something you like, the more time you will have for it.

Those who worry that wasting time on non-remunerative "feel good" activities will drain one's bank account, or cause one to abandon one's responsibilities, should have no fear. Remember that raising your emotional level regarding anything will raise your overall vibration, and every area of your life will benefit.

Sometimes people think that if life is ghastly, then raising your vibration will just get you more of the stuff you don't like. But that is not the way it works!

If you hate your ex and you raise your emotional level regarding him or her, it is often thought that you are inviting the hated person more into your life. But what really happens is that you draw to you people with the characteristics that are a match to your raised vibration. If your ex does not possess those characteristics, he or she cannot occupy the same space as you. Vibrational proximity determines proximity in space and time.

If your ex does possess those characteristics, he or she will exhibit, magically, changed behavior. The vibrational universe has the fascinating property that it will mirror to you that which is activated within you. It can seem magical and mysterious, but it is really just vibrational physics.

Because the universe has a function called "Vibrational Matching," finding your passion sets you up to receive the things you want. Most important, it changes the way you feel about yourself. All personal physical manifestations must begin with a change in your personal vibration.

How do you find your passion?

By becoming aware of what you like, and what you don't like.

Many people know pretty clearly what is NOT wanted, but aren't so sure what IS wanted.

To help you find your passion, simply go through the day noticing what makes you feel good. This requires conscious attention, and also requires that you become aware of how you're feeling. (You can also meditate with this idea in mind.) Becoming aware of your feelings is the most important thing you can do in finding your passion, for your feelings are your guidance system. Like one of those levels with air bubbles that carpenters use, your feelings tell you how close you are to aligning with your own life force. They can help you identify goals and establish a rewarding life path.

This process can be undertaken by anyone, at any time. You don't have to be a genius or a saint or somebody "special." You don't even have to be smart, for the vibrational matching property of the universe does not reward a PhD more than a 5th grade dropout. It simply responds to your state of being and your thoughts, which establish the activated vibration to which everything in the universe responds.

Finding your passion uncovers more of the you in you. It is a very rewarding activity and does not require constant diligence; it only requires that you begin to become more mindful, a little bit more conscious, a little bit at a time.

The main rule is, if you're not feeling better, it's not working!

Passion and fun are intimately connected. So find something fun to be and do, and watch what happens.

Is it weird to be different or to live in your own little world?

8.10 Being Different

Have you ever heard the expression: "He is on a different planet than the rest of us" or, "she's living in her own little dream world." I turned on the news the other day and listened for about a minute, and realized it had absolutely nothing to do with my life. Apparently there are all sorts of worries about the economy, and war, and terrorist attacks, but I now see only the good stuff. So I guess someone could say that I was divorced from reality. (Funny thing is, I feel so much better, now that I am no longer a news junkie. I notice that 99% of the news is negative, but when I look around at life, I see 99% positive. Something is a little skewed, I'd say.)

Through the subtle energy transfer of vibration, your thoughts and beliefs about life place you near to those of like mind. This process is sometimes obvious, as you find yourself in a stadium watching a baseball game, and sometimes not so obvious, as you wind up at a job interview with someone who seems predisposed not to like you.

If you are continually worried about cancer for example, you will probably attract something negative into your life sooner or later. Maybe not cancer, but something you don't like. The Law of Vibration guarantees that if you are worried about some-thing, you are activating that feeling within you. When that vibration is activated, you begin to resonate more and more to it, like a tuning fork that is continually struck. Then you begin to find yourself in physical proximity to persons and situations that are a match to the vibration which you have activated. The content of the experiences you have will probably never be identical, but they will all be self-similar, because the carrier wave of your vibrational signal is the same.

Eventually you become so used to hearing the same note, it is not even noticeable anymore. Even though you are continually striking the tuning fork with the vibration of "worry about the economy" or "fear of disease", it just becomes a habit. People get resigned to doing the darndest things! Anyway, the point is, the Universal Operating System guarantees that EVERYONE lives in their own little world, which is orchestrated by them depending upon which thoughts and feelings are being activated.

Essentially, we create our own vibrational islands of personal experience.

Inga's family is into sports, camping, games, and having fun, and so was Inga until a few months ago, when she took a look at her life and didn't like what she saw anymore. Inga quit her job in a sports consulting firm and began taking meditation classes. She now works in a new age bookstore, for far less money, and her family and old friends are confused about where she's at. The vibrations Inga is now activating no longer resonate to those around her. She is on a different wavelength, literally, and so much of what Inga thinks, says and does is no longer real to her family. Eventually, if Inga continues on a vibrational path that is different from that of her family, there will be more and more physical separation between them. This is not good or bad, it is just the way the Universal Operating System works. The law of like attracts like guarantees that Inga will now meet up with people of similar interests. She may lose some of her old friends, because their vibrations now clash with hers.

The idea that people can be on different planets and live next to each other is nothing new. As a child I never even saw my neighbor who lived two doors down from me, even though we lived in that house for eight years! I'll bet many others have experienced similarly. My family was Catholic and theirs were sun worshippers (no kidding!)[22]

The point is, what passes for the common reality in a family or group is usually just what most of the family or group agrees on. What passes for the common reality in a nation is what the majority of the people agree on, which usually means, what is on the news every day. But these realities have no more validity than the reality of any individual. It is just that more people have bought into them. The geniuses, the successful business people, those who prosper in any field are always those who decide to do something and then continue along their path, no matter what anyone

---

[22] If the two families are so opposite, then why do they live next to each other? The main reason is a similar and powerful vibration of financial compatibility. My father and his neighbor were working class, with a similar outlook on life. Our differences were based on religious dogma. Otherwise, the two families were very much alike.

else says. So many of us, when we see the maverick, will be quick to criticize. This is natural, since the vibration the maverick is offering is different from the agreed upon vibration.

What many do is pull back. Inga might say to her family and friends: "Oh, I'm sorry, I guess I am going a little too far with that meditation stuff. I'll behave myself from now on." Inga, like Karl, might quit her job at the bookstore and justify it by telling herself that it was just a whim. She might even get her old job back. She may now feel more comfortable when dealing with family and friends, but if Inga is truly dissatisfied with her life and continues to frequent the same places and deal with the same people, she will become increasingly irritable. The vibrations just aren't meshing anymore.

Being different just means, having your internal vibration set at a different band-width than the people you are hanging around with. You can either stay with the old crowd and be miserable, or march to the beat of your own drummer. If you do decide to change, be assured that the laws of the universe will work for you. You will find yourself, inevitably, meeting up with new people and situations to match your new set of preferences! And if you stay joyful, the process of changing your life will be effortless. You will gradually meet up with people more in tune with you and gradually the others will fade away, with no upset or resentment at all.

Of course Inga doesn't have to lose anyone in her life who is really important to her. By simply doing her thing she will stay cheerful, and by being cheerful, will draw out cheerfulness in others. That's the great thing about maintaining a positive vibration – there is absolutely no downside.

Someone once told me that when you really begin to travel your own unique path through life, you feel alone. Well, this is not necessarily true! You may feel alone if you have suddenly and radically changed your worldview and are now completely out of tune with former associates and loved ones. When you begin to find out who you really are, and discover that unique set of basic desires that you came to earth to fulfill, it feels great! In other words, there is no downside to advancement.

There is a crazy idea on earth that in order to really get any place, you have to work hard, or struggle, or suffer, but this is just another one of those distorted concepts that are floating about in the mass consciousness. If you simply go with whatever feels best to you, you will be inevitably led down the most joyous path to the fulfillment of your true desires. It will feel wonderful. People say there are risks in this approach, and that it really just encourages false hope, and pie-in-the-sky dreaming. "You have to meet your responsibilities," they will say. "You have to pay the bills." The idea is that doing stuff that feels good will lead to financial ruin, but being a drone will at least produce the necessities of life.

Nothing could be further from the truth. There is no risk whatsoever in following your inner voice of inspiration.

There is great risk in feeling lousy, however, because feeling lousy leads to stress, bad health, and more lousy life experiences.

Feeling good leads to good things in your experience, including money. The reason a person can't make money doing things that feel good to him or her is precisely because they do not believe money can be made doing the things they love to do. The economy, the latest world political crisis, government policy, all of these things are irrelevant to your own prosperity and well-being. Of course, if you believe that you have to import the ideas and experiences of others into your personal worldview, then you will begin to experience in that way. But politicians and the news media have got it all bollixed. They have convinced us that their actions are vitally important to us all. And those actions ARE vitally important IF we believe that they are.

No one can create in your experience. You are a sovereign, powerful creator, orchestrating life from the platform of your thoughts, beliefs, and feelings. For example, let's say the government inflates the dollar to the point that it collapses. Now there is a great depression, and all those who believe that dollars are necessary to survival are affected. All those who resonate to the idea of scarcity will experience it. Those who are aligned with abundance, however, will experience abundance. Their portfolios may include investments that are not dollar denominated, or may include tangible assets, whose value will be unaffected. Perhaps they will live like the Amish, completely self-sufficient. There are millions of ways it can work out, each scenario dependent upon individual points of attraction. When massive disruption hits a large group, vibrational entrainment to the "group think" of negative outcomes becomes extremely powerful; but as we've already discussed, completely unnecessary.

Don't give up on your dreams because they happen to be different from the crowd. Blazing your own trail may sometimes result in a clash of vibration, which might feel uncomfortable at first. This does not mean your goals are impossible, or wrong, it is just the Law of Vibration telling you that you are now not resonating to the old ways anymore. That's a good thing, because it means you have truly shifted. It isn't all in your head, you are making it real enough in your vibration for others to respond to. The laws of the universe guarantee that there are plenty of people out there who you can connect up with in your new life. It may take a little time, but if you stick with it, the people and resources you need must come to you.

8.11 The True Meaning of Selfishness

TRUE selfishness is a Divine concept based upon appreciation of self.

A lot of people act selfishly, but many of them are unhappy.

How can this be? They should be feeling good! After all, that is what being selfish means, doesn't it – looking out for your happiness?

Of course, most people would say the reason selfish people are unhappy is BECAUSE of their selfish actions. The common wisdom says that if you are selfish, you will probably be unhappy because you care little for anyone but yourself.

But perhaps this statement is the exact opposite of the truth; perhaps the me-me selfishness people often display is an inversion of a true, divine impulse.

Those who sacrifice their own needs for the good of others are admired and respected. Society believes that allowing people to follow their inner desires will inevitably lead to chaos or, at the very least, imbalance. "If we allowed children to study what they wanted, there'd be a million artists and no engineers," a teacher said to me once. But this is nonsense! Although the parameters of our culture might change, we would have a highly motivated and productive population who loved their work, instead of a struggling and stressed-out one.

By the time a significant section of the population finishes school, a student has regurgitated so much data on so many subjects that he or she has either been bored to death or lost direction. The standard educational curriculum exercises our intellectual muscles and teaches students to disregard their feelings, which, unfortunately, suppresses the subtle inner voice.[23] Intuition is no help on a math test or an engineering problem of course, but losing touch with your feelings is a bad idea, for it disconnects you from yourself, like a ship without a rudder. Now you are subject to the whims of weather, tides, and water conditions and life looks like a series of coincidences and probabilities. A variety of other factors, especially the economic necessity to "make money" or "get a good job" supersedes the living of our dream. Sadly, by the time we reach adulthood many of us don't even know what we are passionate about. We are just trying to make our way as best we can in a world of scarce resources and in our confusion, we try to grab onto as much as possible.

The problem isn't being too selfish, it's not being Self-ish enough!

True Self-ishness always leads to joy, because it is motivated always by the desire to feel as good as possible. Me-first behavior is an attempt to find joy through the accumulation of physical objects, but that is a poor substitute for the life giving qualities that lie within. It is also energetically backwards, an attempt to alter the reflexive flow from inflow, outflow, or crossflow. The guy who bulls his way to the front of

---

[23] "The intuitive mind is a sacred gift and the rational mind is a faithful servant.
We have created a society that honors the servant and has forgotten the gift."—Einstein

the line is somewhere in the lower ranges of the Emotional/ Vibrational Scale, and even if he gets what he wants, the feeling doesn't last. His vibration is that of scarcity, guaranteeing that he will experience more and more of it. His life will go on a gradually descending spiral until he succumbs, or has a "severe reality adjustment" and a change in attitude.

It is only when we are Self-ish enough to be, do and act in accordance with our desires that balance can be maintained. Energetically speaking, a desire is a rush of life force energy, a connection to the divine inner self, which can never result in actions that are harmful. It is only when true desires are blocked that they become twisted and ugly.

Take Kenny for example. As a little child, Kenny is very eager and curious about life. His soul purpose is to be an architect, and he wants to find out how to build things. Therefore, he is constantly pulling stuff off of shelves, getting into drawers, and trying to take things apart. These are very joyful actions to Kenny, but irritating to everyone else in the family. Consequently, his parents and siblings constantly tell him that his conduct is inappropriate, and Kenny is disciplined accordingly. Eventually Kenny learns to simply damp himself down in order to get along with the rest of the family. Of course by doing this he also shuts off the flow of life force energy, for that is what desire is. After a while he begins to lash out, for he has learned that his creative expression is unacceptable. He becomes cynical about people and unhelpful to others, which just magnifies the difficulty. Kenny grows up to be unmanageable in school and at work.

All of this flows from a lack of true Self-ishness. In his desire to get along, he has mistakenly shut off the flow of his desire, and thus his own life force. Of course it is always Kenny's choice to do this. He can re-connect to his desires at any time. But when you are a child it's pretty hard if the big people are telling you otherwise, as many of us have experienced.

Because Kenny thinks his needs cannot be met, he insists upon his fair share at every opportunity. To Kenny, helping others is a joke. "Nobody ever gave me anything," he says. "Why should I give a bleep about them?"

"You are too selfish, Kenny," people say to him. "You should learn to open your heart and help others. Then you would feel a lot better." This is very good advice, if only Kenny could do it! He has already tried that, without very good results. Kenny has simply not been taught to be appropriately Self-ish — in fact, he has been taught to deny his natural impulses. These natural impulses are supposed to be dangerous because they stem from a primitive survival instinct. After all, just look around at the mess the world is in!

However, that is a delusional assertion, a denial of the basic nature of consciousness itself. The natural impulses of human nature stem from a connection to life force energy; it is resistance to this divine impulse that causes objectionable selfish behavior.

If you observe people you will quickly see that those persons who are most alive are full of desire, and those that look lifeless have little or no desire. Desire = life force. Shut off desire = selfish behavior. It's ironic that selfish behavior actually results from self-denial.

So the most dangerous thing you can do to yourself is "go along to get along," even though following your natural, divine impulses can sometimes lead to embarrassment. It would not be acceptable to walk down the street and proclaim to one and all your love for them, for you are liable to get punched in the nose! However, it is your denial of these feelings that causes unhappiness. Most of us practice self-denial so much that by adulthood, we no longer feel the joy of living. We are just getting along. Then many of us try to substitute for true Self-ishness by the accumulation of things, or the acquisition of power, or perhaps in a relationship where there is hope that the wonderful other can provide for us the joy and love we have denied to ourselves. Unfortunately, this substitution places us at the other end of the vibrational stick; at the negative end, looking out at an energetic chasm toward a positive future that cannot be attained because we believe (and have been taught) that it isn't possible to fulfill our true desires.

"What about the pervert who wants to satisfy his desires to abuse children? Or the murderer who needs to satisfy his blood lust? That's not so divine." True enough, but this twisted desire is just the result of a true desire that has been distorted or suppressed for a long time. Allowing your desires without resistance will always result in balance. It isn't possible for a warped impulse to suddenly spring forth, despite what we see in the movies and read in novels. Like a stream that is diverted to a new course, it takes a lot of time to dig the new water bed.

When a person is truly acting Self-ishly, it is possible to be far more helpful to others. I have noticed that people who, as the song says, "Live the life I love, and love the life I live" are very giving persons. This giving stems not from a societal obligation to do the right thing, but from a personal connection to source. When your cup runneth over, you naturally feel the impulse to give to others with an open heart. Again, this is ironic. True Self-ishness leads inevitably to unselfishness.

Self-ishness does not mean hogging more than your fair share. It means always making sure you are thinking and acting in ways that generate positive emotion within you. That is the surest way to determine whether your present path benefits both you and others.

If true selfishness leads to selflessness, then perhaps receiving must come before giving.

8.12 Giving and Receiving

IN order to give, one must first receive. If you are not yourself feeling joy and love, what you are giving to another may not be of much value. In other words, it's important to feel good yourself before you try to help another! This is a little fact that I have often overlooked, and which has caused me some painful set-downs. I have noticed that when I'm purely resonating to well-being, others come to me voluntarily and are really interested in what I have to say. When I set a vibrational example to others, there is an instinctive, and positive, response. But when I'm helping because I feel that it's required, or when I'm not really into it, or when I'm trying to "fix" someone, I'm not really very effective. I wind up bringing others down to my level.

Receiving before giving doesn't mean refusing to love another until they love you first, or declining to give Uncle Harold a birthday present this year because he forgot yours last year. It doesn't mean grabbing as much of the pie as you can before anyone else. All of these actions are based on a consciousness of scarcity and lack, and are guaranteed to bring more scarcity into your life.

Receiving, as it is defined here, is vibrational. Just as a battery cannot provide power without first being charged, a person cannot give effectively unless he or she is feeling positive emotion.

It turns out that all help is vibrational/emotional help. For example, you join a group that passes out food to the needy. This is a very helpful activity, but without a vibrational movement on the part of the recipients up the scale, conditions for them will not change. You will constantly be catching fish, instead of teaching how to fish. Help in the form of physical assistance only postpones the inevitable vibrational reckoning, for life experiences (inflow, outflow, crossflow) are determined by what occurs on the self-reflexive flow.

Before giving, it is important to fill your tank first.

When you receive, however, you do not deprive another.

It's always possible to fill up at the gas station of positive emotion without harming anyone else. You don't have to come cash in hand and exchange for your share. It's not possible to run out of life force energy, so gorge yourself. The better you feel, the more valuable is your service to others.

Some feel that it is inappropriate to feel happiness when others are sad. Some counselors feel that in order to be there for the client, they must feel the client's pain, but this only serves to stick both client and practitioner in the client's vibration.

8.13   Open Systems vs. Closed Systems

PHYSICAL resources are obviously limited; the supply of oil, once used up, is gone forever. A good example of a closed system is a typical power plant. Electrical generation is accomplished by constantly feeding the generator with more energy (coal, oil, nuclear fuel, etc.) If the generator runs out of fuel, the system shuts down. A closed system like this always requires more energy input than is output. A battery, even if it is rechargeable, will eventually drain and become useless.

An example of an open system is a windmill or a waterwheel which can take huge amounts of "free" energy from the environment. "Free" energy doesn't mean violation of the law of conservation of energy. It just means that it is possible to tap into the energy which already exists in the active environment, so more energy is output than is put in. A water wheel, for example, uses the flow of a river to turn a paddle and generate electricity. A windmill uses the power of the wind. An initial energy investment is necessary to build the paddle wheel or windmill, but once that is done, a continuous source of power exists.[24]

Life force energy, as it has been defined in this book, is in infinite supply; it surrounds and penetrates everything in the universe. Therefore, the earth, in its relationship to life force, is an open system. All beings have the ability to tap into the stream and become an amplifier of it, because consciousness interfaces directly with it. Access to this energy is effortless and without penalty; you do not need permission from authority figures, and it doesn't require complicated machinery or government funding! Receiving your supply of happiness, joy, or well being depends only on how much of it you ask for and how much you allow in.

No harm can possibly come to another if you receive something from a positive vibration of well being. If your brother has been in perfect health all of his life, it would be foolish to accuse him of depriving someone else of health. Stephen Hawking, the world-renowned physicist, is a genius, but it would not be appropriate to ask him to

---

[24] Such a system is said to have a coefficient of performance >1, but it is not a "perpetual motion machine."

dumb down for a while so that someone else can be smart! These examples are exaggerations, but they serve to illustrate the idea that although mankind is very good at dreaming up more and more ways to amplify scarcity, the universe contains an infinite amount of abundance. As with health and clarity, so too with prosperity, no matter what form it takes.

8.14 Is it Really "Better to Give than to Receive?"

GIVING without first receiving drains a person's reserves and causes stress. And it's no wonder that it does, for the idea that it is better to give than to receive is unbalanced. Receiving automatically opens the energy stream not only for you, but for everyone else. Have you ever been in the presence of someone truly joyful? It just feels so good! That is what happens when a person takes the time to give freely, with an open heart.

Receiving must come before giving. Even in a closed system, a battery cannot supply energy unless it is charged.

It's OK to receive, and in fact, it is vitally necessary if one is to be an effective giver.

8.15 Source Point vs. Result Point

Is all that hard work really necessary?
The Universal Operating System works in a counter-intuitive fashion. What manifests in your life has more to do with what is activated vibrationally within you, than with how much effort you put into your action cycles. The only way to discover this for yourself is to begin to apply these principles in your life and see what happens. Once you 'click' on it, things will become a lot easier.

The idea that hard work is not as important as your vibrational alignment just seems wrong to many people, but once you understand the importance of the Law of Vibration and the Law of Attraction, it becomes more obvious. This is not to say that action is unnecessary, it is to say that action is most effective when it is performed along the path of least resistance.

Action cycles place you in physical proximity but not vibrational proximity. Paradoxically, it is vibrational proximity that is more important! Have you ever been accosted by a salesman who talked your ear off about something you had no interest in? Physical proximity is useless unless vibrational alignment is present.

We have all been taught that in order to get something, you have to go out and make it happen. What most people do is immediately get into action on inflow before aligning themselves to the goal on the self-reflexive flow. This is somewhat like pushing on the gas pedal before one has put the car in gear; lots of noise is generated but nothing useful is being accomplished.

Listen to commercial radio for a hour. Commercial after commercial blares forth, each one frantically attempting to engage your attention for a few seconds, screaming "CAN'T MISS SALES EVENTS!" and "SAVE NOW!" Most people I know simply do not listen to these messages at all. They are simply "tuned out." That is because vibrational intent is more important than words, and many advertisements are rooted firmly on the lower end of the emotional/vibrational spectrum. Your advertising department may report that x number of people were reached by the latest ad campaign, but that number is entirely subjective and based solely on a statistic. Sound and light may reach the ears and eyes of the viewer/listener, but that does not mean the message penetrated anyone's awareness!

It is of course necessary to let others know your business is out there, but the primary value of advertisements is to align *yourself* toward prosperity. A feeling that "I've got lots of promotion out there reaching thousands of people" produces the correct vibrational orientation. In other words, a minimal advertising budget and a vibrational attitude of success is a better formula than lots of frantic promotion. A friend of mine has been in business for 25 years and has never advertised at all. This isn't something I feel comfortable with personally, but it works for her.

Action cycles are emphasized as the primary focus for any enterprise because (it is said) the universe is a vast creation in which mankind is just an insignificant speck; if you want something you better get off your butt and earn it, for it's a dog-eat-dog competitive world. That is certainly one way to look at it! Actually, the universe is working with you in every moment, bringing to you the content of your activated vibrational signal, placing you in contact with those who can help you accomplish (or thwart) your goals.

When you are in the attitude of "making it happen," you are usually not receptive enough to recognize the universe's responding signals. Potential opportunities go unrecognized or pushed away because you only see one path to travel. Your focus is often so narrow that, like the radio dial tuned narrowly to 89.1, you cannot recognize other signals in close proximity.

Some people will perform an action over and over and over again, even though results are never forthcoming! "It will work this time," a friend of mine told me while trying to use an adjustable wrench to unscrew a reluctant bolt from his car's water pump. "You need a circular wrench for that," I said, but my friend was having none of it. After stripping the screw, he then had to get a special bit and drill it out.

Some people even think it's cheating to allow the Universal Operating System to work for them! "Just luck, what good is that? You can't depend on luck!" Well, you can't depend on luck, but you can depend on the Law of Attraction.

Here's a true story: An aspiring photographer (let's call her Kris) was looking for an outlet for her work, but had no success whatsoever. One day while driving downtown, Kris saw a camera shop and received the impulse to stop in. After wandering around for a few minutes looking at some expensive equipment (which she couldn't afford to buy) she turned to leave when someone came out from the back of the store and said, "Can I help you?" Kris struck up a conversation and discovered that the proprietor's sister was putting together a show and was actively looking for entrants. Kris's work was eventually accepted for the show.

Kris was receptive enough to recognize the vibrational opportunity presented by the camera shop owner, and took advantage by listening to her inner guidance. In this case, Kris's action cycles were almost trivial. She had already, on the reflexive flow, aligned herself very powerfully towards the idea of promoting her work, and with almost no effort at all accomplished her goal. Here again we have co-incidence, brought about by vibrational interaction. It's a subtle energy phenomenon, and not evident unless you begin to pay attention to how you feel.

You might say, "That's a nice little example but you can't operate a business that way." Well, if you always make decisions based upon a feeling of well being, and never do anything that is accompanied by a feeling of negative emotion, you cannot go wrong, no matter what kind of business you are in, or what kind of life you lead.

In the scenario of "working hard to make it happen," you are never in an attitude of reception, where you have to be in order to receive, for your outflowing of energy is blocking the inflowing vibrational responses that will bring you closer to what you want. In other words, you cannot inflow and outflow at the same time, for two physical energy streams cannot occupy the same place at the same time. In order to get the Universal Operating System to interface properly with you, you have to somehow get off the feeling that your life won't work the way you want it to unless you micromanage everything in it.

If you are working really hard there is probably already a resistance to the goal, otherwise, why would you be expending so much effort? Maybe, deep down inside, you do not really believe it is going to happen so you make up for it with a lot of effort, like the annoying salesman with his spiel. A person who is confident of success is relaxed. When he or she interacts with the world around him, things fall into place much more easily because not only is there physical proximity, but vibrational alignment toward the goal as well.

The point is, in order to receive, you have to be receptive. It's a lot less work that way, and a lot more fun.

8.16 Cause and Effect

Is Cause $\Rightarrow$ Effect invariable?

All actions inevitably have consequences. Throw a stone into the air and it falls to earth every time. Pushing one of a row of dominoes causes the entire row to be knocked over. Science has discovered immutable laws of matter; the entire subject of engineering is based on the cause and effect relationship.

Being mean to another usually results in an equal and opposite reaction. My father used to say, "You may do whatever you please, but you must accept the consequences of your actions."

When an action has consequences, a counter-reaction will inevitably follow. When a scientist says that action A causes result B, he means B inevitably follows from A. When B always follows A, given the same experimental conditions, science says that the statement "B follows A" is a law. There is the law of gravity, which we all know so intimately. Science uses observation of an action and its resultant manifestation to discover laws about the behavior of the physical universe, and, as mere mortals, all of us do the same in daily life.

Scientific laws reflect a mathematical, conceptual model based on empirical observations and experiments, which faithfully attempt to mirror phenomenon as closely as possible. Scientific laws are approximations of Nature. As Einstein once said, "As far as the law of mathematics refer to reality, they are not certain; and as far as they are certain, they do not refer to reality."

Consciousness is ephemeral and invisible and therefore is considered irrelevant. Because consciousness is not a variable in any scientific equation, and because science, and popular culture, considers consciousness to be biologically based, most of us have been brought up to assume that what applies to matter and energy must also apply to consciousness. The physical body is said to be paramount, and only that which can be observed has any significance. However, this idea places the cart before the horse. The consciousness of the horse draws the cart, not the other way around! Phenomena like intuition are considered scientifically invalid (not measurable, not provable), yet people have been using intuition successfully for thousands of years. The problem is, we spend no time studying consciousness and all of our time studying matter and energy. What would happen if we began to study consciousness with the same fervor that we study the material world?

Interestingly enough, science is beginning to discover that even in laboratory experiments the intent of the observer can affect the outcome. The work of Dr. Masaru

Emoto, for example, graphically demonstrates the effect the intent of the experimenter has on water crystals. Dr. Masaru Emoto discovered that crystals formed in frozen water reveal changes when specific, concentrated thoughts are directed toward them. He found that water from clear springs and water that has been exposed to loving words shows brilliant, complex, and colorful snowflake patterns. In contrast, polluted water, or water exposed to negative thoughts, forms incomplete, asymmetrical patterns with dull colors.[25]

Science is showing more and more that the physical universe, which seems so solid to our physical senses, is actually quite fuzzy. At the subatomic level of matter, reality looks more and more like the inside of the mind. For example, Bell's Theorem showed that the universe wouldn't work properly if only local connections (slower than the speed of light) are allowed. According to Dr. Nick Herbert (author of "Quantum Reality"), in the quantum description of two objects, there is an interconnectedness between them which never goes away no matter how far apart they get. At first it was thought that this connection was only theoretical, but according to Herbert, Bell's theorem proves that it actually exists in the real world.[26]

When we speak of an action having consequences, consciousness must be a part of the picture. Therefore, no action A can inevitably produce a result B, unless the consciousness of the observer, or initiator, of the action is taken into account.

In this book we're not so much interested in the behavior of matter and energy, for these things are very adequately described by science; but we are very interested in knowing whether cause and effect is inviolate with regard to how the world responds to the choices of a conscious being. If we model our behavior according to the strictures of scientific law the answer is yes, but this removes the variable of consciousness (and free will) from the equation.

Let's take an example from life.

Marge Smith is known in the office as "that bitch." It has been the experience of everyone that when one interacts with Marge, one will experience a set-down. This pattern of action has become so well established that it could be said to be law. Deal with Marge, and you will get snapped at. Now, say, a new hire that has never met Marge enters the office one day. All of the workers gather round, knowing what's coming. When Pete sees Marge he immediately notices the disapproving frown, and her sarcastic welcome makes him feel for a moment like avoiding her at all costs; but he thinks, "What the hell. It's my first day, let's give the old girl the benefit of

---

[25] See *Messages from Water*, Vol 1 by Masaru Emoto.
[26] See "Consciousness and Quantum Reality with Nick Herbert, Ph.D." from Thinking Allowed. Available at http://www.thinking-allowed.com/

the doubt." So Pete gives her a genuinely pleasant smile, holds out his hand and says "Hello, I'm Pete." Marge is taken aback at first by this unusual behavior, but to be polite, shakes Pete's hand. They get to talking, just pleasantries, but no negative outcome is forthcoming, even though Marge knows only one way to deal with people: hold them off. Marge knows others cannot be trusted because she has experienced it over and over again, but despite herself, she feels a pleasant unthawing in the presence of Pete. So B, a negative experience, does not follow from A, an encounter with Marge, even though this has been firmly established by observation in the past.

In life, we observe the rigid inflexibility of cause and effect and never think to deliberately alter our thoughts, and therefore our vibrational pattern, to invite a different, more pleasant set of circumstances. We say "That's the way it's always been with me. I just don't seem to have any luck with money." Or, "Every time I get into a good relationship, it always falls apart." Or, "They always pass over me for promotions. I must be doing something wrong." These are declarative statements which are based solely upon observation. In these statements there is an assumption: what has been must be. B must follow A. There is no allowance for the deliberate creation of another vibration, which will attract a different result! That is a shame, for we do not exercise the free will that is inherent in all conscious beings. We consider ourselves to be mere ciphers, pawns in a game where others can apparently move us around on the board of life.

In human relationships, no matter what is concluded to be true by observation, no matter how many times it has been observed that B follows A, a different outcome can be produced in the presence of creative will!

The inevitability of cause $\Rightarrow$ effect is an illusion. In fact, what seems to be an unbreakable law by observation is merely the idea that one must continue to create conditions based on what is observed. After all, what is observed is real, is it not? So it's truth. And you're not supposed to mess with the truth.

In human relationships, a behavioral 'law' exists only because all hold the same pattern of vibration relative to each other. So cause $\Rightarrow$ effect is, in the vibrational model of the universe, just the continuation of a mode or pattern of thought and belief, and is therefore alterable.

8.17 The Myth of Objectivity

IT is impossible, and undesirable, to be truly objective.

In Western culture we are taught to weigh both sides of an issue before making a decision, and that rational decision making depends upon having all the facts. Science teaches that in performing an experiment, one should never lean one way or the other in the conduct of it, in order that the results should not be tainted. However, this is unfeasible. True objectivity means total detachment, and that is impossible. Total detachment means you're dead!

Attempting to be objective is being disingenuous with the Law of Attraction, for as soon as a person has ANY thought, desire, or intent the universe begins to respond in a matching fashion to them. It is impossible to go through life thinking no thoughts or having no desires; therefore, each person is like an attracting magnet drawing to him or her people and experiences which are an exact match to their thoughts and desires. So a social scientist, for example, can never claim objectivity. In our model, the experimenter always attracts to him or her, those persons, energies, and data which are a match to their thoughts and desires concerning the experiment. In other words, it is never possible to get an unbiased sample.

Weighing the facts simply muddies your desire or intent. If you want something, and your desire is strong enough, it will come to you. However, by including the "cons" along with the "pros" you include in your vibration frequencies which do not match the frequencies of your desire. Objectivity means you are including just as many opposing facts as those which support your desire. Therefore the universe will respond accordingly, guaranteeing that what you want will not come to you in the form that is desired.

Objectivity, then, is just another way of denying to self, that which is wanted.

Objectivity is denial of self.

Denial of self is irrational.

Therefore objectivity is irrational.

Think about it! Why does anyone live life? They live life to have a good time, to feel good about something, to help another, to create, to love, to have fun, to investigate and figure out the universe around us. All of these things are desires! But objectivity, by its very nature, squelches desire. It requires you to turn on your faucet of desire and turn it down little by little, with every contrary fact that is considered. Desire is life force. Life force energy feels wonderful. Turning down the level of your desire makes you feel worse and worse. That's why so many people agonize over large purchases. By the time they are done including and weighing so many facts both for and against, confusion and anxiety is the result! This happened to a client of mine during a three week period in which she researched and test-drove new cars. In the end, she couldn't make up her mind even after test driving many makes and models.

Objectivity is necessary (to the greatest degree possible) when conducting experiments with matter and energy. However, even in the laboratory, an experiment performed in one location in space/time must be a local phenomenon, for the intent of the experimenter will affect the results. That is true in the laboratory of life as well. In our vibrational model of the universe, a person always has complete control of things on the reflexive flow and on outflow, for action always follows thought. However, you have no control whatsoever concerning what happens on crossflows. That is the only way it can be in a universe where everyone has free will and all thought and action is sanctioned. If it were possible for you to determine the actions of another, then it must be possible for others to make you a victim of their wishes. It would mean that others could dictate your actions, your state of being, even your health, against your will. But that is simply not possible.

The Law of Vibration and the Law of Attraction operate on inflow. Consciousness everywhere is subtly connected through a postulated field of subtle energy which fills the universe. This virtual "background energy" carries the impulses of thought from one end of the universe to the other and operates to match you up with vibrations which precisely match your own. It is not possible to come in contact with something or someone without first establishing a vibrational orientation or proclivity towards it. So why be objective?

Well, humanity believes that what manifests in life is mostly a result of luck, or chance. Some people, it is said, just have a knack for getting things they want, while others are unlucky. Some say the only way to really guarantee success is through hard work. But I have noticed that in my life and in the lives of many others, hard work is no guarantee of anything but hard work. I look around and see prosperous people who hardly work at all, and a lot of poor people who work their tails off!

People think that by lining up all of their facts in a row, both good and bad, that a true picture of what may happen for them has been assembled. But these facts are just the experiences of others. It is thought, for example, that if 100 people go out and buy the XYZ brand computer, and 37 of them say XYZ computers suck, then more than likely XYZ computers are poorly made and you have a good chance to get a crummy one. But this is not how it works at all.

If you wanted a computer that functioned properly and you were vibrationally aligned to it, then if you happened to purchase an XYZ computer, it would function perfectly. Even if the XYZ computer company only made ONE good computer, you would get it! The experience of another has absolutely nothing to do with the experience you might have. The experiences of others are just the way they have molded and transmitted their energy, and the manifestations they have received are a result only of their alignment of energy and the universe's response to it, through the property of 'like attracts like.'

Having said that, you could go out and buy an XYZ computer and have it suck for you. But the only reason you would have a bad experience with an XYZ computer, is if you included all of those "cons" along with the pure intent of your desire. The frequency matching property of the universe simply responds to your mix of vibrational frequencies. It is more likely that if XYZ computers are indeed poorly made, and your intent was for an excellent computer, you would never be drawn to the XYZ brand at all.

People don't want to believe this, because accepting it means that everyone is 100% in control of their lives. If there is something going wrong, it is easier to believe that something "out there" is responsible. Otherwise, the uncomfortable realization hits: "I am causing it." To admit that is to make oneself wrong. But this sort of thinking sets you up to fail. Failure results from simply not going with your pure desire or intent in the first place! It occurs from being objective, from including in your mix all of those ideas you don't like as well as those you do like.

Scientists especially object to this idea. Scientists like to believe there is an objective reality that will respond the same way every time. The idea of science is to figure out the "Theory of Everything," a theory of how the universe operates down to the smallest detail. There is only one problem with this approach: in a dynamic and ever-expanding universe, nothing is static or unchanging. There is always thought and response to thought, everywhere in the universe.

If ever a condition existed in which only one response (or a limited, definable set of responses) was generated for any vibrational signal, there would be stagnation, and death. Death is unchanging response to stimuli. Poke a dead person and see an unchanging response! The secret of this universe is that it is ever-changing, ever-expanding, ever-growing. And that means that there cannot, ever, be a Theory of Everything which explains all-that-is in a nutshell. This universe cannot ever be reduced to a few laws, or thoughts, or ideas, that will explain all phenomena every time. If that ever happened, the universe would die, for it would be responding only within a limited set of parameters, just like a dying organism.

The universe is dynamic and will respond to your every decision and desire. It has the capacity to satisfy your every whim, if only you will let it. Don't limit your experiences by trying to be objective – allow those desires and intentions to flow, create a marvelous life that is changing for the better and is never boring.

8.18 Challenge: An Empowering Look at Overcoming Obstacles

"Challenge builds character." This statement would probably be accepted as truth by many, but what does it really mean? Well, a challenge is an obstacle to be overcome, and the satisfaction of persevering through adversity to completion can be a fantastic feeling. However, in an attempt to encourage personal growth, society says, "it's important in this world to learn to overcome adversity. Things aren't always going to go your way." Observation of the world around us seems to bear this out, but looking at challenge within the context of the Universal Operating System yields a different picture.

Say you wanted to start a new business. You have never been self-employed before, so it seems daunting at first. There are two ways you can approach it: you can envision your new enterprise as something that will require a tremendous amount of work, or something that will naturally fly right. If you approach the venture with the attitude that it will be difficult, you are already resisting all of the people, money, and resources which would come to you, through the universal property of like attracts like. The more you work on your business with this attitude, the harder it gets. Now you are facing challenges every day, probably experiencing anxiety, worry, and some upset along the way. But you persevere and eventually get it done. Now you are happy.

Or, you could approach the new business with a detailed vision, a vision in which you are expending very little effort and the resources you need come to you easily. The more you work on your business with this attitude, the more the universe matches you up with the people, money, and things which you need in order to be successful. The Law of Attraction immediately goes to work for you, just as it did in the previous example. But now, there is very little worry, anxiety, and upset. Things fall into place for you with relative ease. The business starts slowly but becomes very successful.

In both cases, a business was created. But in the first case, there were a large number of obstacles to overcome. You gutted it out, successfully overcame all of the challenges. Now, you talk to your buddies and they all say "Great work! You really stepped up and battled hard. Now, you can enjoy your reward." In the second case there were almost no challenges. Obstacles, yes, but these didn't appear to you as something to worry about. You felt good almost all the time, and when you are done, you feel even better.

Now I ask you two questions: Which scenario would you rather experience? And secondly, which business do you think will be easier to run, and be ultimately more successful? If you are like me, I'll take the second experience. I'll leave the worrying, the anxieties and the upset to the other guys. It would seem to me that the guy who was feeling good the whole time will have a more successful business, because you can't stay happy by treading a path feeling rotten most of the time. The law of "like attracts like" will bring you more of the same, so you will likely experience a lot of difficulties operating your business, if you are an "overcome challenges" kind of person.

The second guy didn't have a lot of resistance to his goal. He did his homework and got together a really good business plan, one he was really excited and confident about. The he just went about executing that plan without a lot of worry about it. Mostly he just had fun along the way. The first guy also had a great business plan, but he worried a lot that maybe the economy would go into a recession. He wondered whether he would be able to get good employees. He read the statistics about the percentage of start-ups that fail. He had doubts about his own ability to get it done. But he went ahead into action anyway, figuring he would "accept the challenge." And that's exactly the experience he got! The second guy had his energies almost completely aligned to his goal before he started. The first guy went into action before he had felt comfortable about his new goal.

You might say, "Well, your second example isn't realistic. It's not possible to start a business and have it go well right from the start. There are too many variables." That is always what *overcoming-challenge* types say. And for them, it is completely true, for what they experience is always a match to their expectations.

We might have a conversation that goes something like this:

"Encouraging people to think that it will all be easy and rosy is not only delusional, it's harmful."

"Why do you say that?"

"Because observation and statistics tell us that only a percentage of startups ever succeed."

"But those observations and statistics are based upon what others have done. With that philosophy, no one should start anything, for it might be a failure."

"One should be informed about the current state of affairs, before one blindly and foolishly rushes in."

"Certainly! You have to know where you are before you can go anywhere. You have to figure out how you're going to market your product or service. But once that's done, you must not import the self-limiting beliefs of others into your operation, otherwise you will fail. If you do not, you will succeed."

"That's crazy. You can't control the actions of others, as you've already said over and over. All of them have free will too! So how can you say that a business, which depends on others buying what you have to offer, can succeed just because you want it to?"

"If you know that it will succeed, it will. The degree of success or failure is proportional to the number of doubts you have regarding it. In all analyses, only the recording of actions is possible. It is not possible to document the thoughts, beliefs and attitudes inside a person which not only determine their activities, but how the world at large responds to them."

"That's not only nutty, it's hallucinatory. You have to offer something that others want. There's no guarantee they will like your product or service."

"The success or failure of your product depends primarily upon the vibration you have regarding it. There is enough diversity of interest for any product, no matter how trivial or useless, to find acceptance. All you have to do is line yourself up with the vibration of success. Worry about failure, or even the possibility of failure, only sets you up for failure. The fact is, no one can say what will happen to you, but you can say what will happen to you. The experiences of your life are a direct reflection of the parameters of your beliefs, for all of your actions will be based on those beliefs. The product or service you sell will be based on your vibrational content, and others will respond in kind. The storekeeper, for example, opens his shop and simply waits for people to come in. The response to his promotion will only reflect the state of his beliefs."

"That's nonsense. We're not living in an esoteric fairyland! You're setting people up to fail."

"As you believe, so shall it be."

"Reality is more important than belief."

"Reality is a reflection of belief. Besides, if you're going to start a business, you begin and continue with the idea of success, not failure. The more you allow the possibility of failure to creep into your vibration, the greater chance for failure. Those who fail *always* allow the creeping rot of "reality" to infect their attitude, thus bringing about the failure they are trying so desperately to avoid. Besides, gambling is a zero-sum game, by definition. Life is a win-win game."

"More delusional thinking."

"Well, all I know is that I wouldn't want you for a business partner!"

Here we simply have opposing worldviews, but in one case, there is a certainty of success, and in the other, a decided possibility of failure. The undertaking of any task should proceed from the former attitude, not the latter, otherwise, why do it at all? The challenges of the creative process are not the impediments you encounter in the physical universe, but the obstacles you set up within yourself, which take you off the rails.

Challenge is a feeling of resistance to the goal and is self-imposed. Obstacles and challenges come about from not completely aligning to what you want before you start!

Overcoming obstacles doesn't build character; it just gets you used to overcoming obstacles. In other words, living a challenging life keeps you in a vibrational orientation that guarantees you will have to overcome more and more obstacles. Not only is that pretty inefficient, but it keeps you in the lower reaches of the Emotional/Vibrational Scale with all of the attendant consequences.

If you LIKE to live this kind of life, go for it! Many athletes and military types love this sort of thing and it is certainly not my place to criticize. However, when those who like challenges attempt to impose their world view and lifestyle on the rest of us, difficulties arise. Now we have a society which puts a premium on struggle and strain, leading to an overworked and stressed-out population.

For some reason, our society looks up to those who overcome huge obstacles and disdains those who effortlessly achieve their goals. It's funny, because our society is so results oriented! It just seems to me that if you want to be successful, it would be smart to do so in the most efficient possible manner.

An example from history is instructive in this regard. In 1911, the Norwegian Roald Amundsen and the Englishman Robert Scott both attempted to be the first to reach the South Pole. Amundsen efficiently organized his expedition and successfully made the run. Scott made poor decisions, choosing ponies and motorized sleighs, (rather than the dog-drawn sledges chosen by Amundsen) which broke down in the fierce cold. As a result of his poor decisions, Scott and his group died along the way. Who do we hear about in our history texts? Amundsen, because he was successful, right? Wrong! We hear about the glory of Scott, how he and his crew suffered, about their sacrifices for each other, about the noble dignity of trying hard and failing. In English history, at least, Amundsen is just a historical afterthought! Resistance is admired, and praised to the skies. The virtue of those who simply ask for success and allow it to effortlessly happen are rarely extolled. Such people, it is believed, have it "handed to them on a silver platter." However, vibrational alignment with the goal can make even the most difficult undertaking look effortless. That is because the operating system of the universe is at your back at all times.

If the goal is strictly a physical activity (as above) then physical *obstacles* are inevitable. But whether these become *challenges* is up to you. Say you are a rock climber and decide to climb a 500-foot mesa. Now you definitely are going to experience a little anxiety! But the principle is the same. If you approach your task with the idea that it will be almost impossible and that you might get killed, you are guaranteed to have a series of near-death experiences on the way up. But if you are really clear on your vision of the climb, you will probably take extra practice, working on your holds and your technique. You won't attempt the climb until you feel excited about it, for when you have that excited feeling, that's the sign you are in alignment with the task at hand. The better you feel about the climb, the easier it will be, again by the property of like attracts like. If you feel good about the climb, you will naturally gravitate to those areas where the holds are optimum, where the rock is solid, and where there are a minimum of difficult passages. If you are anxious about the climb, you will be attracted to those areas where the holds are difficult, the rock is loose, and you will experience some difficult passages.

The first guy gets off the mesa and collapses. The second guy gets off the rock and is still excited. He is really tired, had some difficulties, but feels exhilarated at his experience.

The first guy goes to his buddies, after a week of recovery, and starts bragging to them what a monster he is. He tells them about the times he almost fell off, and all the rest. They look at him in awe. The second guy goes to his friends and he tells them how much fun he had. He tells them about his anxious moments, but he describes how good the rock is, how the climb can be successfully negotiated. He shows them the route.

The first guy's buddies are terrified to attempt the climb. They look at him like a minor deity. The second guy's buddies are all excited to try it for themselves. The energy of the whole group is really high, and they all decide to climb it together with the second guy leading the way.

The first guy overcame big-time challenges. The second guy did as well, but his climb was marked by an excitement that comes from a lack of resistance to the goal.

Challenge is mostly self-imposed, regardless of the activity. Anything that can be done with resistance, can be done easier with a lack of resistance. And with a lot more fun as well!

8.19 Sanity vs. Insanity

HUMAN beings for millennia have not been able to agree upon a satisfactory definition of sanity or insanity. That is because we have been looking at conduct or behavior and judging the validity of it. In a free will universe, all thought and conduct is allowed; therefore, evaluating behavior just results in categories of inappropriateness, without going far to resolve it. For example, it is said that someone who is neurotic may suffer from "obsessive-compulsive disorder", or that someone who is insane suffers from "multiple personality disorder." These categorizations do not lend themselves to finding a happy resolution to the irrational behavior.

It can be observed however, that all insane or irrational people feel bad. Sane or rational behavior always occurs when there is a genuine feeling of well being.

- Neurosis is irrational behavior.

- Psychosis is wildly irrational and sometimes destructive behavior.

What is irrational behavior and why is it irrational? In this book, we don't claim that behavior is irrational because it goes against the commonly accepted range or mode of allowed or lawful conduct. We do not base irrational behavior, either, on whether it agrees with morals, ethics, or religious beliefs. These yardsticks of measurement cannot be agreed upon by everyone because they differ from culture to culture, and therefore cannot guarantee results for everyone. There is a common denominator to irrational behavior, however: in all irrational or insane persons, there is a focus upon that which is not wanted.

A person who has a disagreeable life is not a happy camper. He has many things in his experience which he would rather change, but for one reason or other, has not. Therefore, the focus of his thoughts and feelings are on the unwanted conditions. This focus is the cause of the continual creation of them, or at least, the fact that things never change. Action follows thought, obviously, so in order for anything to change, thought must first be changed.

An unhappy person is not necessarily an irrational or insane person. However, a predominant focus upon uncomfortable things will eventually produce action based upon those predominant thought patterns. For example, a person may hate the fact that he never gets promoted in his job. Say he works as a clerk in a department store, but three others have been promoted to section manager ahead of him. If he focuses his thoughts and feelings predominantly upon his lack of advancement, then eventually he will find a reason for it. More than likely this reason will have nothing to do with his own thought or conduct, because no one wants to believe that he or she is not good enough. Say he focuses on the obvious reason, his boss, who has passed him over. At first, he is just grumpy. He complains to the boss, lightly at first, then more strongly. He becomes angry, bad-mouths the boss to all of his coworkers. We say this guy is just a sourpuss and let it go at that. But if his thoughts predominately go to fighting his boss, he will begin to act neurotically. These actions may range from resentful glances to spilling coffee on the boss's new shirt. If, however, the predominant thought becomes exclusive thought, now we have the condition of psychosis. Psychosis is just exclusive attention to that which is not wanted. Now our friend lives to get even with the boss, and his actions may go as far as physical violence.

In the relief of neurosis or psychosis, attention must be paid to those things the person is resisting. That cannot be known simply by observing behavior, for by definition, that behavior is irrational! Irrational behavior is simply an attempt to get rid of something that is not wanted, but the solutions are usually non-sequitur. It is always something personal to the subject, however, and so with a little probing one may discover the true reasons for it.

Trying to get rid of something is self defeating. It is not possible to rid one's self of anything, because the more one attempts to get rid of the unwanted thing, the more attention is placed upon it. The more attention that is placed upon it, the more it comes into your experience. This can be stated cogently as "what you resist persists." The degree of resistance to unwanted things determines the degree of irrationality or insanity. It also determines how miserable a person will feel. Because what is being resisted is different for each individual, it is usually not possible to judge from conduct what is sane or insane. Irrational conduct runs the gamut of emotions and actions. Only by discovering what it is the person is fighting or resisting, can a solution be found.

From these simple principles, we can make sense of the idea of sanity or insanity.

- Sanity always corresponds with feeling good.

- Insanity always corresponds with feeling bad.

- Anything which encourages a good feeling can be considered sane.

- Anything which encourages a bad feeling can be considered irrational.

- Therefore, punishment is irrational.

The purpose of punishment is to place the offender's attention even more on the thing that is not wanted. This can trigger a neurotic state into a psychotic condition, with bad results for society.

Treatment which suppresses the cognitive function is a little better, but still not very effective. Drugging someone to prevent his or her attention to the unwanted condition can never lead to a cure, only to the suppression of symptoms. In order to effect a cure, the person must begin to cease the resistance or fighting against the unwanted condition, and his attention must be placed on creating the wanted condition. The only reason people don't focus on what they want, instead of trying to get rid of what they don't want, is because they have been taught either that they are unworthy of having anything good, or that destroying something is the only way to get rid of it. Both of these ideas are also irrational.

What is sane or insane can largely be determined by how good or bad a person feels. If a person is creating something, he or she is probably feeling good, for the creative impulse is inherent within all of us. A person who is resisting someone or something or some condition, however, is feeling bad to a greater or lesser degree, otherwise there would be no need for resistance in the first place.

So lets stop pretending that punishing people is a good thing. Drugging people is more benign, but ineffective in effecting a real cure. Sometimes it must be used as a last resort, but I think we can do better than that!

Sanity or insanity is directly linked to how a person feels. Educating a person to focus on desires, instead of fighting adversaries, can lead to more effective treatment.

CHAPTER 9

The Creative Process and Manifestation

9.1 Identifying the Power within the Creative Process

THE world looks a lot different now than it did in the twelfth century. Huts and spears have been replaced by houses, skyscrapers, cars, and electronic equipment. The common, everyday objects of the third millennium are a direct result of how conscious beings have organized thought and thus shaped society. In other words, conscious beings think and dream and then mold their environment to suit. So at any point in time, "reality" is simply the ever changing result of ever changing thought. Personal reality is a direct result of personal thought and belief. If this reality is not a positive one, the chances are we will continue to create our lives negatively, being surrounded by unwanted people, circumstances and things. So our thoughts, naturally, continue on a negative trend. It is easy to say "envision a more positive reality," but the law of like attracts like and the law of vibration are working to reinforce negative thought patterns. Here is where a helpful and very powerful observation can be made: every single thing in our lives comes after the creative process has already run its course.

There is a time lag between the conception of something and the receiving of it. We do not, yet, live in a world of magic where thought manifests instantaneously. So in order to change anything in your life you must not focus on what-is, but on what is wanted. Focusing on what-is is pointless, because it is all after the fact of manifestation. It is impossible to create a new reality by continuing to observe and create from the old one. It is, in effect, using the powerful energy of creation to mimic exactly what you see in front of you!

9.2 What We Are Taught Is Backwards

THE chair you are sitting in didn't appear out of thin air. Your chair can be considered as a concatenation of thoughts and decisions. Before there can be a chair, there must be the thought of a chair. There must be the design of the chair, and then there can be the construction or manufacturing of the chair.

The chair itself is post-manifestation.

The thought, design process and manufacturing is pre-manifestation.

If you wanted a different chair, would you continue to observe the chair you have? That is what human beings are taught to do; to face reality, to consider the facts.

After all, facts are solid, comforting things, it is said. Manifested reality is the truth, and one must always look to the truth to decide the worth of anything. This is of course backwards, for it takes consciousness, the creative principle, out of the creative process!

What you see in front of you is the end of the road of the creative process. When you paint a landscape, you get your easel, brushes and paints and you use your creative energies to make something beautiful. After you are done, you can look at the painting, admire it, and show it off to others. But think of all the energy and inspiration that went into the painting! Although the painting on the easel is the culmination of all of your creative power, it is, energetically, minuscule in comparison to the energy you put into making it.

Everything observable in the world is the result of thought and energy which has been previously directed, in the past. The things we see around us in the physical universe are simply the resultant manifestations, with their attendant time-lags.

Matter itself is the coagulation of energy, but it just sits there in a lump until a conscious being moves it, or another force acts upon it. In our vibrational model, matter and energy is ultimately composed of thought, and therefore, all created by consciousness. So a force is actually an impetus provided by consciousness, no matter how far back in time that impetus originated. In other words, we don't say that a force acts upon an object as if these were completely separate, but we say that matter and energy and consciousness are different aspects of the same thing.[27]

---

[27] The famous double-slit experiment in physics is fascinating in this regard. It turns out that observing the flow of electrons through the two slits changes the pattern of hits on a detector plate, so that it is impossible to determine whether the statement "Each electron either goes through slit 1 or slit 2" is true or false. It is impossible to say whether an electron is a particle or a wave, because it behaves differently when we look at it and when we do not! This is just one way of saying that the conditions of an experiment affect the target of the experiment. For a great description of the double-slit experiment, see Richard Feynman's *Six Easy Pieces*, Chapter 6.

It is already known that matter and energy are convertible, and if consciousness, matter and energy are composed of thought, then they are also aspects of the same "thing" and we have a universe in which everything is not only inter-connected, but made of the same "stuff." If this is so, then there is really no conflict between those who assign a biological basis for consciousness, and those who do not!

In this way, the entire universe and everything in it proceeds from the animating principle, and is under the direction of the animating principle. This is a logical extension of a philosophy that places consciousness in the primary position, and if you begin to live your life this way, you begin to emphasize the powerful creative energies within you!

The creative process occurs in the pre-manifestation phase. That is where ALL the action is, because that's where all of the creative energy is.

The post-manifestation phase is complete, a done deal. Of course, a beautiful creation like Michelangelo's pieta can inspire one to creative heights, but the creative process itself is always in the pre-manifestation stage.

Your ideas, thoughts and dreams are always much more important than anything you observe around you. They contain the creative energy to which the universe responds with the manifestations you desire. The manifestations you receive are proportional to the sophistication and power of your thought and the time lag from envisioning to manifestation is directly proportional to the purity and clarity of your vision. It's all utterly dependent on you, and no one else can interfere, unless you let them. In other words, the universe will respond to your signal, no matter what all of the others are saying or doing, no matter what you or others have manifested in the past. Most of the stuff you see around you is how others have manifested their own personal realities. What others have manifested with their thought has no bearing on what you can do, because the power to mold your own reality lies within you. We all have access to creative life force energy, and there are no limits whatsoever to how much of it each of us may have.

Is it any wonder we have so much difficulty getting the things we want, when we put the majority of our attention on what has already happened? It would be like going on a trip and driving your car backwards. How can you get to where you are going when you are always focused on where you have been? Well, you might get there in this manner, but not without crashing a few times first!

The stuff you see around you is not important. Not important enough to get worried about, anyway. If you want your life to go along a different track, pay no attention to the things you have already manifested, if those things are not what you want. Focus on the pre-manifestation phase, where all of your power is. And certainly pay no attention to the things others have manifested, unless those things are pleasing to you. The law of "like attracts like" only works against you if you focus on what is not wanted. All of that unwanted stuff is in the post-manifestation phase. It has no power. It's like a runner who finishes a 10 mile race. He is exhausted. All of his energy has been spent getting to the finish line.

Here is another analogy: The pre-manifestation phase of the creative process can be likened to a gigantic garden hose 1000 feet long. Say you want to water the garden at the edge of your property. You move the hose, turn on the water, and wait. After what seems a lifetime, the water finally reaches your sprinkler, gushes into the air and moves back and forth gently over your plants. The time that it takes for the water to reach the sprinkler is the pre-manifestation phase. It is analogous to your creative vision and the alignment of energy to your desire. The action taken to get the desired result is trivial: move the hose, turn on the tap. All of the work to provide the water, the water pressure, the construction and delivery of the hose, is already provided by the universe. Everything needed for success is already in place. Success is inevitable IF you simply have a clear vision and maintain it during the time it takes to manifest. If you turn on the tap and don't immediately see the water, you might think "the system is broken." That is what many of us do in our own creative process. We are not aware of universal law and of our own powerful connection to it. We are not willing to endure the inevitable time lag from the pre-manifestation phase to the materialization, so we go to the tap and shut off the flow.

Far from being "pie-in-the-sky", your dreams, ideas and aspirations are the only guarantor of your success. Those who are successful in any field are successful because they keep their eyes on the prize. Their vision does not waver, at least not for very long. Their passion and enthusiasm for the wanted thing assures pure focus, and keeps the energy from the universe in response flowing toward the goal; consequently, most of their action is along the path of least resistance.

9.3 The Importance of Being

"What do you want to be when you grow up?" parents sometimes ask their children. "I want to be an airplane pilot!" "I want to be a basketball player!" "I want to be a great musician!"

When we say, "I want to BE a _____" it is implicit that we really mean DO. In other words, it would be more accurate to ask "What would you like to do when you grow up?" because when someone says "I want to be a pilot" they intend to actually fly airplanes, not just think about flying airplanes.

The phrasing of the question involving various forms of the verb BE is indicative of a powerful truth: you must be something before you can do it. Being always comes before doing and having. The more completely you can assume a *beingness*, the faster you will learn.

For example, the pianist Herbie Hancock played with the Chicago Symphony when he was only twelve years old. Mozart gave his first public performance when he was five years of age and composed his first symphony at the age of eight. Some people assign such genius to past-life knowledge, but Occam's Razor (a principle which states "The simplest explanation is most likely to be correct") tells us that there must be a more elegant solution.

What if an assumption of beingness, purely, leads to rapid development? "Beingness" leads to focusing, for someone who purely wants something is giving his or her undivided attention to the goal. A person who is focused on something very strongly and believes he or she can do it without reservation is a very focus-powerful attracting magnet for inspiration and knowledge. [28] There is no explanation for a child prodigy, for example. How does he or she make such rapid progress at such an early age? Well, let's not make the mistake of assuming that the consciousness of a being in a child's body is retarded, because his or her body is not fully developed. In fact, we often say that a child is closest to God. What does that mean, exactly?

It means that a child has a greater awareness of what we call life force energy or source energy. He or she has a greater awareness of the broader consciousness that a person relinquishes to some degree when he or she incarnates into the bubbles of biology called human bodies. Therefore, a child or even a baby is quite capable of focusing his or her attention on subjects of interest, especially when the child has been exposed to something continuously since birth. Music, for instance. It is easy for even a baby to understand the vibrations associated with music, and gain an understanding of the emotional effect of music on the human spirit. Perhaps that is why, in music, there have been so many prodigies.

There is always a connection between the incarnated personality and the "Higher Self" or "Inner Being." From that connection comes a connection to the powerful thought streams of knowledge on every conceivable subject.

In my attempts at piano playing, I did not consider myself a musician, because I am only a beginner. This is a very truthful statement, but it has also led to very slow progress as a pianist. How can you play piano well, when you don't even consider yourself a piano player? The answer is, you cannot! I know this, so why don't I allow myself to completely assume the beingness of a virtuoso player? I don't know, I just don't!

---

[28] "It's not that I'm so smart, it's just that I stay with problems longer."—Albert Einstein

But Mozart did. And so did Herbie Hancock, and Bill Evans and probably hundreds of men and women who are great keyboard players.

I know that I learn the fastest when I am completely uninhibited in my creative process. When I am totally open and am not counter-creating, I seem to be drawn to the right piece to study, or my lesson goes very smoothly and I learn a bunch of stuff all at once.

Bill Murray (in the movie "Groundhog Day") said, "God isn't that smart. He's just been around a long time." A wise woman once said, "Genius is just attention to a subject."[29] The more you focus on something, the more powerful is your vibrational signal, and the easier it is to learn the subject you are studying. The more you learn, the faster you learn. This is just a consequence of the law of like attracts like.

A genius is intensely focused on his or her subject. A study of Mozart's early life shows this to be the case. Mozart was immersed in music since the day he was born. His father, Leopold, instructed both his children assiduously, so that Mozart was able to publicly perform at the age of 5. He wrote his first symphony at 8 and by the age of 20 was considered a mature composer. He learned his craft by listening and studying the music of the best composers of his day, and had an extraordinary memory, composing entire symphonies in his head. Mozart was a diligent worker and would not write anything until every single note of a new work had been constructed in his imagination.

The ability to build something totally in your head is the hallmark of someone who is thinking about a subject all the time.

It seems reasonable to say then, that genius doesn't come from past life memories. It comes from intense focus and study, and the assumption of a pure state of being with little or no counter intention. Fortunately, TV did not exist in Mozart's day!

The assumption of a pure state of being means that one simply allows oneself to BE that. It is always accompanied by a feeling of what it would be like to actually live it (this is easy to understand: if you want a new Porsche, just imagine yourself driving it, and you will get a feeling). A state of beingness is an alignment of your life force energy with the desire or goal. If you intend to be a pianist, for example, you would simply decide that you are a pianist, right now. Mostly people do not because it is considered delusional. "How can you say you're a pianist right now when you can't play anything but chopsticks?" People think that in order to call yourself a pianist, you have to be able to play like Horowitz. But that is nonsense! You do not have to do anything to assume a state of being! People get intimidated by comparing their ability to DO with the doing of others, which invalidates their state of being, bringing in

---

[29] Esther Hicks

counter thoughts and counter intention, and derailing the creative process. Whenever I thought of myself as a pianist, I inevitably compared myself to Bill Evans or Herbie Hancock and I said, "Now there's a pianist!" Then I felt incompetent. That is self defeating in the extreme!

Because doing proceeds directly from being, any counter intention at all will hinder competence. The young Horowitz, for example, did not let criticism of his playing invalidate his knowing of himself as a pianist, and continued to play and record brilliantly into his 70's (he was especially criticized in his early years for bravura performances which were brilliant, but often loud and not always considered tasteful).

Let's say that our friend Thorpe lives in a trailer park and he has $1,000 in the bank, and has just finished paying off his truck. Could Thorpe consider himself to BE wealthy? Of course he can! "That's crazy," you might say. "Ted Turner is wealthy. Thorpe is anything but wealthy." Well, the amount of money Thorpe presently has is irrelevant to an assumption of a state of consciousness about money.

Is Thorpe, with $1,000 free and clear, in worse shape than Rupert Bentley Harrington VII with $50 million in the bank and $60 million in debt? I don't know; if you have 50 mil you can probably borrow another 50, but if you are worried about the $10 mil you owe, then how rich are you really? Like everything else, "rich" is a state of beingness. That state of being has nothing to do with your physical surroundings! You can *make* it be about the stuff you have or the lack of it of course, but that is only a free will decision that you can change at any time. One thing is for sure: your state of mind, continued long enough, will eventually be reflected in your physical experience; for richer or for poorer, as they say when you get married.

Thorpe, if he chooses to, has an excellent way to feel good about himself by appreciating what he has, rather than dwelling on what he doesn't. "Yes but he's just a fool," says Rupert Bentley Harrington. But he isn't! By appreciating what he has, Thorpe keeps himself vibrationally aligned with the prosperity he seeks. If he listens to those who call him an inevitable loser, his life will never change for the better.

9.3.1 Inspiration

WHEN you approach any task without contradictory thought you will make amazing progress, because your vibration is purely resonating to the wanted thing. You become more aware of those little nudges of inspiration that occur when attention is focused clearly and directly. Inspiration is a result of information from the non-physical part of you, which is connected to the universal field of consciousness within which all data flows.

When you are inspired, more and more brilliant ideas seem to flow right into you; you can hardly keep up with it! And accompanying these ideas is always a feeling of well-being, or some positive emotion. However, this can only happen when you are focused purely on something. I have never been inspired unless I have been in an almost pure state of allowing, or, as some say, going with the flow. And you can't reach this state of consciousness unless you are assuming a state of being without a feeling of doubt or uncertainty.

9.3.2 Probability

Human beings have a saying which goes, "All good things must end." What this means is that when things are going well, there is a greater and greater expectation of impediment, the longer things are on a positive slant. However, it is only the expectation of difficulty that knocks your ship off course, not some inherent property of the universe.

Probability and statistical analysis suggest that you can only go so far in any direction before the odds catch up with you. This idea had its genesis in wagering and gambling (especially dice and cards), and led to the birth of the mathematics of probability. A French nobleman, the Chevalier de Mere, asked his friend, the mathematician Pascal, to calculate why some bets made money over time and some didn't. LaPlace showed how it could be an aid to data analysis. Gregor Mendel used it in his study of genetics. Later, in the 20th century, probability was used to describe subatomic phenomena and was even extended to apply to the prediction of group human behavior. Because science has such a remarkable influence on our society, we have embraced the ideas of probability and uncertainty in our own lives.

Many philosophers have tried to determine the secrets of life by observing nature. Nature seeks balance in all things. Day yields to night, which yields to day once more; the sun is obscured and rain falls, but the sun appears again. The number of examples is limitless. The idea that your life could go well all the time seems to violate a natural law of the universe! Most important, we observe that everyone has good times and bad times. Therefore, it would seem inescapable that bad times are inevitable and you just have to get used to them.

However, it is those very assumptions which destroy the purity of your intent and your state of being, change your vibrational signal to the universe, and eventually, by the law of like attracts like, lead to manifestations which confirm your state of mind, and your feelings, about life. One may find balance at a level of happiness and abundance, or find equilibrium at lower levels of emotion and success. In other words, you may always experience ups and downs, but they may be subtle, and always in a positive range!

9.3.3 Being vs. Doing

What is the difference between being and doing?

Doing involves movement – physical movement. Being also involves movement – the movement of thought impulses. When Tesla conceives his turbines or Mozart his symphony, he is using mental energy, life force energy. One constructs mental blueprints and prototypes, using creative visualization, and that energy is just as real as the building materials in the physical universe. Regardless of your lack of imagination, you are always using thought to guide your action! The clarity and sophistication of your thought will determine the clarity and sophistication of your life.

How does any physical movement begin? With a thought impulse. When you reach for a glass, you first have the thought, "Let's get that glass into my hand." You see the glass in your hand first within your mind before you reach for it with your hand.

What I'm trying to show is that being and doing are not so different – each involves movement of energy. But being comes first, and controls doing and having. It is one of those intellectually obvious principles that is often not consciously applied in life. In other words, it is one thing to know something and quite another to use it. Becoming mindful will lead to greater and greater awareness and self-control.

As thought becomes more developed upon a subject, the thought forms associated with the subject become more sophisticated. Thought forms are just patterns of energy, manipulated within one's consciousness. In order to build a thought template, one designs and moves patterns of thought energy around. The physical object is then constructed directly from the thought templates, moving physical stuff around.

You can buy lathes nowadays which are programmable. One simply inputs the design for an ornately decorated stile, for example, inserts a piece of wood, and the machine spews out the finished product. Thought templates translated almost instantly to the physical universe! It's exciting.

Being is about consciousness. It's about thought and decision making. In our model, surrounding all living things is a field of life force energy, and in that nurturing cocoon are the templates, or the 'etheric blueprint,' which programs the cellular material of the body. This is how the cells know how to grow into a dog instead of a cat, or an amoeba instead of a tree. In this representation, DNA is itself the physical representation of such 'etheric' programming.

Just as an engineer works from a blueprint to construct a building, consciousness operates from the design templates of thought. Don't laugh! Some scientists are coming around to this idea, even if grudgingly. In his paper "Precursor Engineering: Directly Altering Physical Reality," Dr. T Bearden describes a set of mass-free, 4-spatial dynamics which he calls a precursor engine. By separating the massless component from the observable masses and forces, one can, theoretically, directly engineer the precursor engine and change the structure of physical matter and energy.

Of course this idea is out of the mainstream, but so what? Pioneers of new thought and new technology are often criticized. As Max Planck, the famous physicist said, "A new scientific truth does not triumph by convincing its opponents and making them see the light, but rather because its opponents eventually die, and a new generation grows up that is familiar with it."—Quoted in T.S. Kuhn, *The Structure of Scientific Revolutions*.

Einstein also said, "Whoever undertakes to set himself up as judge in the field of truth and knowledge is shipwrecked by the laughter of the Gods."

A conscious being does this all the time within his or her own human energy field, through the process of thought. A thought proceeds directly from consciousness, so it interfaces directly with the life force energy within the human energy field. In this analogy, the "precursor engine" of a human being is the human energy field, and the programming is done by thought itself!

It may not be possible to levitate chairs but all of us have the ability to directly engineer how we feel.

We have looked at the universe as a set of vibrations, and have said that the solid objects of our world appear so because of the vibrational receptors of the human senses. These are precisely tuned into the minuscule portion of the electromagnetic spectrum which is perceived as visible light, and the tiny range of vibrations which the ears perceive as sound.[30] The point is, our personal worlds are self-created. Have you ever noticed how two people can look at the same thing and disagree about the reality of it? One time my wife and I were looking at a deep-blue tinted glass urn. I thought it would function perfectly as a drinking glass, and was going to purchase it for that purpose. She was astounded and said, "Drink out of it! It would be perfect for a flower arrangement." As we continued to discuss the object it became apparent that her view of it was much different than mine. Even its physical shape was open to dispute! Of course, we could say that our differences were the result of the limitations of language, and that our eyes perceived the same reflected light off the object. That is what a scientist might say, relegating our differences to personal opinions about an objectively perceivable object. But I'm not so sure about that. I believe that two people never see the same thing, and that differences of opinion are at least somewhat based upon differences in perception! That would mean that we are all largely at the center of our own personally created universes. This is the idea behind the universal interface to consciousness which I call the Universal Operating System, and why I say that the UOS can only be described and experienced from an individual perspective.

---

[30] The human eye perceives frequencies at 10^{14} cycles per second (visible light) but the ear perceives sounds at only 10^4 cycles per second. That is a huge disparity!

In this model, each one of us interfaces directly with the universe at large and is constantly interacting vibrationally with the rest of existence. Each of us is in his or her own little bubble of consciousness. Within that bubble, our thoughts and feelings generate pulses of energy, which vibrate out to the rest of the universe. Through the law of like attracts like, our vibrational signal is constantly, in every moment, being matched up with other signals like it. Being, then, is a dynamically changing situation, for it is a good bet that the sum total of a person's thoughts, beliefs and feelings are never precisely the same from moment to moment.

(If one had the ability to see the human energy field, what would it look like? In Chapter 2 we took a stab at it, by saying it has the shape of a torus. Whatever shape it is, I imagine the human aura as a multicolored light show, a sophisticated, intricate and breathtakingly beautiful tapestry of energy in complex patterns and shapes. I see it as billions of tiny filaments of energy, interweaving in complex and beautiful geometries. The body lies within this field of energy, completely surrounded and nurtured by it. Of course the human senses only perceive the body and not the aura, so we never recognize what truly magnificent beings we all are. In a sense, being human hides the greater part of our being.)

9.4 Establishing a State of Being

WHAT precisely is a state of being?

A state of being is a fundamental decision that reflects a person's conception of himself or herself. This is expressed in language with an "I AM" statement.

How do you establish a state of being?

The first step is deciding TO BE something. "I am a musician." "I am a healer." "I am an engineer." "I am a warrior." It is possible to assume multiple states of being all at once. My friend Dave is a musician, a keyboard designer and builder, an instrument designer, an oil painter, a writer, a teacher, a tool builder, and a philosopher.

The next step is the visualization of what you want. Needless to say, without first deciding what you want, you cannot visualize it; furthermore, the clarity and firmness of your decision determines the power and clarity of your visualization. Creative visualization essentially creates a thought prototype. The sophistication of your thought template determines the sophistication of your creation in the physical universe: a child's drawing, for example, is a mirror of its primitive thought pattern.

Moreover, the clearer your decision, the more powerful is your platform of attraction. How can you tell whether your decision is clear and powerful, with no counter-intention? First and foremost, by the way you feel.

A state of being serves three purposes: It creates a vibrational platform of attraction, interfacing with the Universal Operating System. It aligns your own life force energy toward the goal, resulting in positive emotion, and it begins the creative process. A state of being provides motivation and inspiration for action cycles in the physical universe, and eventually leads to manifestation.

This system will work with ANY decision. If there are five possible joyful paths, don't agonize over which one to choose, just pick one of them! That's what my friend Dave does. First it was music, then keyboards, then teaching, then instrument design, then turbine and engine design, then oil painting, then welding and casting, then tool making, then music…he just goes from one to the other, on the inspiration of the moment. To live like that, always in the middle of creative energy, ah…that's living! Any joyful path you tread will bring joy, it's just that simple.

The greatest experts at being are children. It is very instructive to watch a child at play. First, he is an airplane pilot. He takes his plane and zooms it through the air and you can tell he is inside, feeling just what it's like to be that. Next, he is an engineer, putting blocks one on top of the other. Then he decides to be a soldier, shooting a gun; then he's an athlete, running around as fast as he can. The child is practicing for life, and a smart parent will encourage the child's imagination. Often however, when he is older, parents and teachers will criticize an overactive imagination. "It's time to grow up, Joe," they will say. "Get off your butt and make something of yourself." When you beat the imagination out of a child, you hinder his or her creative process and the connection to source energy, things that are vital for success and joy in life.

Is it possible to assume a negative state of being? Yes it is, and there probably isn't one of us who has not. Free Will permits us to Be and then Become anything, even if it feels rotten. Because humanity operates a lot of the time on the equation "bad = good," it is thought beneficial to endure pain and suffering, despite the strong protest of our emotional guidance system. The guidance system assumes rationality; in other words, it assumes that if something feels bad, it is not in a person's best interest. It is an elegant system that, if followed, keeps us always lined up with positive goals. Many of us blithely ignore these sometimes very uncomfortable protests, even when they result in illness. Feeling crummy and acting irrationally are not only acceptable modes of behavior in many human societies, such behavior is considered inevitable, and it is even glorified.

Life force energy is the animating principle of the universe, and it can be used for any purpose whatsoever. This might seem completely contradictory to the positive theme of this book, but it is pretty obvious that (on earth anyway) people will act in the most ghastly ways. However, as we have said before, all outcomes are ultimately positive, for at "death" one returns, unadulterated, to the native, non-physical state of consciousness. Since all actions are permitted, then perhaps even activities that produce discomfort and horror are also part of our divine nature. Consider those who deliberately risk death and experience the most severe hardships. What is the motivation? Adventure! Those who "risk death" really understand, deep down inside, that death is an illusion, a big earth joke. A person who free climbs (without ropes) might laugh off questions about his or her sanity by saying, "I might die but I'll have fun doing it!"

Freedom comes from the assumption of a state of being and following that path, wherever it leads. Being true to yourself is just having the courage to always listen to your own guidance system despite what others say.

9.5 Aligning Energy

Vibrationally speaking, the creative process is all about aligning to your desire, and keeping your focus there. If you do this, success is guaranteed, and if you don't, failure is probable, for reasons already given. Success does not depend on what others think, say, or do. If you are experiencing opposition from any quarter, you are already out of alignment, for you have attracted such into your experience. Life is a self-fulfilling prophecy. You always experience precisely according to your activated vibrational content. The ideas presented in this book are absurdly simple, and understood by everyone at the most intimate level of being: the only being who can determine the outcome of your life is you.

All individuals are sovereign in their experience. The way to success is to find something you want, and keep lined up to it!

All desires begin as thoughts. Very often, a rush of positive emotion accompanies this thought. "Wouldn't it be great to write a bestselling book?" "I want to learn karate and kick ass." "Starting my own company would be fantastic." "I want a new house, this one is too small." "I want to be a more loving person." Etc. However, in most cases, your present vibration (reflected in the conditions of your life) is nowhere near the vibration of your desire. That's because desire is often strongest when you are living just the opposite! The new desire is a little packet of energy that, at present, represents an unfulfilled gap or a potential relative to your present vibration. When that gap is completely bridged, it will be reflected in the physical universe.

"Aligning energy" is simply a vibrational matching to your desire, in accordance with the Law of Vibration and the Law of like attracts like. Thought, action, and manifestation are symbiotically linked, thought being the driving force that determines the nature of the other two. The creative process is, essentially, keeping yourself lined up with what you want while you complete the necessary steps toward manifestation.

Failure to do so must result in falling short of the goal. In fact, what happens in the physical universe (or within yourself, if the goal is strictly personal) will be a precise reflection of the design templates of thought that you keep alive in your consciousness.

9.5.1 Introduction

Until you are purely in harmony with your desire, there will be conflicting vibrations present within you. This means that your efforts will result in some of what you do want as well as some of what you don't want. This is OK, because the results you are getting will be a good gauge of exactly where your vibration is, relative to your desire. You can look at what is appearing in your life and if there is something you are getting you don't like, there is a belief that exactly matches it. Now you can precisely identify old beliefs and release them, making the action cycles you perform much more efficient and aligned with the goal.

How many times have you begun something with the hope that it will work out? "Well, I'll try this way, and see what happens." With an intention like that, the results will very likely not be satisfactory. Here, there is a kernel of desire but the sophistication and power of your thought is not yet congruent with the desire. The actions you take reflect the somewhat amorphous quality of your thought and therefore, what you receive is amorphous as well. Of course, it is impossible to immediately perform at a high skill level without working at your craft. Nevertheless, a powerful and confident vibration, combined with a clear vision, establishes a compelling platform of attraction.

My piano teacher told me that the great saxophonist Charlie Parker would practice 14 hours a day 7 days a week but for me, that is absolutely ridiculous. If I get 30 minutes every other day at the piano I'm doing well. But then I asked myself, "what are you doing the rest of the time?" Writing! I write every day, sometimes for 16 hours at a time with a few breaks for eats. Apparently, it all depends on where your interest is, and where you are focused. My vibration is powerfully focused on writing, as Mr. Parker's was on music. In 5 years I've gone literally from zero, to four books. And it wasn't work at all, it was just fun the whole time. That is probably how Charlie Parker felt about his music.

The universe you perceive is a mirror of your vibration. It is your helpful servant, delivering to you exact matches to where you place your focus. It is constantly pointing out to you where you are on the roadmap of life. This is not only very logical, it is very helpful, for, if you are honest with yourself, you may observe your manifestations and benchmark your progress. In other words, if there is something continually recurring in your life, then clearly you have an activated pattern of thought or belief supporting it. Operating from the assumption that consciousness is cause, you can then stop blaming luck, chance, or other people for your misfortune, and get yourself back on the rails.

Many people think that it is impossible to consciously create the life they want. That is because almost everyone gets some of what is wanted and some of what isn't wanted, so it seems like a crap shoot. Or luck. Or coincidence. It seems to most that the earth is a very chaotic place, and even a cursory glance at the news seems to confirm that.

Far from being a chaotic place, the planet earth is perfectly ordered and balanced! It just seems chaotic sometimes, because so many people do not consciously focus and direct their thoughts. Their vibration is all over the place, and so that is what they receive! The key is to clearly identify what you really want.

9.5.2 Stages in the Manifestation Process

The First Stage

THE first and most important stage in aligning your energy is to have a clear idea of what your goal or desire is. Most people don't get exactly what they intend, because their vision is not crystal clear! Often this step is neglected in favor of action cycles. "Well, I don't really know what I want, but maybe if I hope enough and work hard enough, something good will happen." Yeah, maybe it will, but one of the purposes of this book is to describe the process of conscious creation. It's a lot more fun to have control of your life than to just go on hoping!

Sometimes necessity demands that you plunge in before you are ready, but it is vitally important that you clarify where you are going along the way. If your thoughts are amorphous, the results you obtain will be as well. Here is where creative visualization comes into the picture.

Creative visualization is the process of building a template of thought and emotion which will establish your point of attraction and guide your action. It establishes the being portion of the be-do-have process. Creative visualization utilizes a balance of heart and mind. When it is done correctly, creative visualization alters your personal vibration, results in a change of feeling within you, and lines you up to the goal. That is why so many athletes use it.

You will know you have achieved clarity when you can recreate, at will, the feeling of what it would be like to have, or be living, your desire. By clearly visualizing your new life, or the thing that is wanted, you will generate a positive emotional response within you. These positive feelings are your vibrational platform of attraction from the rest of the universe, via the law of like attracts like. The feeling of positive emotion indicates successful vibrational alignment with the goal.

This is not trivial! Go through your life and list goals, and then identify your position on the emotional/vibrational scale regarding each one. You will find that your progress is directly proportional to how you feel about them. The progress (or lack of it) you have made is a direct reflection of the amount of counter-thought you have regarding it.

Very often your mental picture will change during the creative process. You will get new inspiration, or decide to do something differently. That's totally OK. In fact, it's one of the excitements of creating something. In a novel I'm currently writing, for example, I didn't have a clue how it was going to end until I was halfway through.

Of course, a book, a painting or a sculpture is something you can control every step of the way but in life you don't have that luxury. However, the UOS will respond dynamically to your changing vibrational requests. A painting or a musical composition will clearly follow the thought template. The more you understand about music, for example, the more sophisticated your compositions can be.

I'm currently listening to Herbie Hancock's piano voicing on a Miles Davis CD and I'm blown away by their beauty and complexity. Although my level of musical creation could never compare to Herbie Hancock's I can create much more sophisticated compositions than my friend Larry, who knows nothing about music and hits the keys almost at random. What he can create is very limited because the development of his thought is simplistic. The more evolved are your thought templates, the greater is your creative palette; the more powerful is your creative engine and the greater is the potential for creating and attracting the things you need.

While it is obvious that a painting, a musical composition, or a sculpture must first begin with a template of thought, and will reflect the artist's vision, it is not so obvious that the same is true for a relationship, a business project, or any manifestation that involves the decisions and actions of other people. Life, in other words! While it is true that one cannot buck the current of the Law of Free Will, it is also true that the UOS will respond to your choices and your focus. Others of like mind with different skill sets and interests will be drawn to you. The clarity and development of your personal thought templates, combined with your position on the scale of emotion, will determine how quickly and accurately you link up with the people and resources you need to complete your project. The system works in part because there are 7 billion human beings on our planet and that is enough diversity to supply just about every need.

The important thing to understand is that manifestation is always the result of your personal creative process, and you have complete control over that.

The Second Stage

THE second stage is staying in the present moment while deliberately envisioning what you want. Go through life as much as possible living in "now" time. The "now" moment is always the moment of creation. It is always the moment of experiencing, when the vibrations from the outside world reach your senses. Therefore, envision having what you want NOW. You envision what you want in the now, and when it comes to you, it will be in the now. Life is lived now! It is hard to communicate this concept, because we perceive time as linear – past, present, future.

But the linearity of time is an illusion. The present moment is the platform for creation, because effective creation occurs when one is fully conscious. And one can only be fully conscious by being fully present NOW. Those who detach themselves from the present become less and less attuned to reality, as most of us have probably noticed. My friend's mother had Alzheimer's, and her contact with the now was tenuous at best. My sister-in-law is in a nursing home. She thinks she sees her dead parents all the time, and goes out to lunch with them a lot. Maybe she does, who knows, but wherever she is eating, it isn't on planet earth!

The past is just a mental picture and a bunch of feelings connected to something that occurred in a now moment. The future is a creative visualization of something you want to occur in a now moment. The past and the future are the same thing! We distinguish past from future by saying that the past was an actual incident and the future is a visualization, but both are composed of thought forms. Therefore, both are controllable from the present moment.

If you have ever experimented with past incidents, you know that by changing your version of what happened, you can change the present situation even when it involves another person. If you had a fight with your brother, you can reinvent what happened and pretend the conversation was a cheerful one. Besides making yourself feel better, you alter your vibrational signal and are no longer a match to any of the negative emotions of the other person. If you were truly successful in your vibrational alteration and you called your brother, he might not even be mad anymore.

At the subatomic level of matter, experimentation has discovered that the position of a previously recorded entangled photon will change if, later, we learn more information about its twin! In other words, the first photon will be at one place if, later on in time, we learn more information about its twin, and it will be in another position if we don't have that information. To a physicist this is unremarkable, because he or she understands the mathematics behind the phenomenon. For us laymen, however, it seems fantastic, for it seems to be physical evidence that changing the present can alter the past. It does not seem so strange, then, to say that altering the past can have an effect on the present.[31]

Although this might seem delusional and even dishonest, the actuality of all past incidents have vanished. What remains are mental images and any new decisions stemming from the past event, continually carried forward into the present. In this way a human being accumulates layers of decision-making about life events, and can build up considerable resistance, amassing a host of self-limiting beliefs which inhibit happiness, success, and even health. The past is a self-created phantom, but one which has a vice-like grip on the lives of so many. Creative visualization is an excellent way to "unstick" a person from beliefs which are no longer serving that person.

We may look upon such a "past altering" procedure as a gedanken (thought) experiment. This may seem ludicrous to those who have not experimented with the power of thought, but I assure you that a properly performed "life gedanken experiment" can bring remarkable results. The power of purely resonating to something within your own consciousness is astonishing, and can have almost magical effects on other people (and yourself of course).

It's funny. In physics, "thought experiments" which attempt to understand the mechanics of matter and energy are permitted, but such experiments when applied to life are often scorned as pointless daydreaming or "magic think." However, in this book, we are turning that on its head and using it for our benefit!

Interestingly enough, the Copenhagen Interpretation of quantum mechanics already assigns a role to consciousness in the interpretation of reality. It basically says that in the micro-world of subatomic particles, the only way to determine an object's reality is to observe it, implying to some that a particle does not exist until it is perceived (Einstein once asked Neils Bohr, CI's chief proponent, if the moon exists when no one is looking at it). In this interpretation, which has survived for almost a century since it was first formulated in the late 1920's, it is not possible to say anything at all about a particle before it is observed. The very existence of the particle is undetermined until someone perceives it.

The point is, never dwell on negative events of the past. What's done is done and by far your most powerful point of attraction, by many orders of magnitude, is in the present. When you dwell on the negative past you bring it into the now, activating the vibration of it.

---

[31] See "A Delayed Choice Quantum Eraser" at http://xxx.lanl.gov/pdf/quant-ph/9903047. Ross Rhodes' excellent explanation of this experiment can be found at his website, www.bottomlayer.com.

The Third Stage

THE third stage is gradually gaining the ability to focus on what you want, despite all the reasons not to.

If you have an office job that you hate, but would like to be self-employed, you must align your energies to being self-employed, despite your present reality that is all about the office. You get up every morning and spend the entire day there. You can't align yourself to being self-employed if your every thought and experience is about the office! So what to do?

Imagine as many times as you can during the day, what it would feel like to be on your own. Visualize what you would be doing. Play with it. You'd be surprised how often you can do this if you really want to. I am not encouraging anyone to daydream at work, but there are always breaks during the day in which you can exercise your creative imagination. I often take some time at the end of the day, or in the morning just before work or before I sit down to write, and spend some time at creative visualization. I tried meditating and that helped to calm me down a little, but in meditation there is a releasing of desire, whereas in creative visualization there is a conscious focusing, a distinct vibrational orientation on what is wanted. Besides, I like the idea of harnessing my mind and putting it to work, instead of trying to shut it up!

As you imagine yourself where you want to be, you will probably discover uncomfortable, resistive thought patterns or feelings. This phenomenon is perfectly natural because in the attempt to create something that has not yet manifested, you naturally stir up the thoughts and feelings that have created the unwanted condition. The solution is to keep going, and not give up, despite what "reality" is telling you. You have to make the reality of your vision more important than the reality you have already created. You have to violate the teachings of society, which insists that what has already manifested is more important than your creative vision. This is simply not true! If you take a drive from snowy Chicago to sunny Florida, you have to get out of Chicago first! You don't stop halfway in Tennessee and say "it's still snowing, we're never going to get there," and turn back. But that's precisely what a lot of people do on their route to self-improvement. When traveling along a well-marked highway in your car, you know that if you just keep going, you will eventually arrive. However, the same applies to vibrational distances. You may pass by some crummy sights on your car excursion, but that does not stop you. A few yucky thoughts and feelings should not halt your vibrational progress either.

When unwanted thoughts and feelings come up, release them. Do not dwell on them or try to get rid of them, for doing so will activate them even more strongly. Remember, thoughts and feelings are vibrational and respond to your focused attention! The way to release an unwanted vibration is to keep focused on your visualization and any positive feelings it generates; the unwanted vibrations will gradually die away.

Creative visualization is most effective when engaged in lightly and joyfully. If you get too serious, you are just putting up resistance and contaminating your vibe. It should be fun! Avoid obsessing on the result and neglecting the means, for such focus often comes from a "must have." Now there is an element of desperation involved in the creative process, which sticks you in the present. This is often the case when a person first begins to discover the principle of conscious creation and can't wait for the manifestation. Here there is a genuine element of "magic think," for one cannot achieve any goal without first genuinely altering one's vibration to match it.

Pretend that whatever you thought would magically appear in the physical universe. Say you wanted a new Porsche. It is clear that you would need to understand the design of every part and how it fit together with the whole. In short, you would have to understand, in the minutest detail, everything about the car before it would work! Even in magic, there are levels of proficiency, for the physical Porsche is a direct reflection of the templates of thought from which it manifests. That is why, in life, what you get may not match your desire, but it always matches your creative vision of it. The origin of the saying "Be careful what you ask for, you might get it" is based on an understanding of this idea.

That requires some work! However, it is work that is entirely under your control. Artists understand that a painting or a composition must proceed step by step, and so too in life.

If you want something too desperately, an energetic chasm is created that inevitably separates you from the wanted thing. (I'm not talking about a strong desire, which generates passion. When you feel passionate about something you are on the right track! I'm talking about a desperate reaching that results in one of the lower emotions. Anyone who is paying attention to his or her feelings can tell the difference.) That energy chasm involves yourself at Pole A, not having what you want, and the desired thing off in the distance at Pole B. Sort of like the mule who is motivated to move by a carrot dangling at the end of a stick. When the animal moves, the stick moves as well. The idea is to just *be* at Pole B!

Positive focus on the goal avoids this difficulty. Robert Fritz says that the gap between Pole A and Pole B creates a potential that provides energy for thought and action, somewhat like the voltage a battery provides to a circuit, enabling electrical current to flow. So even though your reality is presently at Pole A, the visualization of Pole B creates energy you can use to get there. Without the visualization, there is no potential and, like an uncharged battery, no way to generate power.

"Yes," you say, "but here at Pole A it's real and solid, and at Pole B there's just a bunch of invisible thought. You can't move a ten ton boulder with a pea shooter!" Well, consider the idea that Pole B is just as powerful as Pole A. Remember that you are continually creating the current conditions with your creative energy; now all you have to do is create Pole B in the same way, and the situation will begin to change. It will change not only because you are lining yourself up vibrationally with others who may be able to help you, but also because, *while being at Pole B*, you come up with new ideas and the actions you take will be supportive of your new vibration. And remember that the "solid" stuff of your physical reality is fundamentally vibrational in nature, as are your thoughts and your creative visualizations. In the vibrational universe concept, matter, energy, and thought are all made of the same "stuff."

To summarize: When you are being at Pole A, you create Pole A; the only way to get something different is by being at Pole B! Obvious, simple and powerful.

The Fourth Stage

THE fourth stage in aligning your energy is gaining the ability to purely focus upon what is wanted. This is a major step, because you have to be clear enough not to have old beliefs and feelings impinging on you every time you attempt to place yourself in your new vibration. When I first began the process of writing, I'd wind up fighting with editors and publishers, explaining to them why my stuff was worth reading. Instead of envisioning what I wanted, I was overcoming obstacles. I struggled with myself and others every time I began to reach higher. It was discouraging, for things seemed to be getting worse, not better.

Eventually I understood that activating new beliefs agitated the old thought structures I had built up over the years. In order to emerge from the stagnant pond of my old beliefs, I had to disturb the waters a little!

If you are like me, it may take quite a bit of work before you can do this step easily (but it does not have to!). I learned that *the only way to deactivate an unwanted thought, belief, attitude or feeling is to cease to pay attention to it.* That is the theme of this book: focus on the wanted thing and ignore the unwanted thing. The unwanted vibration dies off and the desired vibration gets stronger. The now moment is, in every instant, an opportunity to focus your attention. Wherever you place your focus is what will grow bigger for you.

Sometimes this is difficult at first but it will become easier and easier, because the nature of your consciousness, and life itself, is inherently positive. You are perfectly free to screw your life up any way you like, but it is comforting to know that the system is designed for success, not failure.

A good test of your ability is to try holding your visualization purely for 60 seconds at a time without contradictory thought or feeling. Don't laugh! It is a lot harder than you think. I dare you to purely envision something you want (but do not yet have) for a full minute, feeling positive the entire time, with no counter-thought. If you can do this, you are on your way to a much smoother creative process, more effective action cycles, and quicker manifestation. Counter-intention and resistant thought in your vibration will reduce the effectiveness of any action you take, no matter how frenzied it is!

The having of something only serves to help maintain a vibration, a feeling, a state of consciousness, that was already there in the first place. That's because in order for something to manifest in your life, you already had to be a vibrational match to it! Seems strange to say it, but it's true. It's all a result of the powerful law of like attracts like. *Manifestation is just a by-product of the alignment of your energy to your visualization.*

In other words, you cannot have something unless you are already being it! And when you get it, you were already there. And you were there during the process of creating, because that's what provided the inspiration to keep going. The actions you take are joyful, or difficult, in proportion to how you are feeling about the project. Your personal creative process begins, continues, and ends within you.

That's why when you finally get something you want, it's often not as exciting as you thought it was going to be. Artists know that the fun is in the painting of the picture or the writing of the book – once it's done, they are looking towards the next creation, and the next. If you're assigning all of the importance to having, instead of being and doing, you'll never get there, because you're always noticing the gap between where you are and where you want to be. It is always the alignment of your energy towards the goal that causes you to feel good.

In the creative process, you have to have a clear idea where you are going in order to manifest anything worthwhile. Hoping for a miracle is not going to get you where you want to go! Someone may splash a bunch of paint at random on a canvas and call it art, but the truly great artists in any field know exactly where they are going in every moment. Their creations may change from the original conception, but the great artist is one with a wonderful imagination and great technique. My piano teacher and I listened to two fantastic solos by the late great Kenny Kirkland. Dave pointed out the chord structure and said, "This pianist is deliberately and consciously creating his solo note by note, even on the most complex voicing." The same was true on a phenomenal saxophone solo by Sonny Rollins. "The great artists know every note they're playing, and how it relates to the music, in every moment," Dave said. The guy who throws a bunch of stones together couldn't sculpt the pieta. To do that, you have to have technique, and technique comes from a sophisticated template of thought which can be used as your creative palette. It comes from taking the time to work at your craft and get good at it. It comes from the creation of something meaningful to you.

Just as one practices meaningfully as an artist, so too does it take practice to shift vibrationally in life. This is what some call "growth" as a person. Personal growth is changing one's personal vibration to match one's desires. This process is fully supported by the universe's operating system.

The Fifth Stage

THE fifth stage is creating "from the inside out." By that is meant, feeling the creative power originating within you, and understanding that it interfaces with the world to bring you what is wanted. The reflexive flow is primary.

Although this is obvious when creating a work of art, it is not so obvious in life. Many people see the creative energy outside of themselves, and so feel the need to struggle and work inordinately hard. The larger and more elaborate is the goal, the more work it will be, is the thinking. This seems reasonable, because a more expensive car costs less than a cheap one, and since money is energy, a cheaper car should be easier to get. A company-wide restructuring should be more difficult than an individual team or cell. But this isn't true at all. In the vibrational model, an alignment to the goal is all that is needed.

Properly aligned, action cycles will follow effortlessly and resources will become available as necessary; the scope of the project is irrelevant. The scope of your beliefs must be congruent to the scope of your project, however! The energy you are aligning, to which others will respond, is all from inside of you. You are the creator! Feel the creative power coming from within you, radiating outwards into the universe. You are sending out a vibrational beacon, a homing signal that beckons those things you want to come to you, and aligns your energy with them. And in the process the most important thing of all happens: you feel fantastic!

Feeling the creative power coming from inside of you is indescribable. The energy of creation fills every cell in your body, and expands to encompass your entire energy field. It is a rush of exquisite, powerful, blissful energy which fills you with joy and awe. Once you have experienced this, you will never ingest substances to get high. That stuff is pitiful and pathetic in comparison to creative energy. Creative energy is the energy of life, of consciousness itself, which fills the universe and composes everything in the universe. It is always available to you in your creative process.

The Sixth Stage

THE sixth stage is the realization that your new vibration now feels more comfortable than did the old one. At this stage, you have clarified, purified and aligned your energy to your desire so well that it feels natural to live in this new way. There are now no (or almost no) conflicting counter-thoughts or doubts which cause you to feel negative emotion.

The Seventh Stage

THE seventh stage is observation in the physical universe of your goal or dream manifesting. This step actually occurs little by little along the way. It may start out in the early stages with little things that remind you of where you are going. Then, as you get further along, manifestations that are more concrete will occur, until finally, the goal is achieved. Again, this is quite obvious when engaging in an artistic project, but it is not so obvious when trying to change the conditions of your life, or in a business setting.

For example, one day I was writing my third book and I understood that I was fully a writer, doing the things that writers do. The process of change was so gradual I hardly noticed it, for I had so much fun along the way.

Many times, manifestation will not occur in the way you thought it would, or planned it would. The path toward your goal always occurs through the cracks of least resistance in your vibration, so when your life begins to change, it may change in unanticipated ways. Just go with the flow, it will turn out wonderful.

The Eighth Stage

THE eighth stage is the full manifestation. Now you are living your new life, or have the thing that you desired, or have reached your goal. You feel a sense of accomplishment, and expansiveness. It's a great feeling.

The day I got my first two books back from the printer was a special day for me, for in my hands were concrete evidence of my alignment to the goal.

Perhaps what you have created does not live up to your expectations. In this case, realize that what you have created is a precise match to the templates of thought that brought it about. You are not a failure because it didn't happen perfectly the first time! You now have a springboard from which to improve what you have created. For example, my first attempt at writing this book did not meet my expectations, so I started all over again, taking the good parts and rewriting everything else.

Let's say that you are extremely happy with your creation, and you look proudly upon it. But now you find out what was said in step four: having is not all it is cranked up to be! Having is the culmination of the process and when it occurs, you feel magnificent!—for a while. Then the feeling wears off. When I finished my novel I simply put it aside and began the next one! It has been sitting on the shelf for months now, and I've done nothing to promote it. For me, the inspiration and the energy associated with the book (which was considerable while I was writing it) is gone. Sigh. That is the problem for some artists. We are great at the creation stage but not so hot at marketing and promotion.

Why does the excitement of having eventually wear off?

Because you are an ever-expanding being. You are a creator being, and creator beings feel good when they are creating. After something is created and manifests, it is no longer necessary to create it, so there is a kind of let-down.

I'm not saying people don't enjoy playing with their manifestations. It's just that the thrill of playing with anything wears off after a while.

After you have successfully manifested, you will have another desire, and another, and another. Some call this "greed" but guess what, it is not! It is the inherent property of life to expand, to want to be more, feel more, experience more! If you ever run out of desires or goals, you will cease to channel any life force through you, and your body will die. The end of desire is the end of life force, for desire IS life force! Enjoy your manifestation, but don't be surprised if you feel yourself wanting more. It's totally natural. The all-that-is, of which you are an integral part, is set up for continuous growth.

The Ninth Stage

THE ninth and last stage is the next desire. Once you have enjoyed and assimilated the results of your new creation for a while, you have reached a new plateau of perception, and you realize there is more you would like to experience. The process starts all over again, but now you are a more fully realized being. You have knowingly applied your creative process and deliberately manifested a desire. You know that YOU did it. The feeling of power you now have is indescribable, because you know you can do it again! And again, and again, and again. Now life starts to become really exciting. You only have to decide what more you want to be, do, or have and you are on your way.

Geometrically, the creative process can be represented as a spiral. A spiral continues forever upward and outward, reflecting the eternal and expanding nature of consciousness itself.

9.6 Manifestation and Delusion

Most people would define delusion as, "perceiving as true, that which is not real." But this is precisely what you must do in the creative process, in order to manifest anything!

In order to create anything, you have to pay attention to something that is not real for a long enough time until it is created. And you have to believe that it can happen; in other words, you have to consider what you want as totally real, even though it has not yet been translated into the physical universe. An artist who wants to make a painting, for example, will have to hold the idea and the picture of what she wants very clearly in her head, until she has it just the way she wants it. If the artist gives up on her vision, it can never fully manifest.

The energy of thought *is* real, just as real as matter and energy, for matter is mostly space, ephemeral, occupied by fuzzy subatomic particles that oscillate madly about a nucleus composed of other fuzzy subatomic particles. In our model, matter is vibrational in nature, as is thought. Manifestation cannot occur unless there is first a created blueprint of thought that programs action. A construction engineer works from a blueprint, but that blueprint first existed in somebody's head. The invisibility of the thought templates disguises their importance, but neglecting them will inevitably lead to ineffective action cycles.

Consider what would happen if all of your thoughts manifested instantly: that might be a very dangerous thing indeed, for there are very few of us who have complete control of ourselves. We forget that under such a magic scenario, all of our negative thoughts would manifest right alongside the good ones! Many of us would like to think a thought and instantly receive a manifestation, but I have noticed that people who think this way have the least mental control and discipline. As we remarked earlier, if such a person wished for a car, it would materialize non-functional, for in order to materialize a properly working vehicle, everything about the car must be clearly understood. How many parts does the Porsche have, for example? How are each of these parts designed and put together to make the car? We often forget about this little fact when we lazily wish for something, and that is why idle "wishing" never gets you anywhere. It is NOT because wishing is unimportant, but precisely because thought IS so important! As the computer scientists say, "garbage in, garbage out." Whether in a magical realm or in the physical universe, you have to know what you are about. This is why successful people in any endeavor have a vision, and why all things in the physical universe are a direct reflection of the thought forms which manifested them. Paradoxically, it is actually easier to manifest something in the physical universe than it would be if you had the power to instantly make your wishes come true, for someone else has already gone through the painstaking process of design and manufacture. All you have to do is vibrationally line yourself up with an already created object.

What is the main reason people don't manifest what is wanted?

In my personal experience with this material, I can tell you that almost without exception, the main stumbling block is the unhealthy comparison of what you are envisioning to the present reality, and the assessment of how you are faring relative to the accomplishments of others.

In life, it is vital to maintain your state of being in connection with your manifestation, even though there is no evidence of it yet!

Let's take Barb and Olga as an example. Both set up therapeutic massage parlors in the same town. Barb concentrates on creating a beautiful space and ensuring that every customer feels wonderful, but Olga is worried about the competition. She does a marketing survey that tells her there is not enough business to support two establishments, and is resentful of Barb. Olga carefully monitors Barb's customer count, and her own. She tracks improvements and techniques in Barb's shop, comparing them to hers, and follows the economic news carefully, reacting to downturns. Barb is blissfully unaware of Olga, however, and simply concentrates on the joy of running her shop.

Of course, it is impossible to predict whether Barb or Olga will be successful, that is a function of their individual vibrational makeup. Barb may be an airhead with no business sense, and fail miserably! But we can say one thing for sure: Olga isn't helping herself by concentrating on the things that could go wrong. The famous football coach, Bill Parcells, was asked one time about his "predictable" offense going into his first Super Bowl championship with the New York Giants. He said, (paraphrasing) 'I don't care if the other team knows what we're going to do. We know what we can do and we do it better than anyone else.'

How do you keep your focus when reality is completely the opposite?

One way is to simply appreciate what you already have that is in agreement with the vibration of the desired thing.

For example, a person who wants a bigger house, in the woods, might already appreciate the house she has, and the trees that already exist on her property. This process finds the vibrations of the desired thing in the present reality, emphasizes them, gets you resonating to them, and at the same time, deactivates the unwanted vibrations. It is different than looking at black and calling it white, for you'll discover that you are never completely removed from the things you want. If you have desired something for any length of time at all, there will be a slight bit of it already present! Now all you have to do is begin to find that good stuff amongst the stuff you don't want.

In other words, even a poor person has some money. Now all that is required is to emphasize the vibration of more money. A poor person is poor because he or she has been resonating more to lack of money than to a lot of money. A person who wants a new car probably already has a car, even if it's an old junker.

Most people have forgotten how to pretend, mainly because they have been educated out of it, and see no purpose in it. In school, we are taught to assimilate and regurgitate information, feeding the intellect and stifling the imagination. However, pretending is vital to the creative process, and to manifestation; and therefore, it is vital to life itself. If you can regard pretending as a vibrational process, then the whole thing becomes clear, powerful, and purposeful. The process of manifestation is just a change in vibrational orientation and emphasis, and that merely requires placing the attention in different areas and on different things. This shouldn't be hard, because the things you want are fun things! Otherwise you wouldn't want them.

However, if you find that the thing you want makes you feel rotten, then you have to back off. Somehow, you have got crosswise into the stream, and the flow of your desire is hitting you broadside, causing discomfort. However, it is always true that it *is never your desire that is out of position, but your considerations about it.* Even the most twisted "desire" has behind it a positive impulse, because the nature of desire is inherently positive. Even so, your beliefs may be so strong that it is impossible to find anything positive right now. If you want more money, for example, but are certain that it's not possible to get it, then focus on more money isn't a good thing. Try something else that you can feel good about and visualize that. It is better to focus on something you consider trivial and feel positive emotion than it is to struggle with something negative and get nowhere. Eventually you will discover, if you continue to find positive areas in which to focus, the highly resistive areas of your life will begin to thaw like ice exposed to a warm breeze.

All thought, desire, feeling (and eventually manifestation) is vibrational; therefore, bringing yourself to a place of positive emotion is important work. In our model, the distance between where you are and where you want to be is a vibrational distance, not a physical distance in space/time. Therefore, an increase in your vibration relative to *any* subject is beneficial in all areas.

Manifestation is the transfer or translation of a template of thought into physical form.

If you asked ten people "What is the main impediment to manifestation?" nine would probably say "money." But if you can't see a way to come up with the money, then what do you do? What if what you want has nothing to do with money? Like health for instance, or a relationship?

Money is just energy, and it vibrationally lines up with some of the things in this world (like houses and cars), and it doesn't line up with a lot of other things (like good health, or intelligence).

Even if you do not have money, you can still fulfill your desires, for all that is necessary is to line up your vibrational signal with what you want. HOW you manifest is a path that will be different for each and every person. I once knew a guy who desperately wanted a new car. He got a job as a salesman, and along with the job, came his brand-new car! It was not quite what the gentleman wanted though, for the car also came with something he didn't want: being on the road all day. This is an example of the old saying, "Be careful what you ask for, you might get it!" We do know, however, that what manifested for him was a precise match to his state of being, for asking is not a set of words spoken into the air. Although the spoken word is a series of vibrational sound impulses, what the universe responds to, in every moment of NOW, is the sum total of your thoughts, beliefs, attitudes, and feelings about anything. When the spoken word is aligned with what you are resonating to in your mind and heart, then your manifestations will match the spoken word. That is what is so confusing about trying to figure out how to run your life by observing others. What others say may not be their true vibration.

Some people put on a front to hide their intent from others, and even from themselves. Such people are doomed to a life of surprises, for their point of attraction is inconsistent with the mask they are using to live with. And so it may appear that the Universal Operating System is inconsistent or random, when it really isn't.

Most people will find that an application of the principles of the Universal Operating System to their lives will result in a gradual change for the better, as they begin to resonate more and more to what is wanted. The big mistake most people make is to compare their progress with those who are doing better, or who have seemingly manifested more quickly. One can never tell how long someone else has been working on lining up their energy toward something; a manifestation which pops into a person's life may have been the fulfillment of years of vibrational work and action cycles, even though it appears instantaneous to an outsider.

The point is, don't criticize your progress. The only way you can manifest anything is by continually resonating to the desired thing, because the Law of Vibration and the Law of like attracts like never cease to be operational. The laws of the universe, in other words, do not go on vacation.

Let's see what the dictionary says about delusion: "A false belief or opinion." In the synonym study it says, "Delusion implies belief in something that is contrary to fact or reality, resulting from deception, misconception, or a mental disorder (to have delusions of grandeur)." [Webster's New World Dictionary, College Edition, 1962].

The idea is that if you hold true to something in your mind and heart that does not match reality, you are a fruitcake.

Having said that, sometimes there really is a fine line between deliberate creation and delusion. The key to understanding where deliberate creation ends and delusional dishonesty begins is the guiding rudder of your emotions. Where are you on the Emotional Scale? The guy who claims to be abundant but regularly cannot pay his rent at the end of the month had better get some new thoughts! We live in a well-ordered universe however, and universal principles guarantee that as soon as you reach a better vibe not only will you feel better, but the conditions of your life will begin to improve. All you have to do is delusionally focus on the reality you want, and ignore the stuff that irks you. The more conscious you become, the easier it is to be aware of what you are feeling. What you are feeling is paramount, for it tells you the status of your vibration and how much resistant thought you're placing in your own way. Your feelings stem from your thoughts, your beliefs and your attitudes, which is to say, the choices you make and how you decide to BE. When you are down and out, you cannot expect to leap to joy real fast (unless you have practiced) so you are going to spend some time in the nether regions of emotion. However, as long as you are moving upward, it's OK.

Manifestation is a process of continually resonating to something wanted. That means a delusional refusal to acknowledge the things that are not wanted!

Delusion, like many things on this planet, is mis-defined. If I were a conspiracy theorist, I'd say that it was done on purpose, for the things we are taught as children are 180 degrees the opposite of universal principles. Are we just confused? My wife always says, "Never assign to malice that which can adequately be explained by stupidity." Maybe that is true.

The point is, it is truly delusional to continually resonate to unwanted things.

It is said that you have to fail a couple of times before you finally make it. The famous pizza maker, Tom Monaghan (Dominos Pizza ™), is a case history of this idea, but this is just another myth. All failures result from the misalignment of your energy toward the goal. In our culture, many people feel that they have to "pay their dues" first before abundance is deserved.

The cycle of failure and restart is often observed as an exercise in personnel, materials, and action cycles. Business models are developed to aid a person in his or her commercial venture, but really, such analysis is useful as a source of inspiration, but approaches the situation from the wrong angle. The action cycles and the movement of people and resources always results from the vibrational orientation of the participants. The executive or the business owner, if he or she is wise, will recognize that his role is to establish a vibrational orientation among the participants. Although it is impossible to violate the Law of Free Will, it IS possible to set an example that others will want to emulate.

The great leaders understand this either implicitly or explicitly. Gandhi led an entire nation to independence through his pure vibrational example, and became an inspiration to the world as well. He did not fight or protest against those who were opposed to his vision. He allowed, within himself, all thought and action because he was smart enough to realize he could not overcome the free will choices of every conscious being he had to deal with. Yet he was able to effect change on a grand scale. Gandhi understood that in order to change others, one must first change oneself.

We conclude by redefining delusion from "Perceiving as true, that which is not real," to "Paying attention to that which is in alignment with your desires, whether it is real yet or not."

Remaining true to your dreams is a prerequisite for attaining them. As the old song says, "You gotta have a dream, if you want to make a dream come true."

CHAPTER 10

A New Approach to Problem Solving

NOWHERE is understanding of the Universal Operating System more valuable than in dealing with problems. In this chapter we will tackle the subject of problems from a different perspective.

10.1 Handling Problems

A problem is something unwanted that has already manifested in the physical universe. It is something for which you see no immediate resolution, and it soaks up your attention, taking you out of the now moment. The common reaction to all problems is, "How do I find a solution?" However, this is the wrong question! Continuing to proceed in this way will just lead to more problems.

10.1.1 The Physics of Problems

AT first glance, the origin of a problem is clearly in the physical universe. The shipment that does not arrive on time, the lover who does not return phone calls, a lack of money to pay off the overdue loan. In our vibrational model, however, a problem shows up in the physical universe as an exact mirror to that which you have been focusing upon in thought, so a problem could be considered to be entirely self-created. It is a two-pole system, as we talked about before. You are at Pole A, and what you want is at Pole B; but you keep beating the vibrational drum of Pole A, which keeps you stuck at A! However, you are creating the two-pole system energetically. All that is necessary is to collapse one of the poles (preferably A!) and the voltage potential between them will disappear, destroying the conditions that have manifested the difficulty. Any dipole (separation of charges) creates a potential, which then creates a current, or energy flow. This energy flow keeps the problem alive.

What is the difference between having a problem and having a desire or a goal? The answer is, not much! Both involve a separation of energies or vibrations. The only distinction between the two is that a problem involves more focus on Pole A, and having a goal involves focus on Pole B.

Barb finally meets Mr. Right at the office and he agrees to call her that night at 8. Barb, however, does not really believe that he will call, because her previous boyfriends never did. She spends the rest of the day torn between two things: the desire for a good relationship, and the reality of past relationships. She keeps both opposing poles activated within her and by the time she gets home, she's feeling very anxious.

At eight she is nervously awaiting a call, but the phone is silent. When Pete does phone (20 minutes late) she is short with him, causing an uncomfortable conversation. Pete apologizes and says, "I had an international call to my mother in England," but Barb has heard all that before. "Just another excuse," she thinks. "All men really are bums." What has Barb done? She has long ago created Pole B, "a wonderful relationship," but she is right now re-creating Pole A in opposition, through her disbelief that it can happen. Barb sees herself at A once more, even though, through her continual creation of Pole B, she has finally rendezvoused with the perfect guy. As long as Barb stays at Pole A, she will continue to feed energy to the problem. Barb is engaging in a self-fulfilling idiocy, destroying her resonance to what she wants. We have all done it, for it is very difficult to let go of a vibration that has been activated for a long time, and has resulted in unwanted manifestations. Nevertheless, in order to achieve a goal one must focus on the goal, and not the difficulty!

Even though Pete is very interested in Barb, she is unnecessarily creating a problem. Her relationship with Pete will be successful to the degree that she focuses on Pole B, and is able to let go of Pole A.

In the following example we will see how a problem can be transcended by focusing on Pole B and ignoring the current reality at Pole A.

When Jill's big Christmas shipment does not arrive, she is upset. Jill has been promising her clients for weeks that everything is on time. Now she stands to lose 50% of her income for the entire year! It is her worst nightmare. After some reflection, however, Jill does not create Pole A. She calls every one of her customers, informing them of the difficulty and engaging in some creative customer relations. Jill is so cheerful about the situation – even during some angry and personally insulting outbursts from Hank, the volatile ABC Corporation rep – that all turns out well. Jill is so fired up by the end of the day that she gets the impulse to call the shipping company. With her new vibe focused on Pole B, she wangles a special delivery (at extra cost to her) albeit with a 36 hour delay. Tomorrow, however, she can call her clients with the good news. Jill then calls up Barb and takes her out to dinner.

Let's consider what might have happened had Jill remained upset:

Jill: "The %#@ shipment didn't arrive on time, I'm sorry but you're back-ordered."

Customer: "Back-ordered! You promised me! What am I supposed to tell my customers?"

Jill: #$@%!, it's not my fault! XYZ Trucking loaded the wrong pallets at the freight yard and it's going to take another week."

Customer: "That is totally unacceptable, I'm going to cancel and find my stuff elsewhere."

Jill: "You can't do that! We have a contract…." Etc.

After two hours of this, Jill is so stressed she goes home with her problem, and a big headache.

Problems persist (and recur) because you follow action paths that are determined by the vibration of the problem. This seems perfectly logical when you are immersed in the problem, because the solution is not available. Vibrationally speaking, you are nowhere near it. The guy who is working two jobs and still cannot make ends meet desperately thinks about a third job to bring in extra bucks, but he knows this really is not possible. However, he is unable to think of anything else. He is trapped, as long as his attention is within the frequency range of the problem.

Nevertheless, it is always possible to shift your focus, as Jill did (well, maybe after venting a little first!) The fact is, duality is built in to the physical universe; there is always a positive and negative end to every situation. There is no getting around that, and so life experience is just a choice of which end you pay attention to.

When you are stuck in a problem, it is important to understand that *the origin of the problem lies within you.* If you do not assign blame to others, or to circumstances beyond your control, you become empowered to handle it. The elements of the problem appear in the physical universe as a reflection of your vibration, but the problem is defined by which pole you choose to focus on. All problems, no matter how trivial or how significant, are self-created.

10.1.2 The Physics of Handling Problems

THE only way to deal with a problem is to place your attention there. We are all taught that in order to resolve life's difficulties, you have to get in there, look at every component of the problem, and take action to handle it. But what happens? Your focus, or attention, has been around the vibration of the problem for a significant amount of time. If you are like me, even though the problem is now solved, and even if you feel really good about what you have done, there may still be a little bit of your attention on it. You may wonder how the problem manifested itself and whether it might not come back again. And your wondering would have merit, for the reason you had the problem in the first place is because of an activated vibration within you.

The more you place your attention on problems, the more energy you give to them, and the more you draw yourself to the lower end of the Vibrational Scale, where all problems reside.

If another problem arises, you must again focus your attention on it in order to resolve it. You now have a habit of thought which will take you back to the place that is bothering you, every time a new problem arises. Ever so subtly, you develop a habit of fixing things that go wrong. And because it is "common knowledge" that something will always go wrong no matter how diligently you work to prevent them, you begin coping with life instead of enjoying life.

If you continue to operate in this way, the law of like attracts like guarantees that your range of awareness will shift lower. This phenomenon occurs so gradually it is not even noticeable.

When problem-solving leads to more problems like it, it is for this reason. A problem-solution pattern keeps you oscillating in the same range of frequencies – the vibration of problems – and you go from one problem to another.

In other words, by giving your attention to a problem, you place yourself in the vibrational range of the problem. Unless you are the type of person with a uniformly sunny and cheerful disposition – in which case you simply return to your normal place of positive emotion—you may be subject to "vibrational creep." This is how people eventually reach rock bottom.f Attention to problems and their resolution keeps pushing them further and further down the scale. It begins to seem that problems are simply inevitable, but this is not true at all!

I personally experienced this phenomenon during a twenty year period in my life, having been involved in a therapeutic process that was, with good intentions, designed to resolve trauma and erase negative incidents by going over and over them in attempt to discover their origins. Although this process can work miracles when a person is stuck in severe trauma, using it too liberally insidiously drew my vibration, incrementally and slowly, down the scale of emotions. Such a methodology must ultimately defeat itself, and so I began to look for more effective ways of problem solving.

It could be argued that once the problem is resolved you feel better, and you have actually raised your emotional level. That is true, at least temporarily. And in fact, I have noticed that some people like solving problems. Such a person thrives in a crisis, revels in the overcoming of obstacles, and so welcomes problems when they show up. A fellow of this sort has no trouble staying on the high end of his range, because he is approaching problems in a lighthearted manner, using his creative energies in a positive way to solve them. He or she may even be actively looking for problems! But for me, and for others I have observed, continually encountering and solving problems gets tiring.

"Vibrational creep" just means that every time a problem occurs, your natural response is drawn more powerfully to a lower vibration. This is natural, for the physical facts are now unassailable.

You begin training yourself to focus on the bad stuff! That is why problems can steamroll, why your life can get into a big mess. When your life gets like that, it feels like an evil spell. It feels like you are cursed. All that is happening is a simple consequence of the Law of Attraction: you are simply attracting more and more of what you focus on.

The usual method people employ to break this cycle is to take a break. Go on a vacation. Take a nap. Meditate. Get laid. Quit your job. If things get really bad you might even move to another city. However, you may notice that your life gradually begins to assume its old shape. Some of the same problems and difficulties begin to reappear, even though the people and the location has changed. Oh no, you think, I am cursed. The universe does not like me. That is the wrong conclusion – it is just your focus on the same things as before. You may pack up and leave, but you always carry your vibration with you! Your worry or anxiety about your issues will match you up with people and situations that are a direct match to your fears. Like a good and faithful servant, the universe assumes that if your attention is on something, you want it. The vibrational universe is set up to reward mindfulness and conscious awareness. You can't cop out and plea ignorance or stupidity! That might work with mom or dad, or your boss, or your spouse, but the operating system of the universe works 24/7, and it doesn't grant exceptions. Everyone is treated with scrupulous fairness.

10.1.3 A Better Way of Dealing With Problems

L ET's look at a better way, perhaps, of dealing with problems. If solving problems just brings on more problems like it, what can be done?

The first step in handling a problem is of course to be aware that you have a problem. Denying the physical manifestation is delusional, not because what manifests is so important, but because you ignore your own vibrational signal, which has resulted in the physical event. The second step is to ignore the problem as it is currently presented. The third and final step is to find something positive and focus your attention there. In other words, find Pole B instead of Pole A.

Now hold on there! If the bill collectors are coming to throw you out of the house, you had better quickly go out and get some money. These sorts of emergencies require immediate action; however, problems always start out as little ones and graduate to big ones. So there is always plenty of time to do something effective before the problem turns into a crisis. Ignore the difficulty when it first comes up, because that minor irritation is a sign you have been focusing on the negative.

The bigger the problem, the more difficult it is to extricate yourself from the vibration of the problem and the more urgent it will be to take immediate action. If the bill collectors are at your door, your options are limited! You have, in the past, devoted so much of your energy to the lower end that you are vibrationally stuck there. The problem now occupies so much of your attention that you can't even see a way out. It's called the blues, and if you have ever had the blues, you know what I'm talking about.

The first thing we are taught to do when noticing a problem is, "do something about it right away!" This usually involves lots of action cycles in order to erase it, overcome it, or get rid of it. But as we've already seen, this way of handling problems is never permanent.

10.1.4 The Solution

T HE process I am going to describe is not so much dealing with problems, as transcending them. You have to ignore the problem *as it is now presented to you in the physical universe*, even though it is staring you in the face. The problem is not a random event, but a direct result of your activated vibration. Therefore, continuing to focus on the problem is pointless, for you have already been doing so strongly enough to have generated a manifestation.

Even a band-aid fix requires you to come off the problem in order to handle it. The degree to which you do this determines how good your solution is. What usually happens is that the difficulty overwhelms you and you cannot think of anything outside the confining box of the problem. This is perfectly natural because the Law of Attraction is now operating to keep you vibrationally within the box. Your task is to break out!

If you cannot think of a solution, then you have to take your mind off the difficulty and reach for a better *feeling*. Often you cannot think of something because you are feeling upset; therefore, anything that makes you feel better, no matter how trivial, increases the likelihood of a solution.

This idea may seem batty, but that is because the problem and the solution are framed strictly as an intellectual exercise instead of a vibrational one.

"Let's see," you say. "Your solution to difficulty A is to focus on B, C, and D. That's pretty irrational." It does seem that way, doesn't it. But again, focusing on A when the problem is A, just brings you more of A. You have to get off A somehow, so moving your attention elsewhere will unstick you. Here we are advocating a vibrational shift over an intellectual shift of focus. An intellectual shift without a vibrational shift can only bring temporary relief! A desperate plan of action may involve a lot of frenzied activity, but it cannot provide a permanent resolution. That is because you never change the vibrational platform of attraction that caused the problem in the first place.

What did Jill do? After cussing out the shipping company for 15 minutes, she was smart enough to realize that her expression of such lower emotions was useless. Jill knew that shipping schedules were impossibly tight; nevertheless, she forced herself up the emotional scale to the point that a tendril of hope became available. Then she began calling customers with the attitude that *something* good will happen, even though she did not know what it was or how it could possibly occur.

How did Jill accomplish the inflow phenomenon of raising her emotional level? That is to say, how do you place your attention on something good when you are feeling rotten? That is the million-dollar question, and it is the crux of problem solving. It is the subject of countless self-help books and therapeutic procedures. It is impossible to give a pat or systemic answer that will work every time for everyone. That is because at all times, the choices you make will determine how you feel and will mark the trail of your experience. You always have choices, for there is a new moment of NOW every instant! As a conscious being, you have complete control of your personal life force; no one but you has the power to regulate the status of your vibrational signal to the universe at large. Your work, not only in problem solving but also in life itself, is to become more mindful, more aware of who you really are! An understanding of the eternal nature of consciousness and the vibrational universe concept makes the job easier.

The first thing you have to do is accept that the problem is *yours*. Blaming others for your predicament is senseless, for such an orientation cannot lead to a successful outcome.

10.1.5   Raising Your Emotional Level

THE second step is to get off the problem vibrationally, by raising your emotional level.

If you have to vent, then vent, for that can lead to a blowing off of negative emotion and raise you up the scale. In other words, anger is a much higher emotion than apathy, so getting angry is appropriate. But don't spend too much time there!

All positive solutions must first begin with a positive focus. It is not possible to create a positive outcome when you are in a lower emotion; the two are vibrationally incompatible! Remember, the scale of emotion is actually a scale of vibration, and your activated vibration determines your point of attraction. Therefore, raising your emotional level is not some pointless irrelevancy! Going up the scale increases the intellectual function and your ability to dream up a logical and satisfying outcome. It increases the likelihood of a successful plan of action.

You can bootstrap yourself up the emotional/vibrational scale playing a game developed by Esther Hicks, called "What thought feels better." Jill might start with something like this: "That shipment darn well better arrive on time." That didn't do anything, just reminded her of the fact that her customers are really going to be upset, and it made her more upset as well. But it's a place to start! It establishes the vibrational baseline from which to operate. In this case, anger. Jill tries to be optimistic and asserts, "I WILL get that shipment on time," but this doesn't make her feel any better. It is an example of an affirmation about something wonderful, made from a place of feeling rotten. It is "magic think," and it ain't never going to happen. Most people at this stage just give up. "Oh what's the use, this is just making me feel worse." Well, you are feeling rotten anyway, why not carry on a bit more? So Jill tries something else: "DEF Shipping has always come through for me before." That is a good try, but it doesn't help much. It is a shocking reminder that the formerly reliable company let her down at the most crucial point of the business cycle.

Now is the time when it's really tempting to quit, for she isn't getting anywhere. At this point, however, Jill is like the guy pushing a car out of the snow. She has her vibrational vehicle rocking back and forth a little, and even though nothing exciting is happening, the car's inertia is being overcome. Suddenly, Jill remembers something: "Joe Schmoe had the same problem last year, and DEF sent a special truck." That feels a little better, until she remembers that Joe's problem occurred in the middle of August, not at Christmas! But Jill is beginning to jar her emotional vehicle out of the rut. She can feel it. Jill thinks, "I am a very loyal customer of DEF Shipping. That ought to count for something." That feels a little better, but Jill knows that Lazlo at DEF is a hard man to deal with. "I have never asked DEF for a favor before. I am a small customer, but I know my business is appreciated." Now things are starting to move toward the positive. There is less focus on the negative. "There is no reason I can't get a special delivery. A good customer is valued and DEF will want to keep me happy. Otherwise I'll badmouth them to everyone!" Now that is starting to feel good. Jill sees the cigar-smoking Lazlo on his knees, begging her not to leave him, and she laughs out loud. Jill has raised her emotional level to a point where her predicament no longer feels like a problem. She has genuinely (not delusionally) transferred her focus from Pole A to Pole B. She has reached step three, where a rational and effective outcome is possible.

What are you doing here? As Esther Hicks says, giving yourself a sales job. A lot of people would scoff and say "This process lacks integrity. You're just kidding yourself." That is exactly what is happening. You are raising your emotional level in order to alter your point of attraction. Instead of arguing for your limitations, you are breaking free of them!

What difference does it make what excuse you use to feel good? Does feeling good mean you are fooling yourself, even if your present circumstances are not optimum? Would you rather feel rotten, and continue to experience what you don't want? Does integrity mean holding to something that is true, even if that truth is making you miserable? "Well, Jill is just lying to herself. Lazlo is a jerk and DEF already said they haven't got any spare trucks." One thing is certain: Jill cannot get anywhere with that attitude!

The hard part about this process, about any self-help process, is the tendency to focus on the truth, instead of what you want. In other words, if you have a crummy job, what is TRUE is that your job sucks. What you WANT is a better job. Most people can't take their attention off the truth long enough to change their vibe and begin resonating to something better. That is understandable, for our Western societies are based upon the idea of empirical proof. Like the guy from Missouri (the "show me" state) who says, "I'll believe it when I see it," we are taught that only what has already manifested is important. However, by paying attention to the truth (even when it is a rotten truth) we continue to create our lives from what is not wanted! That is a trap. In order to create something better in your life, you have to be more dedicated to feeling good than to observing the truth.

Feeling good is not some meaningless airhead idea. It is the natural tendency for all conscious beings and practicing it produces definable vibrational effects, which can then lead to concrete manifestations. In problem solving, it leads to an avoidance of problems altogether.

It is not possible to change the conditions of your life without first changing your state of being. Therefore, this simple little game, seemingly trivial on the surface, is actually quite powerful if you just give it a shot.

With the "what thought feels better" game, you do not need to wait until you notice something that bugs you. In fact, it is far more effective to play the game when you are feeling good, for then you have access to a much higher vibrational range.

If you play the game when you already feel positive emotion, you can more easily raise your habitual vibration up the scale. Most people will not see the point of practicing feeling good when you already feel good, but I can tell you that it is possible to feel better than you ever imagined, with just a little effort. That is because the higher vibrations are lighter and are easier to change.

The only way to deactivate an unwanted vibration is to activate another in its place. In a vibrational universe, it is impossible to erase, destroy, or eliminate something unwanted. The instant you place your focus on something to deal with it, you have activated it! Like the guy stuck in a bog, the more he struggles to extricate himself, the faster he goes in. Therefore, the most effective way to permanently raise your emotional level (and thus avoid problems altogether) is when you are in the positive emotional range.

Have you ever tried to teach your kids to be nice to each other when they are fighting? The time to teach someone is when he or she is receptive. The time to work on feeling good is when you already feel good. If you can keep your attention more and more on things that please you, the Law of Attraction will go to work for you more often. You can get on a roll that is absolutely awesome.

I have found that a continual application of this process works miracles. Your old problems simply disappear; you do not even need to handle them. They disappear because you are no longer attracting them. You are in a different frequency range and those old difficulties are now out of range. Moreover, the manifestations that accompany such frequencies are no longer matching up with you.

Transcending problems in this manner will lead to a smoother life experience, and difficulties that do arise will be of a milder nature. You will find yourself handling life with more and more aplomb.

If you are aware that consciousness is the senior factor in any problem and that a successful outcome is always possible, you will be able to proceed with confidence. In our model, consciousness created the universe to experience in it, and so a resolution to all problems must begin with conscious choices.

CHAPTER 11

What is Truth?

11.1 What Is Truth, Really?

EVERY thinking person has pondered this question since the dawn of time. It has led to the idea that there is a universal truth or one truth that is consistent throughout the universe. The idea is that once a person discovers universal truth or THE truth, instant enlightenment will follow. There are many avenues to Truth; meditation, science, martial arts, music, the list is almost endless. But how do you know when you have it?

The minimum requirement for a state of enlightenment is a feeling of positive emotion. In other words, if a person is not somewhere in the positive range of the Emotional/Vibrational Scale, it would be hypocritical to claim enlightenment. One might claim great knowledge, but in my experience, knowing lots of data does not make one wise, or happy. In fact, I spent a lot of my life studying books, but it never made me feel much better.

Truth then, whether universal or personal, must be something that feels good. The problem is, is there one Truth that feels good to everyone? Maybe, but identifying it would be very difficult. If you ask ten people about an event, inevitably there will be ten different descriptions. This leads me to think that each person has his or her own, personal, truth. I think we are on safe ground if we describe Truth as personal to each individual, since people can't seem to agree, throughout history, on a Universal Truth. So let us say that Universal Truth, if it exists, is not definable in a way that will make everyone happy. Let's say that Truth, personal or universal, must be something that feels good to you. If we do not make this assumption, then we are forced to admit that ultimate Truth is something that feels rotten, and this is itself an irrational and delusional statement.

Of course, there are plenty of negative people who seem to concentrate on beating themselves (and others) up, in making themselves (and others) feel as miserable as possible. But if you do a little probing you will discover, beneath all of that, uninspected beliefs or ideas. Once a person is aware of these unidentified beliefs, they blow off and he or she feels much better, and the irrational conduct is lessened or goes away.

Persons who feel good act more rationally than those who do not.

The criminal, the neurotic, the insane, are always unhappy people.

Therefore truth (and rationality) must have something to do with positive emotion. There must be a direct connection between rationality and feeling. This means there is a direct connection between logic and feeling. A logician would laugh at this idea. Traditionally logic is defined as purely mental, totally divorced from feeling. But I wonder why the logician delves into logic? I think that if the logician were being truthful, he would have to finally admit that he studies logic because it feels good to him. Ultimately, it is not logic, or rationality, that is the reason for living, but feeling.

How to apply this idea to everyday life?

Let's say that in one month you are going to be laid-off from your present place of employment. You have two job offers, and another choice to be self-employed. One of the job offers, at a large corporation, comes with a 20% increase in salary, but it is administrative and you are not looking forward to the endless meetings and paperwork. The other job offer is with a small company, and the environment is attractive, but requires a 30% cut in pay. The other opportunity is to join a group of friends starting their own company. The risk is enormous because the company might fail, but the upside is also tremendous. After two weeks of intensive thought, you still cannot make up your mind. You are in an agony of indecision. Logic will not work for you in this situation, because the future is not predictable! We have all made decisions based upon logic alone, only to see the future yield a result which was totally unforeseen.

If you apply the idea of personal truth to this situation, you choose the one that makes you feel better. *The truth is always that which makes you feel the best, regardless of the "facts."*

This may seem, itself, to be an irrational suggestion. If all of the facts point to the job with the pay increase, then that's the logical and best choice. But what if you feel your gut tightening at the idea? That crummy feeling is your internal guidance system giving you a warning.

The truth always feels better, because the truth is a connection to your true self.

Sometimes we lose that connection in our daily grind, and when we do, stress, anxiety, and a general sense of the lack of well-being pervades our experiences.

Personal Truth can be defined as "those thoughts and actions that lead to a feeling of well-being."

That is simple, and can be applied on a practical basis to everyday life. Esoteric philosophy, metaphysics, advanced mathematics, abstruse logic, meditation, etc. are all roads to personal enlightenment, but are not applicable to the everyday person. However, even the genius can apply this simple, powerful concept of personal truth.

11.2   What Is Truth Part II — Validity

WHAT do you consider valid? What is your idea of what is important?

I ask these questions because so many people are concerned with the truth, even though attention to the truth is making them miserable.

In part I, we decided that truth must be something that feels good, but were not able to define it. We will say, for the purposes of this discussion, that truth is what can be observed. Not everyone will agree, but it is a definition that most people can understand.

Truth, then, is what is. It's the stuff right in front of your face. The chair the office is truth, so is the desk, the computer, the phone, the building we are in, the sun, etc. The murder on the news last night is truth. It happened, did it not? The polluted stream near the local factory is also truth.

In fact, there are as many truths as there are things to observe. Therefore, we may say that the world is filled to the brim with literally millions of truths, many of them horrible and despicable, many of them beautiful and wonderful. It is up to us, which of these truths we choose to place our attention on. A simple and life-giving solution is to place your attention upon those truths that make you feel good, and ignore the others.

"Hey," your friend Joe says, "did you hear about the earthquake?"

"Yes. Boy I really feel good today!"

"Yeah, but did you see the murder last night on TV? And Danny got his hand stuck in the car door. He had to go to the hospital today."

"Uh huh. Did you see the beautiful sunrise this morning?"

"What's wrong with you?" Joe says, "I'm serious here. You know, oil prices could go up if another war begins in the Middle East."

"Last night I saw a cardinal on the bird feeder," you reply. "He was really beautiful."

Your friend shakes you.

"Wake up! You got your head in the sand. It's time to face reality Johnny boy"!

"I am facing reality!"

"Are you kidding me? We got another war, food and oil prices are going up and you're talking about sunrises and cardinals???"

"It all depends on what reality you want to face."

Joe shakes his head and walks away. You notice him talking to the other office mates and they are all glancing in your direction, shaking their heads worriedly.

Most people like to focus on negative truths.

Even if it is true that a war in the Middle East is imminent, or that food and oil prices might go up, or that there was a murder last night, or that an earthquake killed 5,000 people last week, that is no reason to focus on them. There are thousands of times as many positive truths as negative ones! We just do not notice them. This is called the can't-see-the-forest-for-the-trees syndrome.

When Joe takes a walk outside, he does not really see the beautiful cloud patterns or feel the wind on his face, or see the sunlight falling on the flower garden across the street. He immediately notices the garbage can in the street however, a remnant from the morning's trash pickup. "Damn garbage man," he thinks. "Why can't they just put the empties back on the grass?"

Joe is a good citizen and considers it his duty to stay informed, and diligently watches the news and reads his newspaper, even though he often feels disheartened at the state of world affairs. Joe, like a lot of people, simply does not understand the value of focusing on positive truths. That's probably because, like a sore thumb, the bad stuff sticks out so glaringly.

The earth is a balanced place in which well-being is everywhere. The planet spins on its axis, the sun shines every day, the weather distributes moisture, the apple seed grows to be an apple tree and not a tomato; the list is endless. The forces of nature that assure balance are enormous! While it is true that mankind has created areas of blight, these aren't even a pimple on a pickle in comparison.

But for some reason, people think that anything that *can* be observed deserves attention.

Out of the millions of truths that exist upon our planet, only those that are negative are thought to have real importance. If you do not place your attention on these "important" events, you are considered to be irresponsible. Wars, murders, diseases and disasters are all considered far more important than the unnoticed well-being which surrounds us.

Why is this?

Because we have been trained to think that ignoring the negative stuff will lead to our ruin. In this way, we are taught always to seek out the bad before it can lead to harm. In the United States, there is a saying: "Freedom requires vigilance." However, as we have seen, this philosophy is a self-fulfilling idiocy.

It is important to understand that the mere *belief* in such a philosophy is enough to generate a manifestation. In other words, it is only necessary for such a meme to be inserted into the mass consciousness for it to become an established mode of *behavior.* Then such behavior is reinforced by the concept of *tradition,* and you have the history of planet earth for the past 5,000 years. And in a society which considers that only physical proof establishes legitimacy, one is *required* to assign validity to that which exists! It is now only necessary to *point out* (through mass media) the undesirable actions of others in order to keep the masses imprisoned in a jail of self-limiting thought. Here is a powerful, circular and self-reinforcing system that does not require force for its implementation. In this way, entire populations can be kept on edge, in a state of constant anxiety and fear. It is an elegant system of population control, on a massive scale.

Because mankind looks at the physical world as a zero-sum game with a few big winners, a few big losers and the rest of us lumped in the middle (the famous Bell curve), we have developed congruent philosophies of life. Most feel life events are random; humans are like molecules in a compressed gas, and you can never tell which one you might bump against next. As we said before, solutions are always developed which reflect the dominant vibrational orientation. Our science and our philosophies perfectly mirror the conception of a universe and a life in which individuals are at effect-point, making the best of a world with limited resources. Individual efforts are seen as struggles against the odds, each person battling against universal forces which, if not controlled, will eventually overwhelm us. That is why we form groups; for in our combined efforts we may, perhaps, overcome such larger influences. In probability and statistics, individuals are treated as data points and weighed equally. Individual success is explained as the result of genius (a scarce resource, probably a result of genetic inheritance), hard work, or luck. Consciousness does not appear, cannot appear, in such a system, for it is subjective and immeasurable.

With this mindset, it is obvious that if danger is ignored, then individuals are sitting ducks, unprepared for the assault of randomly generated forces. The reasoning goes, if several murders are committed downtown, then maybe the next time I go downtown I might be killed.

But this sort of thinking is muddle-headed.

The only way you could be murdered downtown is if you had been focusing upon it for a long enough time to have created a strong resonance to it.

All that is necessary is to decide which of the many millions of truths out there you want to have in your experience. Do you want to focus on murders, or beautiful sunsets, on war and rising oil prices, or cardinals, on the good stuff, or the bad stuff?

"But," you say, "If oil prices go up and you are ignorant of it, then you may go to the gas station one day and find it is empty. But I will have stockpiled gasoline."

Well, in the first place, if things got that bad everyone would know about it. In the second place, the price of oil is out of the hands of individuals. Your attention to the possibility of no oil will just make you feel crummy, and orient your thoughts and feelings around that possibility, without doing a thing to affect oil prices or availability. Then, if you do this long enough, you may find yourself in an area that is short of gasoline!

The guy that concentrates on the cardinal and the sunset (and, in general, on pole B instead of pole A) is in perfect alignment with universal energy, and so will always find himself in a place of well-being.

Whatever you pay attention to you eventually experience. So it is actually better to focus on irrelevant truths like cardinals and sunsets than it is to focus on serious and important truths like wars and rising prices.

This idea is exactly backwards of traditional teachings. In the fable "The Ant and the Grasshopper" – which illustrates the pleasure principle vs. the reality principle – the fun-loving grasshopper plays around all summer while the ant works very hard accumulating food for the winter. When the feel-good grasshopper comes knocking on ant's door after the first freeze, begging for food, the ant self-righteously turns him away. The moral of the story is, of course, that positive emotion and fun lead to ruin and serious hard work wins the day. In "The Three Little Pigs," only the third and oldest pig has learned to behave in accordance with the reality principle. He learns to put work first, before play, and is able to protect himself from the big bad wolf, who is not able to blow down his sturdy brick house. (Of course, we don't see what happens next. The wolf, infuriated, waits for the pig to come out of his house and attacks him. That is what eventually happens when you attempt to protect yourself from something).

These idiotic tales, born from mankind's stubborn insistence on scarcity and lack, are just examples of how memes get passed on, stupidly, from one generation to the next.[32] There isn't anything you can do in a lower emotion that you cannot do better in a positive emotion! No one bothers to tell children (at least in fables) that it is possible to work at something you love.

It's up to you! Do you want to choose misery or joy? Pain or happiness?

The world is stuffed full of truths of every description.

Choose those truths that make you feel good, and the world will slowly change around you in a positive direction.

11.3   What is Truth Part III — Prove It!

M ANY practical people would say that truth is what can be observed. If someone asserts something as true, they will say "Prove it!" and what they mean by proof is, "Does it exist?" or "Can it be demonstrated?" which is the same thing.

But this is the wrong question!

What exists is the result of the decisions and conclusions of conscious beings.

On a personal level, a conscious being can affect the conditions of his/her life. By utilizing the infallible law of like attracts like in life, it is possible to prove this assertion to yourself with no great difficulty. Merely by changing your attitude towards an area of life, you may alter an unwanted condition and change it for the better.

If you have not consciously conducted this experiment, it will not be real to you, and if you have, you will never doubt it. Experience is the best teacher.

From the above assumptions, the following is a logical conclusion:

Truth is not what manifests. Truth is not what exists. Truth is not a material object.

Truth is the decisions and conclusions of conscious beings.

---

[32] How about this silly "Nursery Rhyme/lullaby:"
Rock a bye baby, On the tree top, When the wind blows, The cradle will rock
When the bough breaks the cradle will fall, And down will come baby, cradle and all.
Let's see...baby will come crashing down out of the tree...very inspirational!

In other words, *what we observe around us is not the truth. It is the result or product of truth.*

Looking to matter and energy for proof that something is true is like saying the cart draws the horse. It is the consciousness of the horse that directs the cart. Such logic places effect before cause.

Cause is consciousness, the animating principle of the universe; effect is matter and energy.

On planet earth, there is always a time lag between the desire for something, and the manifestation of it. To say, "in order for *A* to be true it must be manifested, and since *A* has not manifested, it is not true" is to ignore the fact that it is the aligning of thought toward the goal (with its accompanying time lag), which is the cause of the manifestation!

When people say, "prove it" they mean "manifest your assertion instantly," or, "indicate an already manifested physical object or condition." Unless you are a very advanced being indeed you will not be able to do the former, and if what you want to create has not yet been created, it will be impossible to demonstrate the latter. However, that is no reason to stop the creative process! To use the idea that "it has not yet manifested" as a reason to give up on your dream, is to cease the process by which that dream will come into physical existence. (A thought form exists; therefore, a creative visualization is already concrete. In our model, even matter and energy is ultimately composed of thought; dreams and visualizations are the blueprint for physical action and eventual manifestation).

The society we live in represents the combined manifestations of all of the thought forms from every conscious being in it. The world looks a lot different now than it did 500 years ago. However, the stuff we see around us has no special meaning other than a demonstration of how consciousness has aligned its energy in the past.

For a conscious being to manifest a desire, it is necessary to align thought toward that desire until manifestation occurs. Manifestation will always occur, and is occurring, as a result of thought. Action always follows thought, and thought is a creation of consciousness.

The vision of a universe that had its growth cycle established from a set of initial conditions at the beginning of the universe doesn't make much sense. In the first place, no cosmologist has ever figured out where all of the energy of the universe came from. Science hasn't even figured out where all of the energy in the universe IS, or even what it is. Feynman has said, in his Lectures on Physics, (p. 4-2) "It's important to realize that in physics today, we have no knowledge of what energy *is*."

They call it dark matter and dark energy but nobody has satisfactorily explained what this is and how it came from those initial conditions at the beginning of the universe. The law of conservation of energy states that energy can neither be created nor destroyed; therefore, the universe must have originated in a singularity, but then of course where did the energy of the singularity come from? Usually this leads to logically prior entities or energies, or parallel universes, but then we must ask how these were created as well. The fact is, something cannot come from nothing! So what passes for truth may not be truth at all; in fact, it may merely be the speculation of conscious beings. Ultimately, all questions about the origin of the universe come back to a causative, creative principle, and so ultimately, truth must be related or associated with that animating principle.

Truth is not only personal, but depends upon one's ability to recognize cause and effect. The source point of all activity in the life of a conscious being is the consciousness of the being! The resulting conditions in which the life is lived is the result.

If someone is telling you that your truth is invalid because it has yet to materialize, do not pay any attention to them! The only way you can manifest is to hold to your vision, which is the same thing as saying, holding your vibration to that of your desire. This is easily done by imagining what it would FEEL like to live your dream. Since a feeling is nothing more than a vibrational pattern of energy, by finding the feeling you are vibrationally matching to your desire. Continuing to do this will eventually result in the manifestation, for a manifestation is more about attaining a vibrational match to the goal than it is a mechanical series of action cycles. Effective action follows effortlessly from a true alignment to the goal.

Persons who demand proof are mixing up cause and effect. It is not necessary to prove anything to anyone. All that is necessary for manifestation is an understanding that a conscious being is the source point, and the manifestation is the result point. Once this is understood, no one will be able to sway you from the realization of your desire.

11.4   What Is Faith?

HAVING been brought up Catholic, I grew weary of hearing the phrase, "You must have faith." Someone would always say that after I had tried and tried to get something I wanted, without success. Having faith became, to me, associated with failure.

"If at first you don't succeed, try, try again." That's another one I always hated to hear.

It seemed people would recommend faith to me after they already knew I was not going to succeed. It was their way to make me feel better, but in my mind, it was recognition of my incompetence.

Yet, faith is a concept that has been with mankind for millennia. In order for something to survive that long in the consciousness of the species, there must be some benefit or survival value to it!

Let's look at faith in relation to the Universal Operating System.

Faith could be defined as: holding to what is desired purely, without allowing thoughts or feelings contradictory to it.

Because the universe will answer your thoughts and feelings with more of the same, it is important to offer them purely, without unnecessary doubt or contradiction.

You just have to begin to apply this idea and watch what happens. Hopefully, you have already begun to practice the alignment of thought towards the positive, and have noticed at least some little improvement. Once you begin to see your life change, you will never doubt it, and having faith will become easier and easier. Faith should be a fun process, because logically, your thoughts (and feelings) will now be geared toward those things that bring you joy.

Here is an example: last winter I was writing full time and not working at all. Although my books were selling at this point, it wasn't enough to pay the bills each month. So I dreamed up a contracting job that would pay well and last a minimum of six months, enough time to finish my book. For the next couple of days I continued to create this idea and then let it go. I even had a dream about it, so it was pretty well established in my consciousness. Two weeks later I received a phone call from a contractor who wanted me to work with him on an exciting project which would pay well and last between six months and two years! This co-incidence was remarkable because I performed no action cycles whatsoever. I made no phone calls, did no promotion; nothing except send out a vibrational signal to the universe and maintain it. It was effortless!

This is the opposite of what I learned in religion classes. I learned that faith is very difficult, achieved only through great diligence. And it IS difficult, if what you are attempting to achieve doesn't line up with what YOU want. If you are trying to achieve goals others have set for you, instead of the ones you've set for yourself, faith can indeed be arduous.

For instance, I was taught in religion class that my elders were always wiser and smarter than I, and that it was the duty of a child to obey parents, teachers, and authority figures. I was taught that helping others is saintly, and doings things for oneself is selfish. So I lived my life like a good little citizen, molding my thoughts and beliefs to others and living in fear of a misstep. I was compliant, helped others, ignored my own needs, and was miserable! But it was OK, I reasoned, because my soul was being purified and a great reward lie waiting for me at the end of my life, if I would only believe.

I know, most people are smarter than that, but it took me a long time to understand the proper role of faith in my life.

It is much better to have faith in yourself than to have faith in another, for you are divine, a little piece of God walking around on earth. So when you have faith in yourself, you have faith in God as well.

I have to admit, it angers me to have swallowed that stuff for so long, while others, like my friend Randy the millionaire, have gone on their merry way since childhood, creating lives of passion, joy and abundance for themselves (and others). Like the hard-working ant, I had only contempt for the happy grasshopper. It took me decades to finally figure out that not only was the grasshopper really having fun, but he was lots more productive than me as well. Oh well. Better late than never, as the saying goes!

There are two flavors of faith, one which is associated with religion, and the other associated with the creative process. My mistake was confusing the former with the latter.

Faith is a powerful concept in any creative endeavor, for it keeps you aligned to the goal. In other words, "having faith" is just holding your vibration in the place you want it. However, in order to make faith work you have to do a little sales job on yourself at the beginning, and get yourself in the right frame of mind to start the ball rolling. In other words, if you have been creating negatively in an area for years, you first have to overcome vibrational inertia. But this inertia is all within the scope of your control, for your vibrational signal is generated on the reflexive flow. The universe's responses come on inflow but are entirely dependent upon the vibrational action on the reflexive flow alone. You are the initiator of everything you experience.

You also have to overcome the fatalistic tendency to regard the solid stuff around you as immovable and unchanging. The unfulfilling relationship, job, or lifestyle seems stuck in place, but it is there only as a consequence of your unchanging vibrational signal. Change that, and your life will change as well.

Having faith is allowing the law of like attracts like to work in your favor. In order to see the vibrational matching property of the law of "like attracts like" at work in your life, begin with something trivial, like finding a model of car you like. I chose Audis because they are not so common. Soon I was noticing Audis everywhere! I had no idea there were so many guys with Audis around. You could say "the Audis were there all the time, you just didn't notice them before." Well, it's a little deeper than that.

The Audis might have been there, but I did not see them. If you are not aware of something, you cannot access or use it. Therefore, it is invisible and does not exist for you. It's like having a database but no index into the database. You may have lots of data, but you cannot get to it. That is how the process of conscious creation works. When you deliberately create your vibrational signal, you become aware of the universe's responses and can take advantage, like Rick did with Bill. Otherwise, you are 'blind' to something that may already be right in front of your nose. Swami Muktananda expressed this idea when he said (paraphrasing) 'In order to know God, you must keep God in the forefront of your consciousness.'

It turns out that the more attention you pay to something, the more of it actually arrives in your experience. You have to find this out for yourself however, by experimentation in the laboratory of life.

11.4.1 Faith vs. Hope

MANY people associate faith with hope. Hope is an entirely different thing from faith. If you have gotten to the stage where you are hoping, you have almost lost the game!

Hope could be defined as trying to get what you want from a place where you are pretty sure you aren't going to get it.

Hope usually comes after you're already discouraged: "Oh, I so much want to buy a house, but the mortgage is too expensive. I hope that one day I can." When you are hoping, you are hanging on to just a thread of desire. This vibration is more about lack of a house than having a house! If you think over times in your life when you were hoping for something, you will find that almost always you weren't very confident of a positive outcome.

I'm not trying to bad-mouth hope! Hope is a lot better than being completely discouraged. When you are hoping, there is still some focus upon what is wanted. It is a good place to start the creative process.

But faith is a much stronger feeling. Faith will never fail to get you where you want to go, because faith means a vibration unsullied and unhindered by contradictory thoughts and feelings. Faith is purely holding your vision so that you may come together in time and space with the people and resources you need in your creative process.

Faith is more consonant with expectation than hope. A feeling of expectation occurs when there is vibrational alignment with something and, even if there is no evidence of it yet, there is confidence that it is just a matter of time.

11.4.2 Holding the Vision

THE hardest part of having faith is continuing to hold the vision through every stage of the creative process, even though the goal has not yet been attained. That only happens, however, when you want something because you think that you cannot be happy without it. This is exactly backwards and will always result in failure, because it places material objects as cause-point and you at effect-point. It uses the creative process wrong-end-forwards, for the creative energy of the universe is the animating principle itself.

In our vibrational model, no goal is ever attained *unless* it is accompanied by a proper vibrational orientation. In fact, it is that vibrational orientation, that wonderful feeling inside you, which is the ultimate goal. That feeling is what makes your action cycles effective, and lines you up with the people and resources you need, for it exists within every one of your advertisements, every one of your creations and will accompany you on every sub-goal in the achievement of the objective. All creation comes forth from consciousness, and is maintained by a conscious orientation towards it. Matter and energy is just the clay, you are the molder and sculptor of the clay!

Worry comes from the idea that you might not get the wanted thing and causes a disconnect from life force energy, which makes you feel worse, which makes you worry some more...this is what happens when you identify your happiness with something outside yourself. When you worry, you focus on something unwanted, thereby becoming an attractor for it.

So why do we worry even though we know that it is irrational, and that it doesn't help? Because we do not understand that a human being is primarily consciousness associated with a physical body, and that consciousness interfaces with other consciousness and the universe's operating system. We do not even acknowledge the importance of the animating principle, even though it has designed and created the universe! We look for proof to matter and energy, and fail to consult the powerful, positive energy of our own life force.

We are told that the basis of life is biological, and anything to do with consciousness is ephemeral and therefore irrelevant, a secondary phenomena of brain function. We have no idea how powerful we are, for our religions and our philosophies assert that man is an irrelevant nothing, living on an isolated planet on the edge of an insignificant galaxy in an infinite universe. Science tells us that life was a happy accident, a random and accidental conglomeration of chemicals, and that the universe will eventually either expand and cool and die, or shrink in on itself, destroying all life within it. When you look at life from the viewpoint of consciousness however, you understand that you are eternally self aware and you connect with your own life force. When you do that it generates a feeling of power and joy within, and you feel like a god! Half the battle of faith is having a proper comprehension of who you really are. Of course, if you have never felt the powerful nature of your own life force, you will not have a clue what I'm talking about. But then you probably wouldn't be reading this book either, so it doesn't matter.

When you are absolutely clear about what you want, when you have a goal and a vision AND you are filled with positive emotion, you are unstoppable, and what you desire is as inevitable as turning on a garden hose. Even if the hose is very long and you have to wait a while, you KNOW the water will eventually find its way to your nozzle.

However, if you are the type of person who just wants the stuff, faith (the Law of Attraction) cannot work, for you will never connect to the feeling of the desire, and therefore you will never, vibrationally, come off of where you're at. "Hey, I want a new car and a lot of money, so if faith really works, I'll just think about it for a while and, by magic, I'll have it." Sorry, it does not work that way! With this attitude, you will always be at A, looking towards B. You will never connect to that life giving feeling of joy and well being that is always associated with a desire that is in alignment with your true Self. And all of your actions will reflect your position at A, looking towards, but never reaching the goal. Like a donkey led on by a carrot and a stick, what you want will always be just out of reach.

The magic is not in the car or the money, the magic is connecting to the life force energy in your desire, and the fantastic feeling that comes with it. Then, as you follow your hunches, as you get inspired to take action, you will inevitably be led down the path of least resistance. The distance to any manifestation, as we've said before, is a vibrational distance, not a distance in time and space which can be overcome solely through action cycles. Without lining yourself up vibrationally toward the goal, manifestation is impossible. The magic of the creative process is the priceless feeling of joy and excitement in the journey! And at the end the satisfaction of a job well done, but traveled along a path filled with enjoyment, excitement, and learning.

In the spirit-mind-body framework the spirit, or consciousness, of a human being is primary. In our vibrational model of the universe, we are more vibrational than we are physical beings. Manifestation is just you and the thing you want existing at the same place and time, and that cannot possibly happen unless there is first a vibrational co-incidence. You can walk into the automobile dealership with $5 in your pocket and stand next to that shiny new Porsche, but you can't drive out with it, unless there is vibrational attunement. Most people will say, "No, it's about the money, stupid." No, it's not about the money. Money represents vibrational alignment. People who have money are aligned to abundance and people who don't, aren't. "No, people are abundant because they have money, you fool." No, that's backwards as well. Money is a physical representation of vibrational alignment with prosperity. Personally, I couldn't care less what I drive, but if you want a Porsche you must first vibrationally align to one.

The meeting in time and space in the physical universe of you and what you want is, according to our model, a meeting and matching of vibration, because the physical object itself has a vibrational footprint. In other words, that Porsche in the dealership started out as a bunch of mud. It was first designed by human beings, and every one of its parts was manufactured by human hands and carries the vibrational imprint of those who have been associated with it. Then the parts were put together under the watchful eyes (hopefully!) of human beings, and finally it is sent to the dealership to be sold by other human beings. At each step of the assembly process, more and more thought energy is associated with the vehicle. The shiny new Porsche sitting in the dealership can validly be regarded as a complex set of vibrational energy, manufactured from a sophisticated template of thought. In our model of the universe, everything is alive!

This may seem silly at first, because we don't normally perceive material things except as lumps that just sit there until we move them about. But once you begin to look at the world from a vibrational point of view, even things like glasses, computer monitors, desks, cars and houses seem to have personalities. You begin to perceive these objects not just on the surface, but "inside" them as well. Call me delusional or over-imaginative, but it's kind of fun.

Having faith is just a continuous process of vibrational alignment to something wanted. Ultimately, faith is a joyous process of constantly paying attention to where you want to be!

11.4.3 Summary

You are not a failure because your desires have not manifested. You are simply involved in an ongoing creative process of lining yourself up with what you want. If you do not believe you can be, do or have something, you cannot, because you never get your vibrational stone in position to roll downhill.

Having unfulfilled desires is what life is all about. There will always be things that you want that you don't have yet. Imagine, if you had everything you wanted, how boring would that be? Once you have painted that painting, written that program, composed or played that music, created anything, do you just sit on your laurels forever? You always feel you can do better, those creative juices are always flowing through you.

It's about the journey, not the manifestation. As Esther Hicks says, you cannot ever get it all done. You don't ever want to get it all done. If that ever happened, you would be dead, because you would not have any more desires.

So have fun. Keep the faith.

Which just means, never let go of your desires, your dreams.

Faith is what keeps you on the true path of joy and knowledge of self, and to the manifestation of your desires.

Sampling and Perception

A vibration can be represented as shown in Figure A.1:

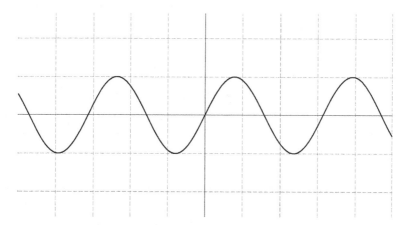

Figure A.1: Wave #1: A simple, repeating vibration

Vibration is motion through a transmitting medium. It can be periodic, like a wave moving up and down along the surface of the water; a sound wave moving through the air; a pendulum swaying back and forth; our ball rotating around the shaft; a planet moving in its orbit about the sun. Alternatively, it can be a sharp burst of sound or a series of non-repeating sounds, as in a musical composition, or "noise."

In Figure A.2 there are non-repeating sharp bursts of sound.

Either way, vibration involves compression and rarefaction of the transmitting medium, or a movement back and forth. For example, the vibrating cone of a speaker creates changes in air pressure, which reach the ear and are translated into the frequencies that were recorded on the playing medium (CD, DVD, tape, LP, etc.)

Figure A.2: Sound file from a music program

Oscillation is an important concept and is the essence of vibration. The electricity that flows through our houses, for example, is alternating current at 60 cycles per second, as a direct result of a rotating coil (armature) within a magnetic field of a generator at the power plant.

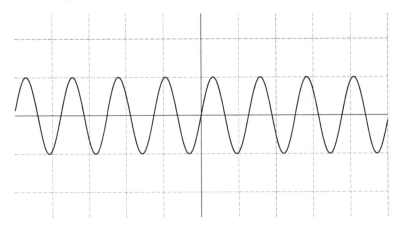

Figure A.3: Wave#2

The closer wave crests are to each other, the higher the frequency. A higher pitched sound will have wave crests closer together and a lower pitched sound will have wave crests further apart. Red light has a lower frequency than blue light, for instance. However, the quintessential nature of perception (or lack of it!) is dependent on the senses of the perceiver, as we've already seen with the dog whistle, or the gamma-ray counter.

Perception and communication are an interfacing of vibration, whether that is biological, electrical, or mechanical. A microphone, for example, takes pressure waves in the air and converts them into electrical signals. A speaker does just the opposite! The photoreactive surface of a CCD (charge coupled device), used in digital cameras, electronically converts light waves into pixel information that gives an accurate image of the target. These devices are all transducers. A transducer is a gadget that converts one type of energy to another, more useful kind. Microphones, speakers, batteries, galvanometers, vinyl record pickup cartridges, light emitting diodes, solar cells, antennas, photocells, thermocouples (temperature sensors), are all examples of transducers.

The human senses are, in a sense, transducers, focusing perception of the vast vibrational bandwidth of the physical universe into very narrow ranges. (Bandwidth is the difference between the highest and lowest frequencies of a transmission channel, or the width of its allocated band of frequencies.) The human eye only sees wavelengths between 400 nm and 700 nm, and we perceive this radiation as various colors of light. The retina, the light sensing portion of the eye, contains a chemical called rhodopsin, which converts light into electrical impulses which are then sent along the optic nerve to the brain. The human ear is a remarkable transducer which has a bandwidth between 20 vibrations per second and 20,000 vibrations per second, converting sound waves into frequency peaks (mechanical patterns of vibration on the basilar membrane) which are then sent, as electrical impulses, along the auditory nerve to the brain. Without getting too complicated, it is accurate to say that the other three senses also translate environmental vibrations into electrical impulses.

A.1 Sampling

IN our model the human senses, being composed of vibrating atoms, "sample" a universe that is itself vibrational in nature.

What is a sample? A sample is a snapshot of an event. In digital technology, a sample is the acquisition of a signal for a predetermined amount of time; in analog-to-digital converters, a snapshot of the signal is taken at every clock pulse. But this concept also applies in analog-to-analog applications, because any signal acquisition is nothing more than an interfacing between two or more vibrations. Imagine that you have a microphone and an amplifier, and begin to sing. You hear exactly what you are playing, continuously in real-time. Well, all of that sound out of your mouth must first get translated electronically. The one thing all microphones have in common is a diaphragm, which vibrates when impacted by the vibration of sound waves in the air, and which then is translated into an electronic signal by various means. How does the sound become a voltage? Through vibrational interaction! The medium of the air interacts with the medium in the microphone, whether that be a diaphragm that moves a coil or a magnet, or whatever. (There are five different technologies commonly used to accomplish this conversion, but all of them do the same thing.) In every instant, the microphone "samples" the pressure waves of your voice. The sampling rate is dependent on the conversion materials used in the microphone.

Analog-to-Digital converters electronically capture an input signal (a sound wave in a recording studio, for example) and turn it into a series of numbers which can then be processed and sent back through a Digital-to-Analog converter, and then through a speaker to re-create the sound wave. That's how the music on CD's gets recorded. We'll see later on that the human body does essentially the same thing!

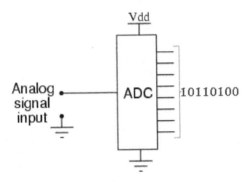

Figure A.4: An Analog-to-Digital Converter

However, this is the same process as analog-to-analog conversion, because those numbers are just representations of analog voltage drops. In other words, the digital 1s and 0s in your computer or sound card are just recorded drops in voltages within the digital circuitry.

Sampling is a concept developed in digital technology, but in a vibrational universe, all perception involves sampling, whether that is accomplished electronically or biologically.

How does sampling affect perception?

In the digital sampling of signals (used in music, in radio and TV broadcasting, and in the analysis of brainwaves and heartbeat), it turns out that a bandwidth limited signal of N cycles per second can be reconstructed without error from samples taken uniformly at a rate which is greater than 2 * N cycles per second (in analog-to-digital signal processing, you often need a higher sampling rate due to the physical limitations of sampling circuitry, but the idea holds). The maximum measurable frequency is therefore equal to half the sampling frequency, which is called the Nyquist limit. So, for example, to digitize a signal with a frequency of 1,000 cycles per second, a minimum sampling frequency of 2,000 cycles per second is required, in order to accurately recover the signal information.

In the above diagram (see Figure A.5), the sampling rate (indicated by the dots) is too low to accurately decipher the vibration indicated by the sine wave, so it looks like a

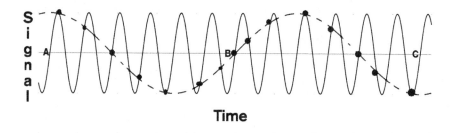

Figure A.5: Insufficient sampling rate demonstration

wave of much lower frequency (the dashed wave). If the sampling rate were reduced so that the signal is sampled once at the beginning (at A), once in the middle (at B), and once at the end (at C), a straight line would result (the line in the middle) which means the actual vibration would be invisible. Failure to sample at a high enough rate also leads to foldover, or aliasing: in the signal there are extra, unanticipated and new low frequency contributions to the sound, causing distortion and noise.

Sampling essentially quantizes a signal into discrete packets of information. One way to understand quantizing is to imagine a line drawn on a piece of paper that is 5.046875 inches long (that's 5 inches plus another 3/64ths of an inch). If you only had a ruler marked out in inches, you would measure its length as "5," but if you had one marked in eighth's of an inch, your measurement would be much closer. The smaller you can quantize the ruler, the more accurate your reading will be.

Quantization occurs in the conversion of analog signals to digital information, because the sampling circuitry needs a little time to process the signal; so the information is acquired is steps. Acquisition of the signal does not begin until a clock pulse is received; so the speed of the clock in the circuitry determines the sampling rate.

It is impossible to continuously measure or perceive anything because it takes time between the receipt of a signal, the processing of it, and re-exposure. During the time it takes for processing, you are missing out on a portion of the signal, as you can see from the above graphic. The digital signal is jerky and shows loss of information.

The input to an analog-to-digital converter is a continuous signal with an infinite number of possible states, but the digital output is a discrete function whose number of different states is determined by the resolution of the converter. Therefore,

analog signal (continuous)

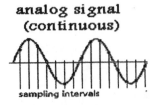

sampling intervals

digital signal (discrete)

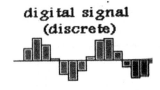

numerical representation of analog signal

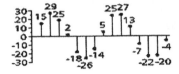

15 29 30 2 -18 -26 -14
5 25 27 13 -7 -22 -20 -4

Figure A.6: Quantization of waves

the conversion from analog to digital loses some information and introduces some distortion into the signal. The magnitude of this error is random, with values up to ±LSB, the least significant bit of the converter's resolution.

In video, undersampling leads to an incorrect impression of an object's behavior. For example, if a rotating wheel is undersampled, its true rotational speed is underestimated, and sometimes it appears to be moving in the opposite direction. This phenomenon is observable in old movies, where a car or wagon wheel appears to be moving in the opposite direction, due to the inadequate frame rate of the recording camera. When the sampling rate is equal to the rotation, the wheel appears to be motionless!

Imagine a darkened room and a one-spoked wheel mounted on a shaft that can be rotated counter-clockwise at predetermined speeds.

Figure A.7: Rotating wheel

The wheel is rotated 7 times, beginning at 1 revolution per minute (rpm) and continuing up to 7 rpm, and the wheel can only be seen every 10 seconds, when a light flashes. Therefore, the sampling rate, or the rate at which the wheel can be perceived, is 6 times per minute. What happens?

When the true rotational frequency is below the Nyquist limit (1 and 2 rpm), the correct frequency and direction of the rotations are observed. When the wheel rotates at the Nyquist limit (3 rpm), the wheel is seen every 180 degrees. Its rotational speed can be deduced, but its rotational direction is ambiguous. When the true rotational frequency is above the Nyquist limit, errors in observation occur. At 4 rpm, an erroneous speed of 2 rpm is estimated, and the apparent rotational direction is also wrong, clockwise instead of counter-clockwise. At 5 rpm, the rotational speed is underestimated still further (1 rpm), and the rotational direction is still incorrect:

Here the wheel appears to be moving clockwise at only 1 rotation per minute, even though it is actually moving at 5 rpm counter-clockwise.

At 6 rpm, twice the Nyquist limit, the wheel is seen every 360 degrees and therefore seems to be motionless:

At 7 rpm, the apparent rotational direction is again correct, but the speed is again underestimated at only 1 rpm:

The rate at which information is gathered determines what is perceived.

In digital signal processing, signals are processed through a low-pass filter, which screens out all frequencies above the Nyquist limit. Such a signal is said to be bandwidth limited. In the physical universe, signals are usually not bandwidth limited (although a wall, for example, essentially operates as a low-pass sound filter, screening out higher frequencies); nevertheless, the perception, analysis, or interpretation of any vibration is always relative to the rate of the sampling vibration.

In audio applications, undersampling can lead to crummy sound quality (but it also has practical uses which we won't go into here); oversampling with digital filtering is used in audio to increase sound quality. Interestingly enough, oversampling (and upsampling[33]) at rates well above the Nyquist limit actually increases sound quality, even though there is no more information in the upsampled signal than in the original!

That is to say, 44.1kHz CD data converted to a 352.8kHz datastream before digital-to-audio conversion (called 8x oversampling) sounds better, even though both data streams have a frequency spectrum within the 20–20,000 cycles per second range of human hearing.

Upsampling has led some to theorize that human hearing is more dependent on rapid changes of sound within the time domain than on the frequency spectrum itself. It is well known that the timbre of a sound (what distinguishes the sound of a drum from that of a piano, for instance) is more dependent on the attack and decay of a sound wave (how fast it gets going and how long it takes to die out) rather than its pitch (highness or lowness). In other words, the difference in the sound of a cymbal and that of an oboe has more to do with the shape of the vibration, rather than its frequency.

Others have said that the improved sound comes from noise shaping and improved filtering of the digital data, reducing the noise floor of the signal before it gets sent out to the speakers.

Whatever the reason, it is clear that what is happening vibrationally within the human ear (and precisely how it interfaces with the brain to produce what is heard) is not fully understood. If, as we've said throughout this book, consciousness as a non-physical phenomena is introduced, then perhaps the subtle vibrational effects of analog and digital sound reproduction equipment may be accounted for.

And even though your ears can't hear infrasound, (sounds below the range of human hearing) it can affect you. Legend has it that the Nazi's used infrasound before WWII to anger and excite crowds gathered to listen to Hitler. A lot of infrasound research has been classified and it is not possible to determine what is fact and what is fiction. However, in the summer of 2003, scientists in Britain conducted an experiment to gauge the effects of infrasound, adding infrasound bass lines to the performed music. It was discovered that infrasound passages caused listeners to experience increased heart rate, feelings of anxiety, shivers on the skin, and fluttering in the stomach. In some participants, the infrasound even evoked sharp memories of emotional losses![34]

It seems that vibration, even if it is beyond the range of human senses, has noticeable psychological effects.

---

[33] According to Wadia Digital, an authority on digital recording, there is no difference between oversampling and upsampling. Both procedures acquire the input signal at rates well above the Nyquist limit.

[34] For a full report on the experiment, go to http://www.infrasonicmusic.co.uk/results.htm.

A.2   Do we Perceive Digitally, or Continuously?

D o human beings perceive the universe in a continuous, uninterrupted manner, or can we extend the sampling concept to the human senses? Sampling is vibrational interaction, and that occurs in both digital and analog applications. Nevertheless, it is interesting to pursue the sampling idea because it turns out that the human senses operate in a sort of biologically digital fashion.

There is experimental evidence to suggest that resolution acuity of the human eye is directly linked to the spatial density of retinal neurons. The sampling theory of visual resolution states that the optical image formed on the retina of the human eye is spatially continuous, whereas the neural image is discrete. According to this theory, the same issues of undersampling, aliasing, etc. that apply in digital signal processing also apply to the human sense of sight.[35]

The human body receives information from the outside world through receptors, which are neurons in the sense organs. Neurons, as we'll see shortly, communicate their information through a series of electrical (electro-chemical) impulses, and send this information through the nervous system and into the brain. The brain is essentially the main switching mechanism of the central nervous system; it receives (and transmits) electrical impulses. A nerve impulse is essentially an interpreted unit of information from the outside world, in the form of an electrical impulse, which makes sense to, and can be used by, the body's organs and systems.

Neurons are the primary cells of the nervous system. The nervous system transmits the information that coordinates the activity of the muscles, monitors the organs, constructs and processes input from the senses. The neuron is an example of what is called an excitable cell. An excitable cell is one that can be stimulated to generate a tiny electrical current. All cells (not just excitable cells) have a resting potential, which is an electrical charge across the plasma membrane. The interior of the cell is negative in relation to the exterior. The size of the resting potential varies, but in excitable cells it runs somewhere around -70 millivolts (mv). External stimuli can reduce the charge across the plasma membrane, which is called depolarization. If the potential is reduced to the threshold voltage (about -50 mv in mammalian neurons), what is called an action potential is generated in the cell. If depolarization at a spot on the cell reaches a threshold voltage, the reduced voltage opens up hundreds of voltage-gated sodium channels in that portion of the plasma membrane. A wave of depolarization sweeps along the cell, which is called the action potential (in neurons, the action potential is also called the nerve impulse).

---

[35] See "Acuity Perimetry and the Sampling Theory of Visual Resolution," The 1997 Glenn Fry Award Lecture, by Larry N. Thibos (School of Optometry, University of Indiana), at http://research.opt.indiana.edu/Library/GlennFryLecture/GlennFryLecture.html#F1

It takes between 0.001 and 0.002 seconds for human neurons to re-polarize and ready itself to transmit another impulse, which is called the refractory period. This means that the neuron can transmit 500-1000 impulses per second,[36] which implies that although the body may be exposed to continuous (analog) signals from the environment, there is a processing delay from the time the signal is received until the neuron is ready to obtain more information. In essence, there is a sampling rate for each individual receptor.

Interestingly, the human neuron operates like a logic gate. It will respond only if the stimulus reaches a threshold level; any stimulus weaker than the threshold will produce no impulse, and any stimulus stronger than the threshold will produce an impulse. However, the impulse is always of the same strength, regardless of the strength of the stimulus. Therefore, a nerve impulse is remarkably like a "bit" of information in computer terminology. It is either "on" or "high" (a 1), or "off" or "low" (a 0). So it seems that digital devices aren't so high-tech after all, merely mimicking human biology!

The human body has billions of neurons sending and receiving information to and from the brain, and the human brain has about 100 billion neurons and 100 trillion connections (synapses) between them. There is a constant stream of electrical impulses reaching the higher cognitive functions from the senses, but this information is discrete, not continuous.[37] We might liken the firing time of a neuron to the "sample and hold" delay time of an ADC (analog to digital converter). In an ADC, it takes time to process the input signal and turn it into a sequence of numbers, just as it takes neurons time to send a nerve impulse and ready itself for the next transmission. Sample and hold just means that the input value must be held constant during the time that the converter turns the signal input into a bunch of numbers.

Whether a system is biological or mechanical, interpretation, conversion, or transduction is imperfect. That is why, in engineering, there is always a tradeoff between efficiency and performance. The body itself can be regarded as an engineered system (even if we often don't really understand what's going on!) so perhaps our digital analogies are not so far-fetched.

In concluding this section, we can say that, in our model, physical perception must be, first and foremost, a vibrational translation or interpretation. Now we extend this concept out on the electromagnetic spectrum, far, far out, until we reach the realm of

---

[36] This information gathered from a number of sources. I have borrowed mainly from the excellent on-line biology textbook of Dr. John W. Kimball, which can be found at http://users.rcn.com/jkimball.ma.ultranet/BiologyPages/. This is copyrighted information and is used with permission. My inclusion of this data does not imply the author's approval of any of my assertions!

[37] It is possible to have a continuous digital output from an analog input stream; however, there is always some loss of information.

subtle energy. Subtle energy is so refined and of such a high vibration that it cannot be measured with the instruments of science. Subtle energy is the energy of thought, of life force. It is a product of consciousness itself, and it fills the universe.[38] It is, on the subtle level of thought, an instantaneous communication medium, invisible, yet tangible. With these assumptions, it is possible to use the vibrational concept to explain non-local phenomenon such as ESP, intuition, remote viewing, and other psychic phenomena.[39] The vibrational concept allows us to integrate the material world with the spiritual. Rather than viewing the material and the spiritual as separate, we can view them as part of the same vibrational continuum.

---

[38] See Appendix B

[39] "The only real valuable thing is intuition."—Albert Einstein

Thought Is the Basic Quantum Unit

In the book we speculated that the basic unit or quanta of energy in the universe is thought. We might liken a thought to a particle like the photon, which has no mass, but non-zero momentum, given in physics by hv / c, where c is the speed of light, v is the frequency of the photon, and h is Planck's constant, referred to in the physics literature as the fundamental constant of nature.

Or perhaps, a thought may be considered as having just the tiniest bit of mass, something so tiny that it can be regarded as virtual. Regardless, a thought, like a photon, has existence. Even though it has no mass, a photon is the basic unit (quantum) of electromagnetic radiation (light), and we can perceive it with our eyes (well, maybe not an individual photon, but a whole bunch of them) and even measure it with instruments.

In this way we sort of disingenuously get around the idea of something from nothing, for a thought is so ephemeral it can be considered to be (almost!) a pure potential.

We can reason like physicists and mathematicians sometimes do. They will look at the math and say, "our calculations show that black holes are required in order for our theory and experimental evidence to be congruent." And so they will advance the idea of black holes, not because anyone has ever seen one before, but just because it seems to fit. In this spirit (although this is purely speculative, with no math to back it up) we can say that a thought is a mapping between consciousness and the physical universe. We can define a virtual function f, which maps a thought ò into the physical universe.

We can write $f(\grave{o}) \Rightarrow q$. Since both f and $\grave{o}$ are virtual and unobservable, we cannot define precisely how this is done. We say simply that the virtual function f operates on a virtual thought $\grave{o}$, translating it into a recognizable physical quantum, q.

Q must, by definition, have both the properties of a particle and a wave, for the following reasons:

q is alive, therefore it is internally in motion. All things in existence are in motion, this is a simple conclusion from the fact that all things are composed of subatomic particles and all subatomic particles are in motion within themselves. Therefore q has the property of a vibration, or a wave.

q, by definition, must be discrete. q is discrete because it exists. q occupies a unique point in space and it was created at a unique moment in time. Therefore it has identity and is distinguishable from other quanta. Discreteness is a simple fact of the definition of existence. If q were not discrete, it would be something else, and therefore not q. In other words, for a thing to have physical existence at all it must have a unique space for it to exist in, for nothing physical can occupy exactly the same space at exactly the same time as another physically identifiable thing. In physics this is known as the principle of complementarity and is the basis of Heisenberg's uncertainty principle.

Wave (vibration) / particle is the fundamental duality of physical existence. In order to have a physical universe at all, duality is a requirement. However, duality is contradictory, because it is clear that all quanta are the same (isotropic), yet in order to have existence, they must somehow be different. That is why geometry is the most fundamental subject in the universe, for there is no difference in the energy of an electron and that of a proton. An atom of iron and an atom of copper are not different because they are composed of "copper" energy and "iron" energy. They are different because the geometry of their elements (atoms) combines in different ways.

B.1   Comments:

CONSCIOUSNESS is a static, something with no mass and no moving parts. A static, in other words, is a pure potential and cannot, by definition, have movement. Therefore consciousness, in its native state, is not IN the universe at all. Consciousness is the creative principle; by definition it has the ability to create a "something" from a "nothing."

The function f, speaking in computer language, returns a quanta q from the virtual realm of consciousness; q is therefore conscious.

We can say that q, along with all other quanta created by consciousness, is simply an aspect of the same energy, which is isotropic (the same everywhere) because all quanta are the creations of consciousness.

Does Like Really Attract Like?

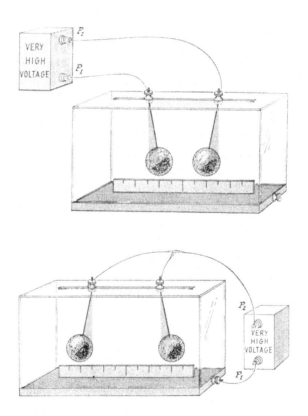

Fig. C.1. Charged spheres attraction demonstration

- When the two spheres are connected to different poles of the battery, they attract.

- When the two spheres are connected to the same pole of the battery, they repel.

Take two spheres of very light weight, each coated with a thin film of metal. The spheres are suspended near each other by fine metal threads in a closed glass box to exclude air drafts. Each suspending thread is connected to a brass terminal. Next to the box is a battery with two terminals. When both spheres are hooked up to different poles of the battery, the spheres come together, and when they hooked up to the same terminal, they move apart. The explanation assigned to this experiment is that (1) there are two and only two types of charge, and (2) opposite charges attract. This convention has been adopted, reasonably, for over 100 years.

However, it contradicts another well-known fact of science: that energy is isotropic (the same everywhere). In other words, the energy that composes a proton is the same as the energy in an electron, or the energy in any subatomic particle. In discussing the difference between iron and copper, we do not postulate a "copper energy" and a separate "iron energy." The difference is entirely geometric. What makes the two elements unique lies in the arrangement of the particles, all of which are composed of the same energy. My understanding is that "charge" is also explained in this manner: a charged particle is only charged because it has, in its geometric arrangement, a dearth or a surplus of electrons. So the assignment of "positive" and "negative" is convenient, but arbitrary (electrons are assigned a negative charge, and protons a positive charge). If energy is fundamentally isotropic then there is really no such thing as "positive" and "negative" charge or energy, even though it helps us to think in this way. In a battery, the positive pole has a dearth of electrons and the negative pole has a surplus of electrons. The electrons try to find balance by going from one pole to the other. In other words, the electrons at the negative pole want to party with their friends at the positive pole, and the electrons at the positive pole desire their mates to join them. When the system finds balance, the battery is no longer charged.

About the Author

Kenneth MacLean is a freelance writer and researcher living in Ann Arbor, Michigan.

He can be reached at kmaclean@kjmaclean.com

Visit *The Big Picture* website at www.kjmaclean.com. For inspirational movies visit http://www.sunrise-production.org

Other Books by the Author

Dialogues: Conversations with my Higher Self

Beyond the Beginning

The End of the Universe

The Manchild

Miracles Can Happen

A Geometric Analysis of the Platonic Solids and Other Semi-regular Polyhedra. With a Discussion of the Phi Ratio

I Love You Dad

Available at http://www.kjmaclean.com/Products/MainProductPage.php, or from Loving Healing Press at www.LovingHealing.com or from bookstores via Ingram Book Group and New Leaf Distributing.

Dialogues:
Conversations with my Higher Self

"*Dialogues: Conversations with my Higher Self* gives the reader a good deal of food for thought."
– Tami Brady, Blether.com.

What is consciousness? How does consciousness become self-aware? Is there really a God? Who or what created the universe? What happens after you die?
Read the Dialogues and find out!
What is time? Are there universal laws, or do the laws of science regarding matter and energy also apply to spiritual beings? What's it like living as a non-corporeal entity?
In a fascinating and wide-ranging discussion, the author, with the help of several non-corporeal entities, provide the answers. Even if you don't believe in channeling, *Dialogues: Conversations With My Higher Self* contains information you just don't want to miss.
"The simple and powerful truth of life is that utter, total, and complete well being, health, prosperity, and joy is the order of the day, in every moment and all that is necessary to experience it is to let it in!"

Book #2 in the *Potentials of Consciousness* Series
Dialogues: Conversations with my Higher Self is a compilation of the author's reflections about a number of metaphysical and scientific matters. Each section takes the form of a question and answer session between the author and a group of individuals that he describes as his Higher Self. These Higher Self individuals reflect various personality traits that the author possesses ranging from the gentle feminine Sweet to the overbearing Dragon. In these sessions, the author learns about topics ranging from the truth about science and the power of thought through the cyclical nature of living and the ultimate beginning of awareness to an understanding about life purpose and the a little about the Higher Self.
"*Dialogues: Conversations with my Higher Self* gives the reader a good deal of food for thought. It is not the author's intention to reveal ultimate truth. The purpose of this book is not to wholeheartedly agree or stubbornly disagree with the reflections presented in this compilation. Instead, the author directs readers to think about their own questions. He also urges readers to create their own reality and be aware of their own thoughts"

Loving Healing Press
5145 Pontiac Trail
Ann Arbor, MI 48105
(734)662-6864
info@LovingHealing.com

300 pp trade/paper
ISBN-10 1-932690-01-
ISBN-13 978-1-932690-01-9
$18.95 Retail
Learn more or buy at
Amazon.com

CPSIA information can be obtained at www.ICGtesting.com
Printed in the USA
BVOW06s2150241115

428425BV00021B/128/P